# Beyond Order

ALSO BY JORDAN B. PETERSON

*Maps of Meaning: The Architecture of Belief*

*12 Rules for Life: An Antidote to Chaos*

# Beyond Order

## 12 MORE RULES
## FOR LIFE

Jordan B. Peterson

ALLEN LANE
*an imprint of*
PENGUIN BOOKS

ALLEN LANE

UK | USA | Canada | Ireland | Australia
India | New Zealand | South Africa

Allen Lane is part of the Penguin Random House group of companies
whose addresses can be found at global.penguinrandomhouse.com.

Penguin
Random House
UK

First published in the United States of America by Portfolio/Penguin,
an imprint of Penguin Random House LLC, 2021
First published in Great Britain by Allen Lane 2021

The authorized representative in the EEA is Penguin Random House Ireland,
Morrison Chambers, 32 Nassau Street, Dublin D02 YH68

A CIP catalogue record for this book is available from the British Library

Hardback ISBN: 978–0–241–40762–2
Trade paperback ISBN: 978–0–241–40763–9

www.greenpenguin.co.uk

*To my wife, Tammy Maureen Roberts Peterson, whom I have loved deeply for fifty years, and who is admirable, in my estimation, in all regards, and beyond all reason.*

# Contents

# Table of Illustrations

1. **The Fool:** Inspired by Pamela Colman Smith, *The Fool*, from the Rider-Waite Tarot card deck, Rider & Son (1910).

2. **Materia Prima:** Inspired by Hermes Trismegistus, *Occulta philosophia* (1613). Also from H. Nollius, *Theoria philosophiae hermeticae* (Hanoviae: Apud P. Antonium, 1617).

3. **St. George and the Dragon:** Inspired by Paolo Uccello, *Saint George and the Dragon* (ca. 1458).

4. **Atlas and the Hesperides:** Inspired by John Singer Sargent, *Atlas and the Hesperides* (ca. 1922–1925).

5. **Fallen Angel:** Inspired by Alexandre Cabanel, *Fallen Angel* (1847).

6. **In our Communal Farm:** Inspired by B. Deykin, *In Our Communal Farm, There Is No Place for Priests and Kulaks* (1932).

7. **Apprentice:** Inspired by Louis-Emile Adan, *Apprentice* (1914).

**8. Irises:** Inspired by Vincent Van Gogh, *Irises* (1890).

**9. The Temptation of St. Anthony:** Inspired by Martin Schongauer, *The Temptation of Saint Anthony* (ca. 1470–1475).

**10. The Love Drink:** Inspired by Aubrey Beardsley, *How Sir Tristram Drank of the Love Drink* (1893).

**11. Satan:** Inspired by Gustave Doré, *Satan*, from John Milton, *Milton's Paradise Lost*, with illustrations by Gustave Doré (London: Cassell & Company, Ltd., 1905).

**12. St. Sebastian:** Inspired by Martin Schongauer, *Saint Sebastian* (ca. 1480).

# A Note from the Author in the Time of the Pandemic

It is a perplexing task to produce a nonfiction book during the global crisis brought about by the spread of COVID-19. It seems absurd, in some sense, even to think about anything else but that illness during this trying time. Nonetheless, binding all the thoughts contained in any current work to the existence of the pandemic—which too shall pass—seems like an error, as the normal problems of life will return at some point (and thankfully) to the forefront. That all means that an author of the present day is inevitably going to make one mistake (concentrating too much on the pandemic, which has an uncertain life span, and producing a book that is instantly dated, in consequence) or another (ignoring the pandemic, which is very much like failing to attend to the proverbial elephant under the rug).

After considering this, as well as discussing the issues with my publishers, I decided to write *Beyond Order: 12 More Rules for Life* according to the plan laid out for it several years ago, and to concentrate on addressing issues not specific to the current time (thus, to risk the second error rather than the first). I suppose it may also be the case that those who have chosen to read this book or listen to the audio version might be relieved to turn their attention to something other than the coronavirus and the devastation it has wrought.

# Overture

On the fifth of February 2020, I awoke in an intensive care ward in, of all places, Moscow. I had six-inch tethers attaching me to the sides of the bed because, in my unconscious state, I had been agitated enough to try to remove the catheters from my arm and leave the ICU. I was confused and frustrated not knowing where I was, surrounded by people speaking a foreign language, and in the absence of my daughter, Mikhaila, and her husband, Andrey, who were restricted to short visiting hours and did not have permission to be there with me at my moment of wakening. I was angry, too, about being there, and lunged at my daughter when she did visit several hours later. I felt betrayed, although that was the furthest from the truth. People had been attending to my various needs with great diligence, and in the wake of the tremendous logistic challenges that come about from seeking medical care in a truly foreign country. I do not have any memory of anything that happened to me during the most recent weeks preceding that, and very little between that moment and my having entered a hospital in

Toronto, in mid-December. One of the few things I could recall, looking back to the earliest days of the year, was the time I had spent writing this book.

I wrote much and edited almost all of *Beyond Order* during a time
when my family was plagued by sequential and overlapping bouts of
seriously impaired health, much of which was the subject of public discussion, and for that reason requires some detailed explanation. First,
in January 2019, Mikhaila had to seek out a surgeon to replace much
of her artificial ankle, implanted about a decade earlier, as the initial
installation was never perfect, causing her serious pain and trouble
with movement as a consequence, and then came near to failing. I
spent a week with her at a hospital in Zurich, Switzerland, for the
week of that procedure and her initial recovery.

At the beginning of March, my wife, Tammy, underwent routine
surgery in Toronto for a common and eminently treatable kidney cancer. A month and a half after that surgery, which involved the removal
of one third of the organ in question, we learned that she was actually
suffering from an extremely rare malignancy, which had a one-year
fatality rate of close to 100 percent.

Two weeks later, the surgeons involved in her care removed the
remaining two thirds of her afflicted kidney, along with a substantial
proportion of the related abdominal lymphatic system. The surgery
appeared to bring the progression of the cancer to a halt, but produced
leakage of fluid (up to four liters, or one gallon, a day) from her now-
damaged lymphatic system—a condition known as chylous ascites—
which rivaled the original condition in danger. We journeyed to see
a medical team in Philadelphia, where within ninety-six hours of the
initial injection of a poppy seed oil dye, whose practical purpose was
the enhancement of images derived from CAT or MRI scans, the complete cessation of Tammy's fluid loss was achieved. This breakthrough

occurred on the very day of our thirtieth wedding anniversary. She recovered rapidly and, to all appearances, completely—a testament to the luck without which none of us can live, and to her own admirable strength and resistance.

Unfortunately, while these events unfolded, my health fell apart. I had begun to take an antianxiety agent at the beginning of 2017, after suffering from what appeared to be an autoimmune reaction to something I had consumed during the Christmas holiday period of 2016.* The food reaction made me acutely and continually anxious, as well as freezing cold, no matter what clothes I was wearing or how many blankets I layered upon myself. Further, it lowered my blood pressure so dramatically that whenever I tried to stand I would gray out and be forced into a crouch half a dozen or more times before trying again. I also experienced insomnia that appeared near total. My family physician prescribed a benzodiazepine as well as a drug for sleeping. I took the latter a mere handful of times before ceasing its use entirely; the terrible symptoms I was experiencing, including the insomnia, were almost immediately and entirely eradicated by the benzodiazepine treatment, making the sleep agent unnecessary. I continued the benzodiazepine for almost exactly three years, because my life did seem unnaturally stressful during that time (the period when my life changed from the quiet existence of a university professor and clinician to the tumultuous reality of a public figure), and because I believed that this drug was—as is often claimed of benzodiazepines—a relatively harmless substance.

Things changed, however, in March 2019, at the onset of my wife's

---

*The illness that had destroyed Mikhaila's ankle, necessitating its replacement, as well as her hip, was also immune related, and my wife had some arthritic symptoms that were similar to hers. I am mentioning this to shed some light on why the assumption of an immune response program sprang to mind and made a certain sense.

medical battle. My anxiety spiked noticeably after Mikhaila's aforementioned hospitalization, surgery, and recovery. In consequence, I
asked my family physician to increase my dose of benzodiazepine,
so that I would not be preoccupied by nor preoccupy others with my
anxiety. Unfortunately, I experienced a marked increase in negative
emotion following the adjustment. I asked to have the dosage raised
yet again (by this time, we were attempting to deal with the second of
Tammy's surgeries and its complications, and I attributed my even
more severe anxiety to that problem), but my anxiety increased even
further. I attributed all of this not to a paradoxical reaction to the
medication (which it was later diagnosed as), but to the recurrence of
a tendency toward depression that had plagued me for years.* In any
case, I ceased using the benzodiazepine entirely in May of that year,
trying two doses of ketamine within a week, as suggested by a psychiatrist with whom I consulted. Ketamine, a nonstandard anesthetic/
psychedelic, sometimes has overwhelming and sudden positive effects
on depression. It produced nothing for me but two ninety-minute trips
to hell. I felt to my bones as if I had everything to feel guilty and
ashamed about, with nothing gained by my positive experiences.

A few days after the second ketamine experience, I began to suffer the effects of acute benzodiazepine withdrawal, which were truly
intolerable—anxiety far beyond what I had ever experienced, an uncontrollable restlessness and need to move (formally known as akathisia), overwhelming thoughts of self-destruction, and the complete
absence of any happiness whatsoever. A family friend—a physician—
enlightened me as to the dangers of sudden benzodiazepine withdrawal. I therefore started to take a benzodiazepine once again—but a

---

*I had taken serotonin reuptake inhibitors such as Celexa for nearly two decades, greatly
benefiting from their administration, before stopping in early 2016, because a dramatic
dietary change seemed to render them unnecessary.

smaller dose than I had climbed to previously. Many, but not all, of my symptoms abated. To deal with those that remained, I also began to take an antidepressant that had been of great use to me in the past. All it did, however, was make me exhausted enough to require an additional four or more hours of sleep a day—which was not helpful in the midst of Tammy's serious health issues—as well as increase my appetite two- or threefold.

After about three months of terrible anxiety, uncontrollable hypersomnia, viciously torturous akathisia, and excessive appetite, I traveled to an American clinic that claimed to specialize in rapid benzodiazepine withdrawal. Despite the good intentions of many of its psychiatrists, the clinic managed only a slow cessation or tapering of my benzodiazepine dosage, the negative effects of which I was already experiencing and which were not and could not be controlled to any significant degree whatsoever by the inpatient treatment offered.

I resided at that clinic, nonetheless, from mid-August, a mere few days after Tammy had recovered from her postsurgical complications, to late November, when I returned home to Toronto, much the worse for wear. By this time, the akathisia (the disorder of uncontrollable movement alluded to earlier) had increased to the point where I could not sit or rest in any position for any length of time whatsoever without severe distress. In December I checked in to a local hospital, and it was at that point that my awareness of events prior to my awakening in Moscow ends. As I later learned, Mikhaila and Andrey removed me from the Toronto hospital in early January 2020, believing that the treatment I received there was doing me more harm than good (an opinion I concurred with entirely once I learned of it).

The situation I found myself in upon reattaining consciousness in Russia was complicated by the fact that I had also developed double pneumonia in Canada, although that was neither discovered nor treated until I was in the Moscow ICU. However, I was there primarily so that the clinic could facilitate my withdrawal from benzodiazepines, using a procedure either unknown or regarded as too dangerous in North America. Since I had not been able to tolerate any decrease in dosage whatsoever—apart from the initial reduction, months before— the clinic placed me in a medically induced coma so that I might remain unconscious during the very worst withdrawal symptoms. That regimen started January 5 and lasted nine days, during which I was also placed in a machine so that my breathing was mechanically regulated. On January 14, I was taken off the anesthetic and the intubation. I woke up for a few hours, and indicated during this time to Mikhaila that I was no longer suffering from akathisia, although I remember nothing of this.

On January 23, I was moved to another ICU specializing in neurological rehabilitation. I can recall waking up on the twenty-sixth for a short period, until my more complete return to consciousness, as previously related, on February 5—ten days during which I passed through a period of delirium of vivid intensity. Once that cleared, I moved to a more homelike rehabilitation center in the outer suburbs of Moscow. While there, I had to relearn how to walk and up and down stairs, button my clothes, lie down in bed on my own, place my hands in the proper position on a computer keyboard, and type. I did not seem to be able to see properly—or, more accurately, see how to use my limbs to interact with what I perceived. A few weeks later, after the problems in perception and coordination had essentially abated, Mikhaila, Andrey, their child, and I relocated to Florida for what we hoped would be some peaceful time of recuperation in the sun (very much welcome after the cold grayness of midwinter Moscow). This was immediately before worldwide concern erupted over the COVID-19 pandemic.

In Florida, I attempted to wean off the medication prescribed by the Moscow clinic, although I was still experiencing numbness in my left hand and foot, trembling of those two extremities as well as the muscles in my forehead, seizure activity, and crippling anxiety. All these symptoms increased quite markedly as my intake of medication decreased, reaching the point where about two months later I returned to the dosages initially prescribed in Russia. This was a material defeat, as the process of lessening their use had been fueled by an optimism that was consequently shattered, as well as returning me to a state of medication usage that I had paid a heavy price for trying to eliminate. I had family members and friends stay with me during this time, thankfully, and their company helped me stay motivated to continue while the symptoms I was experiencing grew unbearable, particularly in the morning.

By the end of May, three months after leaving Russia, it had become obvious that I was worsening instead of improving, and relying on the people I loved and who reciprocated that emotion was both untenable and unfair. Mikhaila and Andrey had been in touch with a Serbian clinic that practiced a novel approach to the problem of benzodiazepine withdrawal, and they made arrangements to move me there, only two days after that country had reopened after the pandemic closure.

I am not going to make a claim that the events that befell my wife, me, and those who were closely involved in her care added up, in the final analysis, to some greater good. What happened to her was truly awful. She experienced a severe and near-fatal crisis of health every two or three days for more than half a year, and then had to cope with my illness and absence. I was plagued, for my part, with the likely loss of someone whom I had befriended for fifty years and been married to for thirty; the observation of the terrible consequences of that on her other family members, including our children; and the dire and dreadful consequences of a substance dependence I had unwittingly stumbled into. I am not going to cheapen any of that by claiming that we became better people for living through it. However, I can say that passing so near to death motivated my wife to attend to some issues regarding her own spiritual and creative development more immediately and assiduously than she might otherwise have, and me to write or to preserve while editing only those words in this book that retained their significance even under conditions characterized by extreme suffering. It is certainly thanks to family and friends (who are named specifically in the Coda of this book) that we are still alive, but it is also true that the meaningful immersion in what I was writing, which continued during the entire time I have related—excepting my unconscious month in Russia—provided me both with a reason to live and a means of testing the viability of the thoughts with which I wrestled.

I do not believe I have ever claimed—in my previous book or, indeed, this one—that it would be *necessarily* sufficient to live by the rules I have presented. I think what I claimed—what I hope I claimed—was this: When you are visited by chaos and swallowed up; when nature curses you or someone you love with illness; or when tyranny rends asunder something of value that you have built, it is salutary to know the rest of the story. All of that misfortune is only the bitter half of the tale of existence, without taking note of the heroic element of redemption or the nobility of the human spirit requiring a certain responsibility to shoulder. We ignore that addition to the story at our peril, because life is so difficult that losing sight of the heroic part of existence could cost us everything. We do not want that to happen. We need instead to take heart, and to take spirit, and to look at things carefully and properly, and to live the way that we could live.

You have sources of strength upon which you can draw, and even though they may not work well, they may be enough. You have what you can learn if you can accept your error. You have medications and hospitals, as well as physicians and nurses who genuinely and bravely care to lift you up and help you through every day. And then you have your own character and courage, and if those have been beat to a bloody pulp and you are ready to throw in the towel, you have the character and courage of those for whom you care and who care for you. And maybe, just maybe, with all that, you can get through. I can tell you what has saved me, so far—the love I have for my family; the love they have for me; the encouragement they have delivered, along with my friends; the fact that I still had meaningful work I could struggle through while in the abyss. I had to force myself to sit down at the computer. I had to force myself to concentrate, and to breathe, and to keep from saying and meaning "to hell with it" during the endless months that I was possessed by dread and terror. And I was barely able to do it. More than half the time I believed that I was going to die in one of the many hospitals in which I resided. And I believe that if I had fallen prey to resentment, for example, I would have perished once and for all—and that I am fortunate to have avoided such a fate.

Is it not possible (even though it may not always deliver us from the terrible situation that we find ourselves in) that we would all be more able to deal with uncertainty, the horrors of nature, the tyranny of culture, and the malevolence of ourselves and others if we were better and more courageous people? If we strived toward higher values? If we were more truthful? Wouldn't the beneficial elements of experience be more likely to manifest themselves around us? Is it not possible, if your goals were noble enough, your courage adequate, your aim at the truth unerring, that the Good thereby produced would . . . well, not justify the horror? That is not exactly right, but it still comes close. Such attitudes and actions might at least provide us with meaning sufficient to stop our encounter with that terror and horror from corrupting us

and turning the surrounding world into something all too closely resembling hell.

Why *Beyond Order?* It is simple, in some regard. Order is explored
territory. We are in order when the actions we deem appropriate produce the results we aim at. We regard such outcomes positively, indicating as they do, first, that we have moved closer to what we desire, and
second, that our theory about how the world works remains acceptably
accurate. Nonetheless, all states of order, no matter how secure and
comfortable, have their flaws. Our knowledge of how to act in the
world remains eternally incomplete—partly because of our profound
ignorance of the vast unknown, partly because of our willful blindness, and partly because the world continues, in its entropic manner,
to transform itself unexpectedly. Furthermore, the order we strive to
impose on the world can rigidify as a consequence of ill-advised attempts to eradicate from consideration all that is unknown. When such
attempts go too far, totalitarianism threatens, driven by the desire to exercise full control where such control is not possible, even in principle.
This means risking a dangerous restriction of all the psychological and
social changes necessary to maintain adaptation to the ever-changing
world. And so we find ourselves inescapably faced with the need to
move beyond order, into its opposite: chaos.

If order is where what we want makes itself known—when we act
in accordance with our hard-won wisdom—chaos is where what we do
not expect or have remained blind to leaps forward from the potential
that surrounds us. The fact that something has occurred many times
in the past is no guarantee that it will continue to occur in the same
manner.[1] There exists, eternally, a domain beyond what we know and
can predict. Chaos is anomaly, novelty, unpredictability, transformation, disruption, and all too often, descent, as what we have come to
take for granted reveals itself as unreliable. Sometimes it manifests it-

self gently, revealing its mysteries in experience that makes us curious, compelled, and interested. This is particularly likely, although not inevitable, when we approach what we do not understand voluntarily, with careful preparation and discipline. Other times the unexpected makes itself known terribly, suddenly, accidentally, so we are undone, and fall apart, and can only put ourselves back together with great difficulty—if at all.

Neither the state of order nor the state of chaos is preferable, intrinsically, to the other. That is the wrong way to look at it. Nonetheless, in my previous book, *12 Rules for Life: An Antidote to Chaos*, I focused more on how the consequences of too much chaos might be remediated.[2] We respond to sudden and unpredictable change by preparing, physiologically and psychologically, for the worst. And because only God Himself knows what this worst might be, we must in our ignorance prepare for all eventualities. And the problem with that continual preparation is that, in excess, it exhausts us. But that does not imply in any manner that chaos should be eliminated (an impossibility, in any case), although what is unknown needs to be managed carefully, as my previous book repeatedly stressed. Whatever is not touched by the new stagnates, and it is certainly the case that a life without curiosity— that instinct pushing us out into the unknown—would be a much-diminished form of existence. What is new is also what is exciting, compelling, and provocative, assuming that the rate at which it is introduced does not intolerably undermine and destabilize our state of being.

Like *12 Rules for Life*, the current volume provides an explication of rules drawn from a longer list of 42, originally published and popularized on the Q and A website Quora. Unlike my previous book, *Beyond Order* explores as its overarching theme how the dangers of too much security and control might be profitably avoided. Because what we understand is insufficient (as we discover when things we are striving to control nonetheless go wrong around us), we need to keep one foot within order while stretching the other tentatively into the beyond. And so we are driven to explore and find the deepest of meanings in standing on the frontier, secure enough to keep our fear under control but learning, constantly learning, as we face what we have not yet made peace with or adapted to. It is this instinct of meaning—something far deeper than mere thought—that orients us properly in life, so that we do not become overwhelmed by what is beyond us, or equally dangerously, stultified and stunted by dated, too narrow, or too pridefully paraded systems of value and belief.

What have I written about, more specifically? Rule I describes the relationship between stable, predictable social structures and individual psychological health, and makes the case that such structures need to be updated by creative people if they are to retain their vitality. Rule II analyzes a centuries-old alchemical image, relying on several stories—ancient and modern—to illuminate the nature and development of the integrated human personality. Rule III warns of the dangers of avoiding the information (vital to the continual rejuvenation of the psyche) signaled by the emergence of negative emotions such as pain, anxiety, and fear.

Rule IV argues that the meaning that sustains people through difficult times is to be found not so much in happiness, which is fleeting, but in in the voluntary adoption of mature responsibility for the self and others. Rule V uses a single example, drawn from my experience as a clinical psychologist, to illustrate the personal and social necessity of attending to the dictates of conscience. Rule VI describes the danger of attributing the cause of complex individual and social problems to single variables such as sex, class, or power.

Rule VII outlines the crucial relationship between disciplined striving in a single direction and forging of the individual character capable of resilience in the face of adversity. Rule VIII focuses on the vital importance of aesthetic experience as a guide to what is true, good, and sustaining in the human world of experience. Rule IX makes the case that past experiences, whose current recall remains laden with pain and fear, can be stripped of their horror by voluntary verbal exploration and reconsideration.

Rule X notes the importance of explicit negotiation to maintenance of the good will, mutual regard, and heartfelt cooperation without which no true romance can be sustained. Rule XI opens by describing the world of human experience in a manner that explains what motivates three common but direly dangerous patterns of psychological response, delineates the catastrophic consequences of falling prey to any or all of them, and lays out an alternative route. Rule XII makes the case that thankfulness in the face of the inevitable tragedies of life should be regarded as a primary manifestation of the admirable moral courage required to continue our difficult march uphill.*

I hope that I am somewhat wiser in my explication of this second set of 12 rules than I was four years ago, when I wrote about the first dozen—not least because of the informative feedback I received in the course of my efforts to formulate my ideas for audiences around the world, in person, on YouTube, and through my podcast and blog.† I

---

*It may be of some interest to note that this book and its predecessor—although each stands on its own—were also designed jointly to represent the balance they both strive to describe. It is for this reason that (in the English-language versions, at least) the first is bound in white and the second in black. They constitute a matched set, like the Taoist yin and yang.

†My YouTube channel can be found at www.youtube.com/user/JordanPetersonVideos. My podcast and blog can be accessed at jordanbpeterson.com.

hope, in consequence, that I have managed to clarify some of the issues that were perhaps left less than optimally developed in my previous work, as well as presenting much that is original. Finally, I hope that people find this book as helpful personally as they seem to have found the first set of 12 Rules. It has been a source of immense gratification that so many people have reported drawing strength from the thoughts and the stories I have had the privilege of bringing forth and sharing.

THE FOOL.

# DO NOT CARELESSLY DENIGRATE SOCIAL INSTITUTIONS OR CREATIVE ACHIEVEMENT

## LONELINESS AND CONFUSION

For years, I saw a client who lived by himself.* He was isolated in many other ways in addition to his living situation. He had extremely limited family ties. Both of his daughters had moved out of the country, and did not maintain much contact, and he had no other relatives except a father and sister from whom he was estranged. His wife and the mother of his children had passed away years ago, and the sole relationship he endeavored to establish while he saw me over the course of more than a decade and a half terminated tragically when his new partner was killed in an automobile accident.

When we began to work together, our conversations were decidedly awkward. He was not accustomed to the subtleties of social interaction,

---

*I have modified the accounts drawn from my clinical practice enough to ensure the continuing privacy of my clients while endeavoring to maintain the essential narrative truth of what I am relating.

so his behaviors, verbal and nonverbal, lacked the dance-like rhythm and harmony that characterize the socially fluent. As a child, he had been thoroughly ignored as well as actively discouraged by both parents. His father—mostly absent—was neglectful and sadistic in his inclinations, while his mother was chronically alcoholic. He had also been consistently tormented and harassed at school, and had not chanced upon a teacher in all his years of education who paid him any genuine attention. These experiences left my client with a proclivity toward depression, or at least worsened what might have been a biological tendency in that direction. He was, in consequence, abrupt, irritable, and somewhat volatile if he felt misunderstood or was unexpectedly interrupted during a conversation. Such reactions helped ensure that his targeting by bullies continued into his adult life, particularly in his place of work.

I soon noticed, however, that things worked out quite well during our sessions if I kept mostly quiet. He would drop in, weekly or biweekly, and talk about what had befallen and preoccupied him during the previous seven to fourteen days. If I maintained silence for the first fifty minutes of our one-hour sessions, listening intently, then we could converse, in a relatively normal, reciprocal manner, for the remaining ten minutes. This pattern continued for more than a decade, as I learned, increasingly, to hold my tongue (something that does not come easily to me). As the years passed, however, I noticed that the proportion of time he spent discussing negative issues with me decreased. Our conversation—his monologue, really—had always started with what was bothering him, and rarely progressed past that. But he worked hard outside our sessions, cultivating friends, attending artistic gatherings and music festivals, and resurrecting a long-dormant talent for composing songs and playing the guitar. As he became more social, he began to generate solutions to the problems he communicated to me, and to discuss, in the latter portion of the hours we shared, some of the more positive aspects of his existence. It was slow going, but he made continual incremental progress. When he first came to see me, we could not sit together at a table in a coffee shop—or, indeed, in any public space—and practice anything resembling a real-world conversation without his being paralyzed into absolute silence. By the time we finished, he was reading his original poetry in front of small groups, and had even tried his hand at stand-up comedy.

He was the best personal and practical exemplar of something I had come to realize over my more than twenty years of psychological practice: people depend on constant communication with others to keep their minds organized. We all need to think to keep things straight, but we mostly think by talking. We need to talk about the past, so we can distinguish the trivial, overblown concerns that otherwise plague our thoughts from the experiences that are truly important. We need to talk about the nature of the present and our plans for the future, so we know where we are, where we are going, and why we are going there. We must submit the strategies and tactics we formulate to the judgments of others, to ensure their efficiency and resilience. We need to listen to ourselves as we talk, as well, so that we may organize our otherwise inchoate bodily reactions, motivations, and emotions into something articulate and organized, and dispense with those concerns that are exaggerated and irrational. We need to talk—both to remember and to forget.

My client desperately needed someone to listen to him. He also needed to be fully part of additional, larger, and more complex social groups—something he planned in our sessions together, and then carried out on his own. Had he fallen prey to the temptation to denigrate the value of interpersonal interactions and relationships because of his history of isolation and harsh treatment, he would have had very little chance of regaining his health and well-being. Instead, he learned the ropes and joined the world.

## SANITY AS A SOCIAL INSTITUTION

For Drs. Sigmund Freud and Carl Jung, the great depth psychologists, sanity was a characteristic of the individual mind. People were well-adjusted, in their views, when the subpersonalities existing within each of them were properly integrated and balanced in expression. The id, the instinctive part of the psyche (from the German "it," representing nature, in all its power and foreignness, inside us); the superego (the sometimes oppressive, internalized representative of social order); and the ego (the I, the personality proper, crushed between those two necessary tyrants)—all had their specialized functions for Freud, who first conceptualized their existence. Id, ego, and superego interacted with each other like the executive, legislative, and judicial branches of a modern government. Jung, although profoundly influenced by Freud, parsed the complexity of the psyche in a different manner. For him, the ego of the individual had to find its proper place in relationship to the shadow (the dark side of the personality), the anima or animus (the contrasexual and thus often repressed side of the personality), and the self (the internal being of ideal possibility). But all these different subentities, Jungian and Freudian alike, share one thing in common: they exist in the interior of the person, regardless of his or her surroundings. People are social beings, however—par excellence—and there is no shortage of wisdom and guidance outside of us, embedded in the social world. Why rely on our own limited resources to remember the road, or to orient ourselves in new territory, when we can rely on signs and guideposts placed there so effortfully by others? Freud and Jung, with their intense focus on the autonomous individual psyche, placed too little focus on the role of the community in the maintenance of personal mental health.

It is for such reasons that I assess the position of all my new clinical clients along a few dimensions largely dependent on the social world when I first start working with them: Have they been educated to the level of their intellectual ability or ambition? Is their use of free time engaging, meaningful, and productive? Have they formulated solid and well-articulated plans for the future? Are they (and those they are close to) free of any serious physical health or economic problems? Do they have friends and a social life? A stable and satisfying intimate partnership? Close and functional familial relationships? A career—or, at least, a job—that is financially sufficient, stable and, if possible, a source of satisfaction and opportunity? If the answer to any three or more of these questions is no, I consider that my new client is insufficiently embedded in the interpersonal world and is in danger of spiraling downward psychologically because of that. People exist among other people and not as purely individual minds. An individual does not have to be that well put together if he or she can remain at least minimally acceptable in behavior to others. Simply put: We outsource the problem of sanity. People remain mentally healthy not merely because of the integrity of their own minds, but because they are constantly being reminded how to think, act, and speak by those around them.

If you begin to deviate from the straight and narrow path—if you begin to act improperly—people will react to your errors before they become too great, and cajole, laugh, tap, and criticize you back into place. They will raise an eyebrow, or smile (or not), or pay attention (or not). If other people can tolerate having you around, in other words, they will constantly remind you not to misbehave, and just as constantly call on you to be at your best. All that is left for you to do is watch, listen, and respond appropriately to the cues. Then you might remain motivated, and able to stay together enough so that you will not begin the long journey downhill. This is reason enough to appreciate your immersion in the world of other people—friends, family members, and foes alike—despite the anxiety and frustration that social interactions so often produce.

But how did we develop the broad consensus regarding social behavior that serves to buttress our psychological stability? It seems a daunting task—if not impossible—in the face of the complexity that constantly confronts us. "Do we pursue this or that?" "How does the worth of this piece of work compare to the worth of that?" "Who is more competent, or more creative, or more assertive, and should therefore be ceded authority?" Answers to such questions are largely formulated in consequence of intensive negotiation—verbal and nonverbal—regulating individual action, cooperation, and competition. What we deem to be valuable and worthy of attention becomes part of the social contract; part of the rewards and punishments meted out respectively for compliance and noncompliance; part of what continually indicates and reminds: "Here is what is valued. Look at that (perceive that) and not something else. Pursue that (act toward that end) and not some other." Compliance with those indications and reminders is, in large measure, sanity itself— and is something required from every one of us right from the early stages of our lives. Without the intermediation of the social world, it would be impossible for us to organize our minds, and we would simply be overwhelmed by the world.

## THE POINT OF POINTING

I have the great good fortune of a granddaughter, Elizabeth Scarlett Peterson Korikova, born in August 2017. I have watched her carefully while she develops, trying to understand what she is up to and playing along with it. When she was about a year and a half old, she engaged in all manner of unbearably endearing behaviors—giggling and laughing when she was poked, high-fiving, bumping heads, and rubbing noses. However, in my opinion, the most noteworthy of all the actions she undertook at that age was her pointing.

She had discovered her index finger, using it to specify all the objects in the world she found interesting. She delighted in doing so, particularly when her pointing called forth the attention of the adults surrounding her. This indicated, in a manner not duplicable in any other way, that her action and intention had *import*—definable at least in part as the tendency of a behavior or attitude to compel the attention of others. She thrived on that, and no wonder. We compete for attention, personally, socially, and economically. No currency has a value that exceeds it. Children, adults, and societies wither on the vine in its absence. To have others attend to what you find important or interesting is to validate, first, the importance of what you are attending to, but second, and more crucially, to validate you as a respected center of conscious experience and contributor to the collective world. Pointing is, as well, a crucial precursor to the development of language. To name something—to use the word for the thing—is essentially to point to it, to specify it against everything else, to isolate it for use individually and socially.

When my granddaughter pointed, she did it publicly. When she pointed to something, she could immediately observe how the people close to her reacted. There is just not that much point, so to speak, in pointing to something that no one else cares about. So, she aimed her index finger at something she found interesting and then looked around to see if anyone else cared. She was learning an important lesson at an early age: If you are not communicating about anything that engages other people, then the value of your communication—even the value of your very presence—risks falling to zero. It was in this manner that she began to more profoundly explore the complex hierarchy of value that made up her family and the broader society surrounding her.

Scarlett is now learning to talk—a more sophisticated form of pointing (and of exploration). Every word is a pointer, as well as a simplification or generalization. To name something is not only to make it shine forth against the infinite background of potentially nameable things, but to group or categorize it, simultaneously, with many other phenomena of its broad utility or significance. We use the word "floor," for example, but do not generally employ a separate word for all the floors we might encounter (concrete, wood, earth, glass), much less all the endless variations of color and texture and shade that make up the details of the floors that bear our weight. We use a low-resolution representation: If it holds us up, we can walk on it, and is situated inside a building, then it is a "floor," and that is precise enough. The word distinguishes floors, say, from walls, but also restricts the variability in all the floors that exist to a single concept—flat, stable, walkable indoor surfaces.

The words we employ are tools that structure our experience, subjectively and privately—but are, equally, socially determined. We would not all know and use the word "floor" unless we had all agreed that there was something sufficiently important about floors to justify a word for them. So, the mere fact of naming something (and, of course, agreeing on the name) is an important part of the process whereby the infinitely complex world of phenomena and fact is reduced to the functional world of value. And it is continual interaction with social institutions that makes this reduction—this specification—possible.

## WHAT SHOULD WE POINT TO?

The social world narrows and specifies the world for us, marking out what is important. But what does "important" mean? How is it determined? The individual is molded by the social world. But social institutions are molded, too, by the requirements of the individuals who compose them. Arrangements must be made for our provisioning with the basic requirements of life. We cannot live without food, water, clean air, and shelter. Less self-evidently, we require companionship, play, touch, and intimacy. These are all biological as well as psychological necessities (and this is by no means a comprehensive list). We must signify and then utilize those elements of the world capable of providing us with these requirements. And the fact that we are deeply social adds another set of constraints to the situation: We must perceive and act in a manner that meets our biological and psychological needs—but, since none of us lives or can live in isolation, we must meet them in a manner approved of by others. This means that the solutions we apply to our fundamental biological problems must also be acceptable and implementable socially.

It is worth considering more deeply just how necessity limits the universe of viable solutions and implementable plans. First, as we alluded to, the plan must in principle solve some real problem. Second, it must appeal to others—often in the face of competing plans—or those others will not cooperate and might well object. If I value something, therefore, I must determine how to value it so that others potentially benefit. It cannot just be good for me: it must be good for me and for the people around me. And even that is not good enough—which means there are even more constraints on how the world must be perceived and acted upon. The manner in which I view and value the world, integrally associated with the plans I am making, has to work for me, my family, and the broader community. Furthermore, it needs to work today, in a manner that does not make a worse hash of tomorrow, next week, next month, and next year (even the next decade or century). A good solution to a problem involving suffering must be repeatable, without deterioration across repetitions—iterable, in a word—across people and across time.

These universal constraints, manifest biologically and imposed socially, reduce the complexity of the world to something approximating a universally understandable domain of value. That is exceptionally important, because there are unlimited problems and there are hypothetically unlimited potential solutions, but there are a comparatively limited number of solutions that work practically, psychologically, and socially simultaneously. The fact of limited solutions implies the existence of something like a natural ethic—variable, perhaps, as human languages are variable, but still characterized by something solid and universally recognizable at its base. It is the reality of this natural ethic that makes thoughtless denigration of social institutions both wrong and dangerous: wrong and dangerous because those institutions have evolved to solve problems that must be solved for life to continue. They are by no means perfect—but making them better, rather than worse, is a tricky problem indeed.

So, I must take the complexity of the world, reduce it to a single point so that I can act, and take everyone else and their future selves into consideration while I am doing so. How do I manage this? By communicating and negotiating. By outsourcing the terribly complex cognitive problem to the resources of the broader world. The individuals who compose every society cooperate and compete linguistically (although linguistic interaction by no means exhausts the means of cooperation and competition). Words are formulated collectively, and everyone must agree on their use. The verbal framework that helps us delimit the world is a consequence of the landscape of value that is constructed socially—but also bounded by the brute necessity of reality itself. This helps give that landscape shape, and not just any old shape. This is where hierarchies—functional, productive hierarchies—more clearly enter the picture.

Things of import must be done, or people starve or die of thirst or exposure—or of loneliness and absence of touch. What needs to be done must be specified and planned. The requisite skills for doing so must be developed. That specification, planning, and development of skills, as well as the implementation of the informed plan, must be conducted in social space, with the cooperation of others (and in the face of their competition). In consequence, some will be better at solving the problem at hand, and others worse. This variance in ability (as well as the multiplicity of extant problems and the impossibility of training everyone in all skilled domains) necessarily engenders a hierarchical structure—based ideally on genuine competence in relation to the goal. Such a hierarchy is in its essence a socially structured tool that must be employed for the effective accomplishment of necessary and worthwhile tasks. It is also a social institution that makes progress and peace possible at the same time.

## BOTTOM UP

The consensus making up the spoken and unspoken assumptions of worth characterizing our societies has an ancient origin, developing over the course of hundreds of millions of years. After all, "How should you act?" is just the short-term, immediate version of the fundamental long-term question, "How should you survive?" It is therefore instructive to look into the distant past—far down the evolutionary chain, right to the basics—and contemplate the establishment of what is important. The most phylogenetically ancient multicellular organisms (that is far enough for our purposes) tend to be composed of relatively undifferentiated sensorimotor cells.[1] These cells map certain facts or features of the environment directly onto the motor output of the same cells, in an essentially one-to-one relationship. Stimulus A means response A, and nothing else, while stimulus B means response B. Among more differentiated and complex creatures—the larger and commonly recognizable denizens of the natural world—the sensory and motor functions separate and specialize, such that cells undertaking the former functions detect patterns in the world and cells in the latter produce patterns of motor output. This differentiation enables a broader range of patterns to be recognized and mapped, as well as a broader range of action and reaction to be undertaken. A third type of cell—neural—emerges sometimes, as well, serving as a computational intermediary between the first two. Among species that have established a neural level of operation, the "same" pattern of input can produce a different pattern of output (depending, for example, on changes in the animal's environment or internal psychophysical condition).

As nervous systems increase in sophistication, and more and more layers of neural intermediation emerge, the relationship between simple fact and motor output becomes increasingly complex, unpredictable, and sophisticated. What is putatively the same thing or situation can be perceived in multiple ways, and two things perceived in the same manner can still give rise to very different behaviors. It is very difficult to constrain even isolated laboratory animals, for example, so thoroughly that they will behave predictably across trials that have been made as similar as possible. As the layers of neural tissue mediating between sensation and action multiply, they also differentiate. Basic motivational systems, often known as drives, appear (hunger, thirst, aggression, etc.), adding additional sensory and behavioral specificity and variability. Superseding motivations, in turn—with no clear line of demarcation—are systems of emotion. Cognitive systems emerge much later, first taking form, arguably, as imagination, and later—and only among human beings—as full-fledged language. Thus, in the most complex of creatures, there is an internal hierarchy of structure, from reflex through drive to language-mediated action (in the particular case of human beings), that must be organized before it can function as a unity and be aimed at a point.[2]

How is this hierarchy organized—a structure that emerged in large part from the bottom up, over the vast spans of evolutionary time? We return to the same answer alluded to earlier: through the constant cooperation and competition—the constant jockeying for resources and position—defining the struggle for survival and reproduction. This happens over the unimaginably lengthy spans of time that characterize evolution, as well as the much shorter course of each individual life. Negotiation for position sorts organisms into the omnipresent hierarchies that govern access to vital resources such as shelter, nourishment, and mates. All creatures of reasonable complexity and even a minimally social nature have their particular place, and know it. All social creatures also learn what is deemed valuable by other group members, and derive from that, as well as from the understanding of their own position, a sophisticated implicit and explicit understanding of value itself. In a phrase: The internal hierarchy that translates facts into actions mirrors the external hierarchy of social organization. It is clear, for example, that chimpanzees in a troop understand their social world and its hierarchical strata at a fine level of detail. They know what is important, and who has privileged access to it. They understand such things as if their survival and reproduction depend upon it, as it does.[3]

A newborn infant is equipped with relatively deterministic re-
flexes: sucking, crying, startling. These nonetheless provide the starting point for the immense range of skills in action that develop with
human maturation. By the age of two (and often much earlier than
that, for many skills), children can orient with all their senses, walk
upright, use their opposable-thumb-equipped hands for all sorts of
purposes, and communicate their desires and needs both nonverbally
and verbally—and this is of course a partial list. This immense array
of behavioral abilities is integrated into a complex assortment of emotions and motivational drives (anger, sadness, fear, joy, surprise, and
more) and then organized to fulfill whatever specific, narrow purpose
inspires the child for the moment and, increasingly, over longer spans
of time.

The developing infant must also hone and perfect the operation of
his or her currently dominant motivational state in harmony with all
his or her other internal motivational states (as, for example, the separate desire to eat, sleep, and play must learn to coexist so each can manifest itself optimally), and in keeping with the demands, routines, and
opportunities of the social environment. This honing and perfecting
begin within the child's maternal relationship and the spontaneous
play behavior within that circumscribed but still social context. Then,
when the child has matured to the point where the internal hierarchy
of emotional and motivational functions can be subsumed, even temporarily, within a framework provided by a conscious, communicable
abstract goal ("let us play house"), the child is ready to play with
others—and to do so, over time, in an increasingly complex and sophisticated manner.[4]

Play with others depends (as the great developmental psychologist
Jean Piaget observed[5]) upon the collective establishment of a shared
goal with the child's play partners. The collective establishment of a

shared goal—the point of the game—conjoined with rules governing cooperation and competition in relationship to that goal or point, constitutes a true social microcosm. All societies might be regarded as variations upon this play/game theme—*E pluribus unum**—and in all functional and decent societies the basic rules of fair play, predicated upon reciprocity across situation and time, come inevitably to apply. Games, like solutions to problems, must be iterable to endure, and there are principles that apply to and undergird what constitutes that iterability. Piaget suspected, for example, that games undertaken voluntarily will outcompete games imposed and played under threat of force, given that some of the energy that could be expended on the game itself, whatever its nature, has to be wasted on enforcement. There is evidence indicating the emergence of such voluntary game-like arrangements even among our nonhuman kin.[6]

The universal rules of fair play include the ability to regulate emotion and motivation while cooperating and competing in pursuit of the goal during the game (that is part and parcel of being able to play at all), as well as the ability and will to establish reciprocally beneficial interactions across time and situation, as we already discussed. And life is not simply a game, but a series of games, each of which has something in common (whatever defines a game) and something unique (or there would be no reason for multiple games). At minimum, there is a starting point (kindergarten, a 0–0 score, a first date, an entry-level job) that needs to be improved upon; a procedure for enacting that improvement; and a desirable goal (graduation from high school, a winning score, a permanent romantic relationship, a prestigious career). Because of that commonality, there is an ethic—or more properly, a meta-ethic—that emerges, from the bottom up, across the set of

---

*"Out of many, one."

all games. The best player is therefore not the winner of any given game but, among many other things, he or she who is invited by the largest number of others to play the most extensive series of games. It is for this reason, which you may not understand explicitly at the time, that you tell your children: "It's not whether you win or lose. It's how you play the game!"* How should you play, to be that most desirable of

---

*Even rats understand this. Jaak Panksepp, one of the founders of the psychological sub-field called affective neuroscience and an extremely creative, courageous, and gifted researcher, spent many years analyzing the role of play in the development and socialization of rats (see J. Panksepp, *Affective Neuroscience: The Foundations of Human and Animal Emotions* [New York: Oxford University Press, 1998], particularly the chapter on play, 280–99). Rats like to play. They particularly enjoy rough-and-tumble play, particularly if they are male juvenile rats. They enjoy it so much that they will voluntarily work—pulling a lever repeatedly, say—to gain the opportunity to enter an arena where another juvenile waits to play. When two juvenile strangers meet for the first time in this situation, they size each other up and then establish dominance. If one rat is only 10 percent larger than the other, he can pretty much win every physical contest, every rat wrestling match—but they still wrestle to find out, and the larger rat almost inevitably pins the smaller. If you were inclined to view the establishment of hierarchy as equivalent to dominance by power, that would be game over. The larger, more powerful rat won. End of story. But that is by no means the end of the story, unless the rats meet only once. Rats live in social environments, and they interact with the same individuals over and over. Thus, the game, once started, continues—and the rules have to govern not so much the single game as the repeating one. Once dominance is established, the rats can play—something they do in a manner very different from genuine fighting (just like play fighting with a pet dog is very different from being attacked by a dog). Now, the larger rat could pin the smaller rat every time. However, that breaks the rules (really, the meta-rules: those that are observable only over the course of repeated games). The purpose of the repeated game is not dominance, but continuing play. This is not to say that the initial dominance is without significance. It matters, not least in the following manner: When the two rats meet a second time, they will both adopt a unique role. The smaller rat is now duty bound to invite his larger friend to play, and the larger rat is duty bound to accept the invitation. The former will jump around playfully, to indicate his intent. The larger rat might hang back and act cool and a bit dismissive (as is now his prerogative); but if he's a decent sort he will join in the fun, as in his heart of hearts he truly wants to play. However—and this is the critical issue—if the larger rat does not let the smaller rat win the repeated wrestling matches some substantial proportion of the time (Panksepp estimated 30 to 40 percent of the time), the smaller rat will stop exhibiting invitations to play. It is just not any fun for the little guy. Thus, if the larger rat dominates with power (like a bully), as he could, then he will lose at the highest level (the level

players? What structure must take form within you so that such play is possible? And those two questions are interrelated, because the structure that will enable you to play properly (and with increasing and automated or habitual precision) will emerge only in the process of continually practicing the art of playing properly. Where might you learn how to play? Everywhere . . . if you are fortunate and awake.

## THE UTILITY OF THE FOOL

It is useful to take your place at the bottom of a hierarchy. It can aid in the development of gratitude and humility. *Gratitude:* There are people whose expertise exceeds your own, and you should be wisely pleased about that. There are many valuable niches to fill, given the many complex and serious problems we must solve. The fact that there are people who fill those niches with trustworthy skill and experience is something for which to be truly thankful. *Humility:* It is better to presume ignorance and invite learning than to assume sufficient knowledge and risk the consequent blindness. It is much better to make friends with what you do not know than with what you do know, as there is an infinite supply of the former but a finite stock of the latter. When you are tightly boxed in or cornered—all too often by your own

---

where the fun continues for the longest possible time), even while he "wins" more frequently at the lower. What does this imply? Most important, that power is simply not a stable basis upon which to construct a hierarchy designed to optimally govern repeated interactions. And this is not just true for rats. Alpha males among at least certain primate groups are far more prosocial than their lesser comrades. Power doesn't work for them, either (see F. B. M. de Waal and M. Suchak, "Prosocial Primates: Selfish and Unselfish Motivations," *Philosophical Transactions of the Royal Society of London: Biological Science* 365 [2010]: 2711–22. See also F. de Waal, *The Surprising Science of Alpha Males*, TEDMED 2017, bit.ly/primate_ethic).

stubborn and fixed adherence to some unconsciously worshipped assumptions—all there is to help you is what you have not yet learned.

It is necessary and helpful to be, and in some ways to remain, a beginner. For this reason, the Tarot deck beloved by intuitives, romantics, fortune-tellers, and scoundrels alike contains within it the Fool as a positive card, an illustrated variant of which opens this chapter. The Fool is a young, handsome man, eyes lifted upward, journeying in the mountains, sun shining brightly upon him—about to carelessly step over a cliff (or is he?). His strength, however, is precisely his willingness to risk such a drop; to risk being once again at the bottom. No one unwilling to be a foolish beginner can learn. It was for this reason, among others, that Carl Jung regarded the Fool as the archetypal precursor to the figure of the equally archetypal Redeemer, the perfected individual.

The beginner, the fool, is continually required to be patient and tolerant—with himself and, equally, with others. His displays of ignorance, inexperience, and lack of skill may still sometimes be rightly attributed to irresponsibility and condemned, justly, by others. But the insufficiency of the fool is often better regarded as an inevitable consequence of each individual's essential vulnerability, rather than as a true moral failing. Much that is great starts small, ignorant, and useless. This lesson permeates popular as well as classical or traditional culture. Consider, for example, the Disney heroes Pinocchio and Simba, as well as J. K. Rowling's magical Harry Potter. Pinocchio begins as a wooden-headed marionette, the puppet of everyone's decisions but his own. The Lion King has his origin as a naive cub, the unwitting pawn of a treacherous and malevolent uncle. The student of wizarding is an unloved orphan, with a dusty cupboard for a bedroom, and Voldemort—who might as well be Satan himself—for his archenemy.

Great mythologized heroes often come into the world, likewise, in the most meager of circumstances (as the child of an Israelite slave, for example, or newborn in a lowly manger) and in great danger (consider the Pharaoh's decision to slay all the firstborn male babies of the Israelites, and Herod's comparable edict, much later). But today's beginner is tomorrow's master. Thus, it is necessary even for the most accomplished (but who wishes to accomplish still more) to retain identification with the as yet unsuccessful; to appreciate the striving toward competence; to carefully and with true humility subordinate him or herself to the current game; and to develop the knowledge, self-control, and discipline necessary to make the next move.

I visited a restaurant in Toronto with my wife, son, and daughter while writing this. As I made my way to my party's table, a young waiter asked if he might say a few words to me. He told me that he had been watching my videos, listening to my podcasts, and reading my book, and that he had, in consequence, changed his attitude toward his comparatively lower-status (but still useful and necessary) job. He had ceased criticizing what he was doing or himself for doing it, deciding instead to be grateful and seek out whatever opportunities presented themselves right there before him. He made up his mind to become more diligent and reliable and to see what would happen if he worked as hard at it as he could. He told me, with an uncontrived smile, that he had been promoted three times in six months.

The young man had come to realize that every place he might find himself in had more potential than he might first see (particularly when his vision was impaired by the resentment and cynicism he felt from being near the bottom). After all, it is not as if a restaurant is a simple place—and this was part of an extensive national organization, a large, high-quality chain. To do a good job in such a place, servers must get along with the cooks, who are by universal recognition a formidably troublesome and tricky lot. They must also be polite and engaging with customers. They have to pay attention constantly. They must adjust to highly varying workloads—the rushes and dead times that inevitably accompany the life of a server. They have to show up on time, sober and awake. They must treat their superiors with the proper respect and do the same for those—such as the dishwashers—below them in the structure of authority. And if they do all these things, and happen to be working in a functional institution, they will soon render themselves difficult to replace. Customers, colleagues, and superiors alike will begin to react to them in an increasingly positive manner. Doors that would otherwise remain closed to them—even invisible—will be opened. Furthermore, the skills they acquire will prove eminently portable, whether they continue to rise in the hierarchy of restaurateurs, decide instead to further their education, or change their career trajectory completely (in which case they will leave with laudatory praise from their previous employers and vastly increased chances of discovering the next opportunity).

As might be expected, the young man who had something to say to me was thrilled with what had happened to him. His status concerns had been solidly and realistically addressed by his rapid career advance, and the additional money he was making did not hurt, either. He had accepted, and therefore transcended, his role as a beginner. He had ceased being casually cynical about the place he occupied in the world and the people who surrounded him, and accepted the structure and the position he was offered. He started to see possibility and opportunity, where before he was blinded, essentially, by his pride. He stopped denigrating the social institution he found himself part of and began to play his part properly. And that increment in humility paid off in spades.

## THE NECESSITY OF EQUALS

It is good to be a beginner, but it is a good of a different sort to be an equal among equals. It is said, with much truth, that genuine communication can take place only between peers. This is because it is very difficult to move information up a hierarchy. Those well positioned (and this is a great danger of moving up) have used their current competence—their cherished opinions, their present knowledge, their current skills—to stake a moral claim to their status. In consequence, they have little motivation to admit to error, to learn or change—and plenty of reason not to. If a subordinate exposes the ignorance of someone with greater status, he risks humiliating that person, questioning the validity of the latter's claim to influence and status, and revealing him as incompetent, outdated, or false. For this reason, it is very wise to approach your boss, for example, carefully and privately with a problem (and perhaps best to have a solution at hand—and not one proffered too incautiously).

Barriers exist to the flow of genuine information *down* a hierarchy, as well. For example, the resentment people lower in the chain of command might feel about their hypothetically lesser position can make them loath to act productively on information from above—or, in the worst case, can motivate them to work at counterpurposes to what they have learned, out of sheer spite. In addition, those who are inexperienced or less educated, or who newly occupy a subordinate position and therefore lack knowledge of their surroundings, can be more easily influenced by relative position and the exercise of power, instead of quality of argumentation and observation of competence. Peers, by contrast, must in the main be convinced. Their attention must be carefully reciprocated. To be surrounded by peers is to exist in a state of equality, and to manifest the give-and-take necessary to maintain that equality. It is therefore good to be in the middle of a hierarchy.

This is partly why friendships are so important, and why they form so early in life. A two-year-old, typically, is self-concerned, although also capable of simple reciprocal actions. The same Scarlett whom I talked about earlier—my granddaughter—would happily hand me one of her favorite stuffed toys, attached to a pacifier, when I asked her to. Then I would hand it, or toss it, back (sometimes she would toss it to me, too—or at least relatively near me). She loved this game. We played it with a spoon, as well—an implement she was just beginning to master. She played the same way with her mother and her grandmother— with anyone who happened to be within playing distance, if she was familiar enough with them not to be shy. This was the beginning of the behaviors that transform themselves into full-fledged sharing among older children.

My daughter, Mikhaila, Scarlett's mother, took her child to the outdoor recreational space on top of their downtown condo a few days before I wrote this. A number of other children were playing there, most of them older, and there were plenty of toys. Scarlett spent her time hoarding as many of the playthings as possible near her mother's chair, and was distinctly unimpressed if other children came along to purloin one for themselves. She even took a ball directly from another child to add to her collection. This is typical behavior for children two and younger. Their ability to reciprocate, while hardly absent (and able to manifest itself in truly endearing ways), is developmentally limited.

By three years of age, however, most children are capable of truly sharing. They can delay gratification long enough to take their turn while playing a game that everyone cannot play simultaneously. They can begin to understand the point of a game played by several people and follow the rules, although they may not be able to give a coherent verbal account of what those rules are. They start to form friendships upon repeated exposure to children with whom they have successfully negotiated reciprocal play relationships. Some of these friendships turn into the first intense relationships that children have outside their family. It is in the context of such relationships, which tend strongly to form between equals in age (or at least equals in developmental stage), that a child learns to bond tightly to a peer and starts to learn how to treat another person properly while requiring the same in return.

This mutual bonding is vitally important. A child without at least one special, close friend is much more likely to suffer later psychological problems, whether of the depressive/anxious or antisocial sort,[7] while children with fewer friends are also more likely to be unemployed and unmarried as adults.[8] There is no evidence that the importance of friendship declines in any manner with age.* All causes of mortality appear to be reduced among adults with high-quality social networks, even when general health status is taken into consideration. This remains true among the elderly in the case of diseases such as hypertension, diabetes, emphysema, and arthritis, and for younger and older adults alike in the case of heart attacks. Interestingly enough, there is some evidence that it is the provision of social support, as much or more than its receipt, that provides these protective benefits (and, somewhat unsurprisingly, that those who give more tend to receive more).[9] Thus, it truly seems that it is better to give than to receive.

Peers distribute both the burdens and joys of life. Recently, when my wife, Tammy, and I suffered serious health problems, we were fortunate enough to have family members (my in-laws, sister and brother;

---

*This makes the July 30, 2019, poll from YouGov, "Millennials Are the Loneliest Generation" (bit.ly/2TVVMLn), indicating that 25 percent have no acquaintances and 22 percent no friends, particularly ominous, if true.

my own mother and sister; our children) and close friends stay with us and help for substantial periods of time. They were willing to put their own lives on hold to aid us while we were in crisis. Before that, when my book *12 Rules for Life* became a success, and during the extensive speaking tour that followed, Tammy and I were close to people with whom we could share our good fortune. These were friends and family members genuinely pleased with what was happening and following the events of our lives avidly, and who were willing to discuss what could have been the overwhelming public response. This greatly heightened the significance and meaning of everything we were doing and reduced the isolation that such a dramatic shift in life circumstances, for better or worse, is likely to produce.

The relationships established with colleagues of similar status at work constitute another important source of peer regulation, in addition to friendship. To maintain good relationships with your colleagues means, among other things, to give credit where credit is due; to take your fair share of the jobs no one wants but still must be done; to deliver on time and in a high-quality manner when teamed with other people; to show up when expected; and, in general, to be trusted to do somewhat more than your job formally requires. The approval or disapproval of your colleagues rewards and enforces this continual reciprocity, and that—like the reciprocity that is necessarily part of friendship—helps maintain stable psychological function. It is much better to be someone who can be relied upon, not least so that during times of personal trouble the people you have worked beside are willing and able to step in and help.

Through friendship and collegial relationships we modify our selfish proclivities, learning not to always put ourselves first. Less obviously, but just as importantly, we may also learn to overcome our naive and too empathic proclivities (our tendency to sacrifice ourselves unsuitably and unjustly to predatory others) when our peers advise and encourage us to stand up for ourselves. In consequence, if we are fortunate, we begin to practice true reciprocity, and we gain at least some of the advantage spoken about so famously by the poet Robert Burns:

> O wad some Pow'r the giftie gie us
> To see oursels as ithers see us!
> It wad frae mony a blunder free us,
> An' foolish notion:
> What airs in dress an' gait wad lea'e us,
> An' ev'n devotion![10]

## TOP DOG

It is a good thing to be an authority. People are fragile. Because of that, life is difficult and suffering common. Ameliorating that suffering— ensuring that everyone has food, clean water, sanitary facilities, and a place to take shelter, for starters—takes initiative, effort, and ability. If there is a problem to be solved, and many people involve themselves in the solution, then a hierarchy must and will arise, as those who *can* do, and those who *cannot* follow as best they can, often learning to be competent in the process. If the problem is real, then the people who are best at solving the problem at hand should rise to the top. That is not power. It is the authority that properly accompanies ability.

Now, it is self-evidently appropriate to grant power to competent authorities, if they are solving necessary problems; and it is equally appropriate to be one of those competent authorities, if possible, when there is a perplexing problem at hand. This might be regarded as a philosophy of responsibility. A responsible person decides to make a problem his or her problem, and then works diligently—even ambitiously—for its solution, with other people, in the most efficient manner possible (efficient, because there are other problems to solve, and efficiency allows for the conservation of resources that might then be devoted importantly elsewhere).

Ambition is often—and often purposefully—misidentified with the desire for power, and damned with faint praise, and denigrated, and punished. And ambition is sometimes exactly that wish for undue influence on others. But there is a crucial difference between *sometimes* and *always*. Authority is not mere power, and it is extremely unhelpful, even dangerous, to confuse the two. When people exert power over others, they compel them, forcefully. They apply the threat of privation or punishment so their subordinates have little choice but to act in a manner contrary to their personal needs, desires, and values. When people wield authority, by contrast, they do so because of their competence—a competence that is spontaneously recognized and appreciated by others, and generally followed willingly, with a certain relief, and with the sense that justice is being served.

Those who are power hungry—tyrannical and cruel, even psychopathic—desire control over others so that every selfish whim of hedonism can be immediately gratified; so that envy can destroy its target; so that resentment can find its expression. But good people are ambitious (and diligent, honest, and focused along with it) instead because they are possessed by the desire to solve genuine, serious problems. That variant of ambition needs to be encouraged in every possible manner. It is for this reason, among many others, that the increasingly reflexive identification of the striving of boys and men for victory with the "patriarchal tyranny" that hypothetically characterizes our modern, productive, and comparatively free societies is so stunningly counterproductive (and, it must be said, cruel: there is almost nothing worse than treating someone striving for competence as a tyrant in training). "Victory," in one of its primary and most socially important aspects, is the overcoming of obstacles for the broader public good. Someone who is sophisticated as a winner wins in a manner that improves the game itself, for all the players. To adopt an attitude of naive or willfully blind cynicism about this, or to deny outright that it is true, is to position yourself—perhaps purposefully, as people have many dark motives—as an enemy of the practical amelioration of suffering itself. I can think of few more sadistic attitudes.

Now, power may accompany authority, and perhaps it must. However, and more important, *genuine authority constrains the arbitrary exercise of power.* This constraint manifests itself when the authoritative agent cares, and takes responsibility, for those over whom the exertion of power is possible. The oldest child can take accountability for his younger siblings, instead of domineering over and teasing and torturing them, and can learn in that manner how to exercise authority and limit the misuse of power. Even the youngest can exercise appropriate authority over the family dog. To adopt authority is to learn that power requires concern and competence—and that it comes at a genuine cost. Someone newly promoted to a management position soon learns that managers are frequently more stressed by their multiple subordinates than subordinates are stressed by their single manager. Such experience moderates what might otherwise become romantic but dangerous fantasies about the attractiveness of power, and helps quell the desire for its infinite extension. And, in the real world, those who occupy positions of authority in functional hierarchies are generally struck to the core by the responsibility they bear for the people they supervise, employ, and mentor.

Not everyone feels this burden, of course. A person who has become established as an authority can forget his origins and come to develop a counterproductive contempt for the person who is just starting out.

This is a mistake, not least because it means that the established person cannot risk doing something new (as it would mean adopting the role of despised fool). It is also because arrogance bars the path to learning. Shortsighted, willfully blind, and narrowly selfish tyrants certainly exist, but they are by no means in the majority, at least in functional societies. Otherwise nothing would work.

The authority who remembers his or her sojourn as voluntary beginner, by contrast, can retain their identification with the newcomer and the promise of potential, and use that memory as the source of personal information necessary to constrain the hunger for power. One of the things that has constantly amazed me is the delight that decent people take in the ability to provide opportunities to those over whom they currently exercise authority. I have experienced this repeatedly: personally, as a university professor and researcher (and observed many other people in my situation doing the same); and in the business and other professional settings I have become familiar with. There is great intrinsic pleasure in helping already competent and admirable young people become highly skilled, socially valuable, autonomous, responsible professionals. It is not unlike the pleasure taken in raising children, and it is one of the primary motivators of valid ambition. Thus, the position of top dog, when occupied properly, has as one of its fundamental attractions the opportunity to identify deserving individuals at or near the beginning of their professional life, and provide them with the means of productive advancement.

## SOCIAL INSTITUTIONS ARE NECESSARY— BUT INSUFFICIENT

Sanity is knowing the rules of the social game, internalizing them, and following them. Differences in status are therefore inevitable, as all worthwhile endeavors have a goal, and those who pursue them have different abilities in relationship to that goal. Accepting the fact of this disequilibrium and striving forward nonetheless—whether presently at the bottom, middle, or top—is an important element of mental health. But a paradox remains. The solutions of yesterday and today, upon which our current hierarchies depend, will not necessarily serve as solutions tomorrow. Thoughtless repetition of what sufficed in the past—or, worse, authoritarian insistence that all problems have been permanently solved—therefore means the introduction of great danger when changes in the broader world makes local change necessary. Respect for creative transformation must in consequence accompany appropriate regard for the problem-solving hierarchical structures bequeathed to us by the past. That is neither an arbitrary moral opinion nor a morally relative claim. It is something more akin to knowledge of twin natural laws built into the structure of our reality. Highly social creatures such as we are must abide by the rules, to remain sane and minimize unnecessary uncertainty, suffering, and strife. However, we must also transform those rules carefully, as circumstances change around us.

This implies, as well, that the ideal personality cannot remain an unquestioning reflection of the current social state. Under normal conditions, it may be nonetheless said that the *ability* to conform unquestioningly trumps the *inability* to conform. However, the *refusal* to conform when the social surround has become pathological—incomplete, archaic, willfully blind, or corrupt—is something of even higher value, as is the capacity to offer creative, valid alternatives. This leaves all of us with a permanent moral conundrum: When do we simply follow convention, doing what others request or demand; and when do we rely on our own individual judgment, with all its limitations and biases, and reject the requirements of the collective? In other words:

How do we establish a balance between reasonable conservatism and revitalizing creativity?

First and foremost on the psychological front is the issue of temperament. Some people are temperamentally predisposed to conservatism, and others to more liberal creative perception and action.[11] This does not mean that socialization has no ability to alter that predisposition; human beings are very plastic organisms, with a long period of preadult development, and the circumstances we find ourselves in can change us very drastically. That does not alter the fact, however, that there are relatively permanent niches in the human environment to which different modes of temperament have adapted to fill.

Those who tend toward the right, politically, are staunch defenders of all that has worked in the past. And much of the time, they are correct in being so, because of the limited number of pathways that produce personal success, social harmony, and long-term stability. But sometimes they are wrong: first, because the present and the future differ from the past; second, because even once-functional hierarchies typically (inevitably?) fall prey to internal machinations in a manner that produces their downfall. Those who rise to the top can do so through manipulation and the exercise of unjust power, acting in a manner that works only for them, at least in the short term; but that kind of ascendance undermines the proper function of the hierarchy they are nominally part of. Such people generally fail to understand or do not care what function the organization they have made their host was designed to fulfill. They extract what they can from the riches that lie before them and leave a trail of wreckage in their wake.

It is this corruption of power that is strongly objected to by those on the liberal/left side of the political spectrum, and rightly so. But it is critically important to distinguish between a hierarchy that is functional and productive (and the people who make it so) and the degenerate shell of a once-great institution. Making that distinction requires the capacity and the willingness to observe and differentiate, rather than mindless reliance on ideological proclivity. It requires knowing that there is a bright side to the social hierarchies we necessarily inhabit, as well as a dark (and the realization that concentrating on one to the exclusion of the other is dangerously biased). It also requires knowledge that on the more radical, creative side—the necessary source of revitalization for what has become immoral and outdated—there also lurks great danger. Part of the danger is that very tendency of those who think more liberally to see only the negative in well-founded institutions. The further danger stems from the counterpart to the corrupt but conservative processes that destabilize and destroy functional hierarchies: there are unethical radicals, just as there are crooked administrators, managers, and executives. These individuals tend to be profoundly ignorant of the complex realities of the status quo, unconscious of their own ignorance, and ungrateful for what the past has bequeathed to them. Such ignorance and ingratitude are often conjoined with the willingness to use tired clichés of cynicism to justify refusal to engage either in the dull but necessary rigors of convention or the risks and difficulties of truly generative endeavor. It is this corruption of creative transformation that renders the conservative—and not only the conservative—appropriately cautious of change.

A few years before writing this, I had a discussion with a young woman in her early twenties—the niece of someone who emailed me after watching some of my online lectures. She appeared severely unhappy, and said that she had spent much of the past six months lying in bed. She came to talk to me because she was becoming desperate. The only thing that stood between her and suicide, as far as she was concerned, was the responsibility she still maintained for an exotic pet, a serval cat. This was the last remaining manifestation of an interest in biology that once gripped her, but which she abandoned, much to her current regret, when she dropped out of high school. She had not been well attended to by her parents, who had allowed her to drift in the manner that had become disastrous over the span of several years.

Despite her decline, she had formulated a bit of a plan. She said she had thought about enrolling in a two-year program that would enable her to finish high school, as a prerequisite for applying to a veterinary college. But she had not made the necessary detailed inquiries into what would be required to carry out this ambition. She lacked a mentor. She had no good friends. It was far too easy for her to remain inactive and disappear into her isolation. We had a good conversation, for about three quarters of an hour. She was a nice kid. I offered to discuss her future in more detail if she would complete an online planning program designed by my professorial colleagues and me.*

All was going well until the discussion twisted toward the political. After discussing her personal situation, she began to voice her discontent with the state of the world at large—with the looming catastrophe, in her opinion, of the effects of human activity on the environment. Now, there is nothing wrong, in principle, with the expression of concern for planet-wide issues. That is not the point. There is something wrong, however, with overestimating your knowledge of such things—or perhaps even considering them—when you are a mid-twenty-year-old with nothing positive going on in your life and you are having great difficulty even getting out of bed. Under those condi-

---

*This is part of the Self-Authoring Suite, a set of individual programs designed to help people write about the troubles of their past (Past Authoring), the faults and virtues of their present personality (Present Authoring, in two parts), and their desires and wishes for the future (Future Authoring). I specifically recommended the latter.

tions, you need to get your priorities straight, and establishing the humility necessary to attend to and solve your own problems is a crucial part of doing just that.

As the verbal exchange continued, I found myself no longer engaged in a genuine conversation with a lost young woman who had come to speak with me. Instead, I became a hypothetically equal partner in a debate with an ideologue who knew what was wrong, globally speaking; who knew who was at fault for those global problems; who knew that participating in the continuing destruction by manifesting any personal desire whatsoever was immoral; and who believed, finally, that we were all both guilty and doomed. Continuing the conversation at that point meant I was (1) speaking not with this young woman so much as with whatever or whomever took possession of her while in the grip of generic, impersonal, and cynical ideas, and (2) implying that discussion of such topics under the circumstances was both acceptable and productive.

There was no point in either outcome. So, I stopped (which did not mean that the entire meeting had been a waste). It was impossible for me not to conclude that some of what had reduced her to her monthslong state of moral paralysis was not so much guilt about potentially contributing to the negative effects of human striving on the broader world, as it was the sense of moral superiority that concern about such things brought her (despite the exceptional psychological danger of embracing this dismal view of human possibility). Excuse the cliché, but it is necessary to walk before you can run. You may even have to crawl before you can walk. This is part of accepting your position as a beginner, at the bottom of the hierarchy you so casually, arrogantly, and self-servingly despise. Furthermore, the deeply anti-human attitude that often accompanies tears shed for environmental degradation and man's inhumanity to man cannot but help but have a marked effect on the psychological attitude that defines a person's relationship to him or herself.

It has taken since time immemorial for us to organize ourselves, biologically and socially, into the functional hierarchies that both specify our perceptions and actions, and define our interactions with the natural and social world. Profound gratitude for that gift is the only proper response. The structure that encompasses us all has its dark side—just as nature does, just as each individual does—but that does not mean careless, generic, and self-serving criticism of the status quo is appropriate (any more than knee-jerk objection to what might be necessary change).

## THE NECESSITY OF BALANCE

Because doing what others do and have always done so often works, and because, sometimes, radical action can produce success beyond measure, the conservative and the creative attitudes and actions constantly propagate themselves. A functional social institution—a hierarchy devoted to producing something of value, beyond the mere insurance of its own survival—can utilize the conservative types to carefully implement processes of tried-and-true value, and the creative, liberal types to determine how what is old and out of date might be replaced by something new and more valuable. The balance between conservatism and originality might therefore be properly struck, socially, by bringing the two types of persons together. But someone must determine how best to do that, and that requires a wisdom that transcends mere temperamental proclivity. Because the traits associated with creativity, on the one hand, and comfort with the status quo, on the other, tend to be mutually exclusive, it is difficult to find a

RULE I                                    35

single person who has balanced both properly, who is therefore comfortable working with each type, and who can attend, in an unbiased
manner, to the necessity for capitalizing on the respective forms of
talent and proclivity. But the development of that ability can at least
begin with an expansion of conscious wisdom: the articulated realization that conservatism is good (with a set of associated dangers), and
that creative transformation—even of the radical sort—is also good
(with a set of associated dangers). Learning this deeply—truly appre-
ciating the need for both viewpoints—means at least the possibility of
valuing what truly diverse people have to offer, and of being able to
recognize when the balance has swung too far in one direction. The
same is true of the knowledge of the shadow side of both. To manage
complex affairs properly, it is necessary to be cold enough in vision to
separate the power hungry and self-serving pseudoadvocate of the status quo from the genuine conservative; and the self-deceptive, irre-
sponsible rebel without a cause from the truly creative. And to manage
this means to separate those factors within the confines of one's own
soul, as well as among other people.

And how might this be accomplished? First, we might come to understand consciously that these two modes of being are integrally inter-
dependent. One cannot truly exist without the other, although they
exist in genuine tension. This means, first, for example, that discipline—
subordination to the status quo, in one form or another—needs to be
understood as a necessary precursor to creative transformation, rather
than its enemy. Thus, just as the hierarchy of assumptions that make
up the structure that organizes society and individual perceptions is
shaped by, and integrally dependent on, restrictions, so too is creative
transformation. It must strain against limits. It has no use and cannot be
called forth unless it is struggling against something. It is for this reason
that the great genie, the granter of wishes—God, in a microcosm—is

archetypally trapped in the tiny confines of a lamp and subject, as well, to the will of the lamp's current holder. Genie—genius—is the combination of possibility and potential, and extreme constraint.

Limitations, constraints, arbitrary boundaries—rules, dread rules, themselves—therefore not only ensure social harmony and psychological stability, they make the creativity that renews order possible. What lurks, therefore, under the explicitly stated desire for complete freedom—as expressed, say, by the anarchist, or the nihilist—is not a positive desire, striving for enhanced creative expression, as in the romanticized caricature of the artist. It is instead a negative desire—a desire for the complete absence of responsibility, which is simply not commensurate with genuine freedom. This is the lie of objections to the rules. But "Down with Responsibility" does not make for a compelling slogan—being sufficiently narcissistic to negate itself self-evidently—while the corresponding "Down with the Rules" can be dressed up like a heroic corpse.

Alongside the wisdom of true conservatism is the danger that the status quo might become corrupt and its corruption self-servingly exploited. Alongside the brilliance of creative endeavor is the false heroism of the resentful ideologue, who wears the clothes of the original rebel while undeservedly claiming the upper moral hand and rejecting all genuine responsibility. Intelligent and cautious conservatism and careful and incisive change keep the world in order. But each has its dark aspect, and it is crucial, once this has been realized, to pose the question to yourself: Are you the real thing, or its opposite? And the answer is, inevitably, that you are some of both—and perhaps far more of what is shadowy than you might like to realize. That is all part of understanding the complexity we each carry within us.

## PERSONALITY AS HIERARCHY—AND CAPACITY FOR TRANSFORMATION

How, then, is the personality that balances respect for social institutions and, equally, creative transformation to be understood? It is not so easy to determine, given the complexity of the problem. For that reason, we turn to stories. Stories provide us with a broad template. They outline a pattern specific enough to be of tremendous value, if we can imitate it, but general enough (unlike a particular rule or set of rules) to apply even to new situations. In stories, we capture observations of the ideal personality. We tell tales about success and failure in adventure and romance. Across our narrative universes, success moves us forward to what is better, to the promised land; failure dooms us, and those who become entangled with us, to the abyss. The good moves us upward and ahead, and evil drags us backward and down. Great stories are about characters in action, and so they mirror the unconscious structures and processes that help us translate the intransigent world of facts into the sustainable, functional, reciprocal social world of values.*

The properly embodied hierarchy of values—including the value of conservatism and its twin, creative transformation—finds its expression as a personality, in narrative—an ideal personality. Every hierarchy has something at its pinnacle. It is for this reason that a story,

---

*You can see this played out, for example, in the proclivity of American evangelical Protestants to ask, when faced with a novel existential problem, "What would Jesus do?" It is an easy approach to parody, but indicates precisely the values of stories: Once a narrative has been internalized, it can be used as a template to generate new perceptions and behaviors. It might seem naive or presumptuous to imagine what actions the archetypal Savior Himself might undertake in the confines of a normal life, but the fundamental purpose of religious narratives is in fact to motivate imitation.

which is a description of the action of a personality, has a hero (and even if that someone is the antihero, it does not matter: the antihero serves the function of identifying the hero through contrast, as the hero is what the antihero is most decidedly not). The hero is the individual at the peak, the victor, the champion, the wit, the eventually successful and deserving underdog, the speaker of truth under perilous circumstances, and more. The stories we create, watch, listen to, and remember center themselves on actions and attitudes we find interesting, compelling, and worthy of communication as a consequence of our personal experience with both admirable and detestable people (or fragments of their specific attitudes and actions), or because of our proclivity to share what has gripped our attention with those who surround us. Sometimes we can draw compelling narratives directly from our personal experience with individual people; sometimes we create amalgams of multiple personalities, often in concert with those who compose our social groups.

The client whose story was told in part earlier had a life usefully employed as an example of the necessity of social engagement. That tale did not, however, exhaust the significance of his transformed attitudes and actions. While he was reconstructing his social life, becoming an active participant in a range of collective activities, he simultaneously developed a certain creative expertise that was equally unexpected. He had not benefited from formal education beyond the high school level, and did not have a personality that immediately struck the external observer as markedly creative. However, the personally novel social pursuits that attracted him were in the main oriented toward aesthetic endeavor.

He first developed his eye for form, symmetry, novelty, and beauty as a photographer. The social advantages of this pursuit were manifold: he joined a club that had its members attend biweekly photography walks, where they would sojourn as a group of twenty or so to parts of the city that were visually interesting, either for their natural beauty or uniqueness or for the attraction they held as industrial landscapes. He learned a fair bit about photographic equipment, technically, because of doing so. The group members also critiqued one another's work—and they did this constructively, which meant that all of them appeared to indicate what errors had been made but also what of value had been managed.

This all helped my client learn to communicate in a productive manner about topics that might otherwise have been psychologically difficult (touching as they did on criticisms that, because of their association with creative vision, could easily have generated counterproductively sensitive overreactions) and, as well, to increasingly distinguish between visual images that were trite or dull or conformist and those of genuine quality. After a few months, his perception had developed sufficiently so that he began to win local contests and generate small professional commissions. I had believed from the beginning that his participation in the photography club was well advised from the perspective of personality development, but I was genuinely struck by the rapid development of his visual and technical ability and very much enjoyed the times we spent in our sessions reviewing his work.

After a few months of work on the photography front, my client began to produce and to show me other images he had created, as well—which were in their first incarnation decidedly amateurish abstract line drawings done in pen. These essentially consisted of loops of various sizes, joined continuously, on a single page: scribbles, really, although more controlled and evidently purposeful than mere scribbles. As I had with the photographs (and the photography club), I regarded these as psychologically useful—as an extension of creative ability—but not as worthwhile artistic endeavors in their own right. He kept at it, however, generating several drawings a week, all the while bringing what he had created to our sessions. What he produced increased in sophistication and beauty with dramatic rapidity. Soon, he was drawing complex, symmetrical, and rather dramatic black-and-white pen-and-ink drawings of sufficient intrinsic beauty to serve as commercially viable T-shirt designs.

I had seen this sort of development clearly in the case of two other clients, both characterized by intrinsically creative temperaments (very well hidden in one of the cases; more developed, nurtured, and obvious in the other). In addition, I had read accounts of clinical cases and personal development by Carl Jung, who noted that the production of increasingly ordered and complex geometrical figures—often circles within squares, or the reverse—regularly accompanied an increase in organization of the personality. This certainly seemed true not only of my client, as evidenced by his burgeoning expertise at photography and the development of his skill as a graphic artist, but also of the two others I had the pleasure of serving as a clinical therapist. What I observed repeatedly was, therefore, not only the reconstruction of the psyche as a consequence of further socialization (and the valuation of social institutions) but the parallel transformation of primarily interior processes, indicated by a marked increase in the capacity to perceive and to create what was elegant, beautiful, and socially valued. My clients had learned not only to submit properly to the sometimes arbitrary but still necessary demands of the social world, but to offer to that world something it would not have had access to had it not been for their private creative work.

My granddaughter, Scarlett, also came to exhibit behaviors that were indicative of, if not her creative ability, then at least her appreciation for creative ability, in addition to her socialization as an agent of socially valued pointing. When people discuss a story—presented as a movie, or a play, or a book—they commonly attempt to come to a sophisticated consensus about its point (sophisticated because a group of people can generally offer more viewpoints than a single individual; consensus because the discussion usually continues until some broad agreement is reached as to the topic at hand). Now, the idea that a story is a form of communication—and entertainment—is one of those facts that appears self-evident upon first consideration, but that becomes more mysterious the longer it is pondered. If it is true that a story has a point, then it is clear that it is pointing to something. But what, and how? What constitutes pointing is obvious when it is an action specifying a particular thing, or a person by a particular person, but much less obvious when it is something typifying the cumulative behavior, shall we say, of a character in a story.

The actions and attitudes of J. K. Rowling's heroes and heroines once again provide popular examples of precisely this process. Harry Potter, Ron Weasley, and Hermione Granger are typified in large part by the willingness and ability to follow rules (indicating their expertise as apprentices) and, simultaneously, to break them. While those who supervise them are inclined, equally, to reward both apparently paradoxical forms of behavior. Even the technologies used by the young wizards during their apprenticeship are characterized by this duality. The Marauder's Map, for example (which provides its bearer with an accurate representation of explored territory in the form of the physical layout or geography of Hogwarts, the wizarding school, as well as the locale of all its living denizens), can be activated as a functional tool only by uttering a set of words that seem to indicate the very opposite of moral behavior: "I solemnly swear that I am up to no good," and deactivated, so that its function remains secret, with the phrase "Mischief managed."

It is no easy matter to understand how an artifact that requires such statements to make it usable could possibly be anything but "no good"—a tool of evil purpose, apparently. But, like the fact that Harry and his friends regularly but carefully break rules, and are equally regularly and carefully rewarded for doing so, the Marauder's Map varies in its ethical desirability with the intent of its users. There is a strong implication throughout the series that what is good cannot be simply encapsulated by mindless or rigid rule following, no matter how disciplined that following, or how vital the rules so followed. What this all means is that the Harry Potter series does not point to drone-like subservience to social order as the highest of moral virtues. What supersedes that obedience is not so obvious that it can be easily articulated, but it is something like "Follow rules except when doing so undermines the purpose of those selfsame rules—in which case take the risk of acting in a manner contrary to what has been agreed upon as moral." This is a lesson that seems more easily taught by representations of the behaviors that embody it than transmitted by, say, rote learning or a variant rule. Meta-rules (which might be regarded as rules about rules, rather than rules themselves) are not necessarily communicated in the same manner as simple rules themselves.

Scarlett, with her emphasis on pointing, learned soon after mastering the comparatively straightforward physical act, to grasp the more complex point of narratives. She could signify something with her index finger at the age of a year and a half. By two and a half years, however, she could understand and imitate the far more intricate point of a story. For a period of approximately six months, at the latter age, she would insist, when asked, that she was Pocahontas, rather than Ellie (the name preferred by her father) or Scarlett (preferred by her mother). This was a staggering act of sophisticated thought, as far as I was concerned. She had been given a Pocahontas doll, which became one of her favorite toys, along with a baby doll (also very well loved), who she named after her grandmother, my wife, Tammy. When she played with the infant doll, Ellie was the mother. With Pocahontas, however, the situation differed. That doll was not a baby, and Ellie was not its mother. My granddaughter regarded herself, instead, as the grown Pocahontas—mimicking the doll, which was fashioned like a young woman, as well as the character who served as the lead in the Disney movie of the same name, which she had raptly observed on two separate occasions.

The Disney Pocahontas bore marked similarities to the main protagonists of the Harry Potter series. She finds herself promised by her father to Kocoum, a brave warrior who embodies, in all seriousness, the virtues of his tribe, but whose behavior and attitudes are too rule bound for the more expansive personality of his bride-to-be. Pocahontas falls in love, instead, with John Smith, captain of a ship from Europe and representative of that which falls outside of known territory but is (potentially) of great value. Paradoxically, Pocahontas is pursuing a higher moral order in rejecting Kocoum for Smith—breaking a profoundly important rule (value what is most valued in the current culture's hierarchy of rules)—very much in the same manner as the primary Potter characters. That is the moral of both narratives: follow the rules until you are capable of being a shining exemplar of what they represent, but break them when those very rules now constitute the most dire impediment to the embodiment of their central virtues. And Elizabeth Scarlett, not yet three years of age, had the intrinsic wisdom to see this as the point of what she was watching (the Disney movie) and using as a role-playing aid (the doll Pocahontas). Her perspicacity in this regard bordered on the unfathomable.

The same set of ideas—respect for the rules, except when following those rules means disregarding or ignoring or remaining blind to
an even higher moral principle—is represented with stunning power in
two different Gospel narratives (which serve, regardless of your opinion about them, as central traditional or classical stories portraying a
personality for the purposes of evoking imitation). In the first, Christ
is presented, even as a child, as a master of the Jewish tradition. This
makes him fully informed as to the value of the past, and portrays him
as characterized by the respect typical, say, of the genuine conservative. According to the account in Luke 2:42–52,* Jesus's family journeyed to Jerusalem every year at the Jewish holiday of Passover:

> And when he was twelve years old, they went up to Jerusalem
> after the custom of the feast.
>
> And when they had fulfilled the days, as they returned, the
> child Jesus tarried behind in Jerusalem; and Joseph and his
> mother knew not of it.
>
> But they, supposing him to have been in the company, went
> a day's journey; and they sought him among their kinsfolk and
> acquaintance.
>
> And when they found him not, they turned back again to
> Jerusalem, seeking him.
>
> And it came to pass, that after three days they found him in
> the temple, sitting in the midst of the doctors, both hearing
> them, and asking them questions.
>
> And all that heard him were astonished at his understand-
> ing and answers.
>
> And when they saw him, they were amazed: and his mother

---

*All biblical citations are from the King James Version unless otherwise noted.

said unto him, Son, why hast thou thus dealt with us? behold,
thy father and I have sought thee sorrowing.

And he said unto them, How is it that ye sought me? wist
ye not that I must be about my Father's business?

And they understood not the saying which he spake unto
them.

And he went down with them, and came to Nazareth, and
was subject unto them: but his mother kept all these sayings in
her heart.

And Jesus increased in wisdom and stature, and in favour
with God and man.

A paradox emerges, however, as the entirety of the Gospel accounts
are considered—one closely associated with the tension between respect for tradition and the necessity for creative transformation. Despite the evidence of His thorough and even precocious understanding
and appreciation of the rules, the adult Christ repeatedly and scandal-
ously violates the Sabbath traditions—at least from the standpoint
of the traditionalists in His community, and much to His own peril.
He leads His disciples through a cornfield, for example, plucking and
eating the grains (Luke 6:1). He justifies this to the Pharisees who
object by referring to an account of King David acting in a similar
manner, feeding his people when necessity demanded it on bread that
was reserved for the priests (Luke 6:4). Christ tells his interlocutors
quite remarkably "that the Son of man is Lord also of the sabbath"
(Luke 6:5).

An ancient document known as the Codex Bezae,* a noncanonical

---

*A codex is a book composed of sheets of vellum, papyrus, or most commonly, paper.
The term is now generally reserved for manuscripts that have been handwritten, as in
the case of the Codex Bezae. The Codex Bezae contains Greek and Latin versions of

variant of part of the New Testament, offers an interpolation just after
the section of the Gospel of Luke presented above, shedding profound
light on the same issue. It offers deeper insight into the complex and
paradoxical relationship between respect for the rules and creative
moral action that is necessary and desirable, despite manifesting itself
in apparent opposition to those rules. It contains an account of Christ
addressing someone who, like Him, has broken a sacred rule: "On that
same day, observing one working on the Sabbath, [Jesus] said to him
O Man, if indeed thou knowest what thou doest, thou art blest; but if
thou knowest not, thou art accursed, and a transgressor of the Law."[12]

What does this statement mean? It sums up the meaning of Rule I
perfectly. If you understand the rules—their necessity, their sacredness, the chaos they keep at bay, how they unite the communities that
follow them, the price paid for their establishment, and the danger of
breaking them—but you are willing to fully shoulder the responsibility of making an exception, because you see that as serving a higher
good (and if you are a person with sufficient character to manage that
distinction), then you have served the spirit, rather than the mere law,
and that is an elevated moral act. But if you refuse to realize the importance of the rules you are violating and act out of self-centered
convenience, then you are appropriately and inevitably damned. The
carelessness you exhibit with regard to your own tradition will undo
you and perhaps those around you fully and painfully across time.

This is in keeping with other sentiments and acts of Christ described in the Gospels. Matthew 12:11 states: "And he said unto them,
What man shall there be among you, that shall have one sheep, and if
it fall into a pit on the Sabbath day, will he not lay hold on it, and lift

---

Acts and most of the four Gospels that are unique in what they additionally include,
what they omit, and often, the style in which they are written.

it out?" Luke chapter 6 describes Him healing a man with a withered hand on another Sabbath, stating "It is lawful on the Sabbath days to do good, or to do evil? to save life, or destroy it?" (Luke 6:9). This psychologically and conceptually painful juxtaposition of two moral stances (the keeping of the Sabbath versus the injunction to do good) is something else that constantly enrages the Pharisees, and is part of the series of events that eventually leads to Christ's arrest and Crucifixion. These stories portray the existential dilemma that eternally characterizes human life: it is necessary to conform, to be disciplined, and to follow the rules—to do humbly what others do; but it is also necessary to use judgment, vision, and the truth that guides conscience to tell what is right, when the rules suggest otherwise. It is the ability to manage this combination that truly characterizes the fully developed personality: the true hero.

A certain amount of arbitrary rule-ness must be tolerated—or welcomed, depending on your point of view—to keep the world and its inhabitants together. A certain amount of creativity and rebellion must be tolerated—or welcomed, depending on your point of view—to maintain the process of regeneration. Every rule was once a creative act, breaking other rules. Every creative act, genuine in its creativity, is likely to transform itself, with time, into a useful rule. It is the living interaction between social institutions and creative achievement that keeps the world balanced on the narrow line between too much order and too much chaos. This is a terrible conundrum, a true existential burden. We must support and value the past, and we need to do that with an attitude of gratitude and respect. At the same time, however, we must keep our eyes open—we, the visionary living—and repair the ancient mechanisms that stabilize and support us when they falter. Thus, we need to bear the paradox that is involved in simultaneously respecting the walls that keep us safe and allowing in enough of what is new and changing so that our institutions remain alive and healthy. The very world depends for its stability and its dynamism on the subsuming of all our endeavors under the perfection—the sacredness—of that dual ability.

Do not carelessly denigrate social institutions or creative achievement.

---

# IMAGINE WHO YOU COULD BE, AND THEN AIM SINGLE-MINDEDLY AT THAT

## WHO ARE YOU—AND WHO COULD YOU BE?

How do you know who you are? After all, you are complex beyond your own understanding; more complex than anything else that exists, excepting other people; complex beyond belief. And your ignorance is further complicated by the intermingling of who you are with who you could be. You are not only something that is. You are something that is becoming—and the potential extent of that becoming also transcends your understanding. Everyone has the sense, I believe, that there is more to them than they have yet allowed to be realized. That potential is often obscured by poor health, misfortune, and the general tragedies and mishaps of life. But it can also be hidden by an unwillingness to take full advantage of the opportunities that life offers—abetted by regrettable errors of all sorts, including failures of discipline, faith, imagination, and commitment. Who are you? And, more importantly, who could you be, if you were everything you could conceivably be?

Are such questions impossible to answer, or are there sources available to us from which guidance might be derived? After all, we have been observing ourselves behave—in our successes and failures—for tens (perhaps hundreds) of thousands of years. During that time, our shamans, prophets, mystics, artists, poets, and bards have distilled something vital from such observations—some concentrated essence of what makes us human in actuality and possibility. In doing so, they have provided us with representations of that vital essence, presenting itself to us as that which can be neither ignored nor forgotten. Those creative people write and act out the dramas and tell us the stories that capture our imagination, and they fill our dreams with visions of what might be. The deepest and most profound of these are remembered, discussed, and otherwise honed collectively, and made the focus of rituals that unite us across the centuries, forming the very basis of our cultures. These are the stories upon which the ritual, religious, and philosophical edifices characterizing sophisticated, populous, successful societies are built.

The stories we can neither ignore nor forget are unforgettable for this reason (among others): They speak to something we know, but do not know that we know. The ancient Greek philosopher Socrates believed that all learning was a form of remembering. Socrates posited that the soul, immortal in its essence, knew everything before it was born anew as an infant. However, at the point of birth all previous knowledge was forgotten and had to be recalled through the experiences of life. There is much to be said for this hypothesis, strange as it might now appear. There is much that we *could* do—much that our bodies and minds are capable of doing—that remains dormant, right down to the genetic level. Exposure to new experience activates this dormant potential, releasing abilities built into us over the vast span of our evolutionary history.[1] This is perhaps the most basic manner in which our bodies retain past wisdom and draw upon it when necessary. It is in this way, although not only in this way, that human possibility exists. Thus, there is something profound to be said for the concept of learning as remembering.

Obviously, as well as "remembering" (as in the turning on of innate but hidden possibilities), we can learn much that is new. This is one of the primary factors differentiating us from animals. Even complex and intelligent mammals such as chimpanzees and dolphins tend to repeat their species-typical behaviors generation after generation, with very little change. Humans, by contrast, can and continually do seek out and encounter what is new, investigate and adapt to it, and make it part of themselves. We can, as well, translate something we already know at one level of representation into knowledge at another. We can watch the actions of a living creature, animal or human, and then imitate them, translating our perceptions of their movement into new movements of our own. We can even generalize such imitative acts, catching the "spirit" of what or whom we are observing, and producing new ways of seeing and acting that are in some manner similar to that spirit.* This is part of what makes up the basis of the deeply embodied implicit knowledge that forms so much of the basis of our true understanding. We can also observe someone act or something occur and write down what we see, translating action into language that outlasts its utterance— and then communicate it later in the absence of what or whom is being described. Finally, and most mysteriously, we can imagine and then act

---

*Consider the professional impersonator. He or she doesn't necessarily copy the precise behaviors, movement for movement, of those being impersonated, but the spirit—what's common across all the behaviors of the target celebrity. The same is true when children play at being adults. It's the spirit they're after, not the individual behaviors.

out something that has simply not been seen before, something that is truly original. And we can code and represent all that ability—adaptive action and its transformation—in the stories we tell about those we admire, as well as those we hate. And that is how we determine who we are, and who we could perhaps become.

Stories become unforgettable when they communicate sophisticated modes of being—complex problems and equally complex solutions— that we perceive, consciously, in pieces, but cannot fully articulate. It was for this reason, for example, that the biblical story of Moses and the Israelites' exodus from Egypt became such a powerful touchstone for black slaves seeking emancipation in the United States:

> Go down, Moses, way down in Egypt land
>   Tell old Pharaoh
>   To let my people go.[2]

The biblical story of Exodus is properly regarded as archetypal (or paradigmatic or foundational) by psychoanalytic and religious think- ers alike, because it presents an example of psychological and social transformation that cannot be improved upon. It emerged as a product of imagination and has been transformed by constant collective retell- ing and reworking into an ultimately meaningful form that applies politically, economically, historically, personally, and spiritually, all at the same time. This is the very definition of literary depth—something that reaches its apogee in certain forms of ancient, traditional stories. The fact of that depth means that such accounts can be used diversely as a meaningful frame for any process of profound change experienced by any individual or society (stable state, descent into chaos, reestab- lishment of stability), and can lend that process multidimensional real- ity, context, powerful meaning, and motivation.

# THE EMERGENCE OF THE UNFORGETTABLE

How might an unforgettable story come to be? What might precede its revelation? It is at the very least the consequence of a long period of observation. Imagine a scientist monitoring the behavior of a wolf pack, or a troop of chimps—indeed, any group of complex social animals. He or she attempts to identify regularities in the behavior of the individuals and the group (patterns, in a word) and to articulate those regularities—to encapsulate them in language. The scientist might first relate a series of anecdotes about animal actions emblematic of the general behavior of the species. He or she might then abstract even further, attempting to generalize across anecdotes with rule-like descriptions. I say "rule-like" because the animals are not following rules. Rules require language. Animals are merely acting out regularities. They cannot formulate, understand, or follow *rules*.

But human beings? We can observe ourselves acting, as a scientist might—more accurately, as a storyteller might. Then we can tell the stories to each other. The stories are already distillations of observed behavior (if they are not distillations, they will not be interesting; relating a sequence of everyday actions does not make for a good story). Once the story is established, we can analyze it, looking for deeper patterns and regularities. If that analysis is successful, we can generalize across anecdotes with the formulation of rules, and then we can learn, consciously, to follow those rules. Here is how this might happen. We all react judgmentally when a child or adult—or, indeed, a society—is acting improperly, unfairly, or badly. The error strikes us emotionally. We intuit that a pattern upon which individual and social adaptation depends has been disrupted and violated. We are annoyed, frustrated, hurt, or grief-stricken at the betrayal. This does not mean that each of us, reacting emotionally, has been successful at articulating a comprehensive philosophy of good and evil. We may never put our finger on what has gone wrong. However, like children unfamiliar with a new game but still able to play it, we know that the rules are being broken.

Something precisely like this is portrayed in the biblical story of Exodus, the ancient account of the flight of the Hebrew slaves from their Egyptian masters. Moses, who leads the escaping people, is continually called upon by his followers to draw very fine moral distinctions when they struggle with one another and seek his advice. In consequence, he spends a very long time observing and contemplating their behavior. It is as if the desert prophet had to discover what rules he and his Israelite followers were already struggling to act out, prior to his receipt of the explicit commandments from God. Remember: Every society is already characterized by patterned behavior; otherwise it would be pure conflict and no "society" at all. But the mere fact that social order reigns to some degree does not mean that a given society has come to explicitly understand its own behavior, its own moral code. It is therefore no accident that in this story Moses serves as a judge for his followers—and does so with sufficient duration and intensity to exhaust himself—before he receives the Ten Commandments:

> And it came to pass on the morrow, that Moses sat to judge the people: and the people stood by Moses from the morning unto the evening.
>
> And when Moses' father in law saw all that he did to the people, he said, What is this thing that thou doest to the people? why sittest thou thyself alone, and all the people stand by thee from morning unto even?

And Moses said unto his father in law, Because the people
come unto me to inquire of God:

When they have a matter, they come unto me; and I judge
between one and another, and I do make them know the stat-
utes of God, and his laws.

And Moses' father in law said unto him, The thing that
thou doest is not good.

Thou wilt surely wear away, both thou, and this people
that is with thee: for this thing is too heavy for thee; thou art
not able to perform it thyself alone. (Exodus 18: 13–18)

This difficult exercise in discrimination and judgment, observing
and weighing, is an integral part of what prepared the biblical patriarch
for the receipt of divine revelation. If there had been no behavioral base
for those rules—no historical precedent codified in traditional ethics,
no conventions, and no endless hours of observation of the moral
patterns—the commandments simply could not have been understood
and communicated, much less obeyed.

An unforgettable story captures the essence of humanity and dis-
tills, communicates, and clarifies it, bringing what we are and what we
should be into focus. It speaks to us, motivating the attention that inspires us to imitate. We learn to see and act in the manner of the heroes of the stories that captivate us. These stories call to capacities that
lie deep within our nature but might still never develop without that
call. We are dormant adventurers, lovers, leaders, artists, and rebels,
but need to discover that we are all those things by seeing the reflection of such patterns in dramatic and literary form. That is part of
being a creature that is part nature and part culture. An unforgettable
story advances our capacity to understand our behavior, beyond habit

and expectation, toward an imaginative and then verbalized understanding. Such a story presents us in the most compelling manner with the ultimate adventure, the divine romance, and the eternal battle between good and evil. All this helps us clarify our understanding of moral and immoral attitude and action, personal and social. This can be seen everywhere, and always.

Question: Who are you—or, at least, who could you be? Answer: Part of the eternal force that constantly confronts the terrible unknown, voluntarily; part of the eternal force that transcends naivete and becomes dangerous enough, in a controlled manner, to understand evil and beard it in its lair; and part of the eternal force that faces chaos and turns it into productive order, or that takes order that has become too restrictive, reduces it to chaos, and renders it productive once again.

And all of this, being very difficult to understand consciously but vital to our survival, is transmitted in the form of the stories that we cannot help but attend to. And it is in this manner that we come to apprehend what is of value, what we should aim at, and what we could be.

## MATERIA PRIMA: WHO YOU COULD BE (I)

I would like to try my hand at explaining the meaning of the illustration, based on an ancient alchemical woodcut, that opens this chapter. Describing what it signifies reveals how much information can be contained within an image without the viewer possessing any explicit understanding of its contents (such a picture is in fact better considered an early stage in the process by which such explicit understanding develops). The ancient alchemist* who produced the picture was dream-

---

*Alchemy—the search for the philosopher's stone, an artifact that would transform base

RULE II
59

ing, in a very real sense, while doing so—dreaming about what a person could be, and how that might come about.

At the very base of the image is a winged sphere. Atop that perches a dragon. Standing on the dragon is a two-headed human figure—one head male, the other female. The male head is associated with an image of the Sun; the female, with the Moon. In between but also above the two heads is the symbol for Mercury: god, planet, and metal, simultaneously. A variety of additional symbols round out the picture. Everything portrayed is enveloped in an egg-shaped container. This arrangement indicates that the image is of many things inside one thing—a multiplicity in a unity—just as an unhatched chick is encapsulated within a single container but is many increasingly differentiated and complex biological parts, particularly in its later stages of development. In its entirety, the image is labeled materia prima—Latin for the "primal element."

The alchemists regarded the materia prima as the fundamental substance from which everything else—matter and spirit included, equally—emerged, or was derived. You can profitably consider that primal element the potential we face when we confront the future, including our future selves—or the potential we cannot help upbraiding ourselves and others for wasting. It can also be usefully conceptualized as the information from which we build ourselves and the world, instead of the matter out of which we generally consider reality

---

metals into gold, as well as rewarding its bearer with health and immortality—was practiced for thousands of years by the misfits, mystics, magicians, and prescientific practitioners who took the first fantastical steps toward establishing what eventually became genuine science. As alchemy developed, however, the "stone" eventually became conceptualized as something more akin to a personality than a material object, as the alchemists increasingly realized that the development of the psyche was a more important pursuit than mere gold itself. I wrote about this in J. B. Peterson, *Maps of Meaning: The Architecture of Belief* (New York: Routledge, 1999), which contains the relevant references to the work on alchemy conducted by Jung and his students.

composed. Each interpretation—potential and information—has its advantages.

What does it mean that the world can be usefully considered as potential or information? Think about what happens, for example, when you stop by the mailbox and pick up your mail. Consider, as well, what that mail is "made of." Materially speaking, it is merely paper and ink. But that material substrate is essentially irrelevant. It would not matter if the message was delivered by email or voice—or in Morse code, for that matter. What is relevant is the content. And that means that each piece of mail is a container of content—of potential or information, positive, neutral, or negative. Maybe, for example, it is a notification of investigation from your country's tax department. This means that, despite its apparently harmless presence in your hand, the letter is tightly and inextricably connected to a gigantic, complex and oft-arbitrary structure that may well not have your best interests in mind. Alternatively, perhaps it is something joyful, such as an unexpected letter from someone loved or a long-awaited check. From such a perspective, an envelope is a container—a mysterious container, at least in potential—from which an entire new world might emerge.

Everyone understands this idea, even if they do not know it. If you have been having trouble with the tax authorities, for example, and you receive an official piece of mail from their agency, your blood pressure will increase (or drop precipitously), your heart will pound, your palms will sweat, and a feeling of intense fear, even doom, may sweep over you. That is the instinctive response, associated with preparation for action, that accompanies exposure to danger. And now you will have to decide: are you going to open the letter and face what is "inside"? And, having done so, are you going to think your way through the problem, terrible as that might be, and begin to address it? Or are you going to ignore what you now know, pretend that everything is all right (even though you know, emotionally—as a consequence of your anxiety—that it is not), and pay the inevitable psychological and physical price? It is the former route that will require you to voluntarily confront what you are afraid of—the terrible, abstract monster—and, hypothetically, to become stronger and more integrated as a result. It is the latter route that will leave the problem in its monstrous form and force you to suffer like a scared animal confronted by a predator's vicious eyes in the pitch of night.

A winged sphere, inscribed with a square, a triangle, and the numerals 3 and 4 occupies the bottom third of the image in question.* This singular entity or object was known by the alchemists as the "round chaos."[3] It is a container—the initial container of the primordial element—the container of what the world, and the psyche, consists of before it becomes differentiated. This is the potential, or information. This is what attracts your attention unconsciously and compels you to attend to something before you know why it has gripped your interest. This is when and where what is new makes its entrance into what is predictable and certain (for better or worse); what flits about you, with little voluntary control—as if it is something winged—as your imagination and your attention move unpredictably but meaningfully from association to association; and it is what you are looking at when you have no idea what it is you are

---

*We're going to approach the picture from the very bottom upward, as if each element were emerging from the lower. Images of this type (and they are a type) often represent a process of psychological or spiritual development or growth, and appear to employ the basic symbolism of a plant or a tree extending itself upward as it matures. Something similar can be observed in Eastern images of the Buddha, emerging from a lotus flower floating on the surface of placid water, with its stalk extending into the murky deep underneath and its roots grounded far, far below even that, into the mud that composes the lowest level of the depths.

confronting. Finally, it is what you cannot look away from when you are possessed by horror, even as such potential for horror simultaneously adds vital interest to life.

Strangely, the round chaos may be familiar to modern audiences (again, even if they do not know it), because of the Harry Potter series of books and films. J. K. Rowling, the series author, takes some pains to describe a sporting event, Quidditch, which helps to define and unify Hogwarts. The point of Quidditch is to drive a ball (the Quaffle) through one of the three hoops guarded by the opposing team, while flying about the playing pitch on enchanted brooms. Success in doing so gains the scorer's team 10 points. Simultaneously, two separate players (one from each team) play another game—a game within the game. Chosen for their exceptional skill in attention and flight, these two competitors—known as Seekers—attempt to locate, chase, and capture a winged ball, the Snitch, which is identical in appearance to the round chaos that sits at the bottom of the alchemist's image. The Snitch is golden—indicating its exceptional value and purity*—and zips around chaotically, at a very fast rate, darting, weaving, bobbing, and racing the Seekers as they pursue it astride their brooms. If a Seeker captures the Snitch, his or her team gains 150 points (typically enough to ensure victory) and the entire game comes to an end. This indicates that chasing and capturing whatever is represented by the Snitch—and, by implication, the round chaos—is a goal whose importance supersedes any other.† Why is Rowling's game, conjured up for

---

*As gold is both rare and unwilling, so to speak, to combine promiscuously with other elements or compounds.

†It is of some real interest to note—particularly in relationship to the discussion of the dangers of creativity presented in Rule I—that the Seekers chase the Snitch both inside and outside the playing field that provides boundaries for all the other players. While outside, they can career through the wooden foundation of the Quidditch stadium. This would not be a problem, if they weren't simultaneously being chased by a Bludger, a

us by her deep imagination, structured in that manner? What does her narrative idea signify? There are two ways of answering these questions (although both answers relate importantly to each other):

First: In Rule I, we discussed the idea that the true winner of any game is the person who plays fair. This is because playing fair, despite the particularities of any given game, is a higher-order accomplishment than mere victory. Striving to play fair, in the ultimate sense— following the spirit of the rules, as well as the letter—is an indication of true personality development, predicated as it is on concern for true reciprocity. The Seekers of the Snitch must ignore the details of the game of Quidditch, of which they are still a part, while attempting to find and seize the Snitch, just as the player of a real-world game must ignore the particularities of that game while attending to what constitutes truly ethical play, regardless of what is happening on the playing field. Thus, the ethical player, like the Seeker, indomitably pursues what is most valuable in the midst of complex, competing obligations.

Second: Among the alchemists, the round chaos was associated with the winged god Mercury, who served as messenger from the realm of the divine, guide of souls to the underworld, and bringer of good fortune. It is for this reason that the ancient symbol for Mercury is located at the very pinnacle (the most important location) of the image in question. It is an attempt to indicate what guides the process that the picture represents. Centuries ago, prior to the dawn of modern chemistry, the god Mercury represented what inspires or attracts interest involuntarily. He was the spirit who possessed a person when his or

---

solid, massive, flying ball capable not only of knocking them off their brooms, but of crashing through and seriously damaging that same structure. If they succeed in catching the Snitch, as we have indicated, they generally attain victory. But they risk damaging the very foundations of the game while doing so—just as creative people do when they pursue their innovative yet disruptive visions.

her attention was drawn irresistibly to some person, situation, or event. Imagine that there are very complex processes going on in your mind unconsciously, highlighting events of potential worth and distinguishing them from everything else constantly unfolding around you. Imagine that those processes that distinguish value are alive, which is certainly the case, and that they are complex and integrated enough to be conceptualized as a personality. That is Mercury. The draw he exerts on our attention reveals itself in a sense of significance—in the sense that something happening around you is worth attending to, or contains something of value. The Seeker—in real life, as well as in Rowling's Potter series and its Quidditch game—is he or she who takes that sense of significance more seriously than anything else. The Seeker is therefore the person who is playing the game that everyone else is playing (and who is disciplined and expert at the game), but who is also playing an additional, higher-order game: the pursuit of what is of primary significance. The Snitch (like the round chaos) can therefore be considered the "container" of that primary significance—that meaning—and, therefore, something revelatory when pursued and caught. We might in this context remember what has come to be known as the Golden Rule: "And as ye would that men should do to you, do ye also to them likewise" (Luke 6:31). There is nothing more important than learning to strive under difficult and frustrating circumstances to play fair. This is what should be chased, so to speak, during any game (even though it is also important to try to obtain victory in the game).*

---

*It is also of great interest to note, in this regard, that the metal mercury can be used in the mining and purification of gold. Gold dissolves in mercury, and mercury can, therefore, be used to draw out the small amounts of the precious metal typically found in ores. The mercury is then boiled off (it has a low boiling point) so that only the gold remains. The proclivity of mercury for gold has given rise to the symbolic idea that the liquid metal has an "affinity" for what is most precious: that mercury will seek what is noble

Each of us, when fortunate, is compelled forward by something that grips our attention—love of a person; a sport; a political, sociological, or economic problem, or a scientific question; a passion for art, literature, or drama—something that calls to us for reasons we can neither control nor understand (try to make yourself interested in something you just do not care about and see how well that works). The phenomena that grip us (*phenomena*: from the Greek word *phainesthai*, "to appear, or to be brought to light") are like lamps along a dark path: they are part of the unconscious processes devoted to integrating and furthering the development of our spirits, the furtherance of our psychological development. You do not choose what interests you. It chooses you. Something manifests itself out of the darkness as compelling, as worth living for; following that, something moves us further down the road, to the next meaningful manifestation—and so it goes, as we continue to seek, develop, grow, and thrive. It is a perilous journey, but it is also the adventure of our lives. Think of pursuing someone you love: catch them or not, you change in the process. Think, as well, of the traveling you have done, or of the work you have undertaken, whether for pleasure or necessity. In all these cases you experience what is new. Sometimes that is painful; sometimes it is better than anything else that has ever happened to you. Either way, it is deeply informative. It is all part of the potential of the world, calling you into Being, changing you forever—for better or worse—in consequence of your pursuit.

Atop the round chaos perches a dragon. This is because what is

---

and pure and incorruptible—like gold itself, speaking symbolically once again—and concentrate it in usable amounts. So, the fundamental idea is that the pursuit of meaning, guided by Mercury, messenger of the gods (the unconscious, as far as modern people are concerned), will enable the Seeker to collect what is, like gold, of the highest value. For the alchemists who created drawings like the one we are analyzing, that highest value came to be the ultimate development of the psyche, or spirit, or personality.

interesting and meaningful (and novel and unexpected, as those all go together) manifests itself in a form that is both dangerous and promising, particularly when its grip is intense and irresistible. The danger is, of course, signified by the presence of the immortal, predatory reptile; the promise is hinted at, as a dragon archetypally guards a great treasure. Thus, the drawing represents a psychological progression. First, you find yourself interested in something. That something (the round chaos) contains or is composed of potential, or information. If it is pursued and caught, it releases that information. Out of that information we build the world we perceive, and we build ourselves as perceivers. Thus, the round chaos is the container from which both matter (the world) and spirit (our psyches) emerge. There is some numerological indication of this on the spherical body of the round chaos itself: the number 3, accompanied by a triangle, which is traditionally associated with spirit (because of its association with the Holy Trinity), and the number 4, associated with the world of matter (because of its association with the four traditional elements: earth, water, wind, and fire). The dragon, in turn, perched on top of the round chaos, represents the danger and possibility of the information within.

Atop the dragon stands a figure known as a Rebis, a single body with two heads, one male, one female. The Rebis is a symbol of the fully developed personality that can emerge from forthright and courageous pursuit of what is meaningful (the round chaos) and dangerous and promising (the dragon). It has a symbolically masculine aspect, which typically stands for exploration, order, and rationality (indicated by the Sun, which can be seen to the left of the male head), and a symbolically feminine aspect, which stands for chaos, promise, care, renewal, and emotion (indicated by the Moon, to the right of the female). In the course of normal socialization, it is typical for one of these aspects to become more developed than the other (as males are

socialized in the male manner, to which they are also inclined biologically, and females in the female manner). Nonetheless, it is possible—
with enough exploration, enough exposure to the round chaos and the
dragon—to develop both elements. That constitutes an ideal—or so
goes the alchemical intuition.

Out of the unknown—the potential that makes up the world—
comes the terrible but promising form of the dragon, peril and promise united. It is an eternal dichotomy echoed by the presence of the
two remaining symbols to the right and above the dragon's tail: Jupiter,
representing the positive, and Saturn, the negative. Out of the confrontation with peril and promise emerges the masculine and feminine aspects of the psyche, working together in harmony. Guiding the
process is the spirit Mercurius, manifesting itself as meaning in the
world, working through unconscious means to attract exploration to
what will unite the various discordant and warring elements of the
personality. This can all be read, appropriately, as a story of the development of the ideal personality—an attempt, in image, to describe
what each of us could be.

## POLYTHEISM INTO MONOTHEISM, AND
## THE EMERGENCE OF THE VIRTUOUS HERO:
## WHO YOU COULD BE (II)

Now we are going to attempt a description of "who you could be" from
another perspective, taken from one of the earliest stories we have been
fortunate enough to rediscover. In the ancient Mesopotamian *Enuma
Elish* (translation: When on High) we have the oldest near-complete
hero myth known, estimated at four thousand years of age in its written form and, no doubt, far older as an oral tradition. The story begins
when the primordial goddess Tiamat, embodiment of salt water (as

well as a monstrous aquatic dragon), enters into sexual union with her equally primordial male consort, Apsu, the embodiment of fresh water. This union gives rise to the initial realm of being, inhabited by the elder gods, the first children of Tiamat and Apsu.

To understand the beginning of this story, we need to know a few things the ancients held to be fundamentally true. These are markedly different from the truths of modern science. Before the dawn of the scientific worldview, a mere six hundred years ago, *reality* was construed as all that which human beings experience. That which we experience can be distinguished, conceptually, from *reality as objective world*—pure physical being—by its more comprehensive contents, which include subjective experiences such as emotions, dreams, visions, and motivational states such as hunger, thirst, and pain. That which we experience is better compared to a novel or a movie, which concentrates on the communication and sharing of subjective as well as objective states, than is reality as objective world, which we might liken to a scientific description of physical reality. It is the actual, particular, and unique demise of someone you love, for example, compared to the listing of that death in the hospital records. It is the drama of lived experience. It is because our own experience is genuinely literary, narrative, embodied, and storylike that we are so attracted to fictional representations. Movies, plays, operas, TV dramas—even the lyrics of songs—help us deal with our lived experiences, which are something different and broader than the mere material from which our experience hypothetically rises.

Engaging with the first part of the *Enuma Elish* requires us to understand a second fundamental realization of the ancients: the fundamentally social nature of our cognitive categories. That is why everything is personified in children's books: the Sun, the Moon, toys, animals—even machines. We see nothing strange in this, because it so profoundly mirrors our perceptual tendencies. We expect children to view and understand the world in this manner, and we can easily fall back into doing so ourselves. Something should be clarified here: It is not truly accurate to state that the reality portrayed in children's fiction is personified. It is the case, instead (and this is a genuine reversal of the presumption in question), that we directly and naturally perceive reality as personified, and then must work very diligently to strip that personification away, so that we can detect "objective reality."* We understand reality, therefore, as if it is constructed of personalities. That is because so much of what we encounter in our hypersocial reality, our complex societies, is in fact personality—and gendered personality, at that, reflecting the billion years or so since the emergence of sexual reproduction (ample time for its existence to have profoundly structured our perceptions). We understand male, and abstract from that the masculine. We understand female, and abstract from that the feminine. Finally, we understand the child, and abstract from that, most commonly, the son. These basic divisions are clearly reflected in the creation story of the *Enuma Elish*, just as they are reflected in, or more accurately underpin, our understanding of the stories we all know.

Tiamat, the primordial goddess, is chaos, a female monster, a dragon. She is the terror of nature, creative and destructive, mother and slayer of us all. Apsu, her husband, is the eternal father. He is the order that we depend upon for security, and by which we are simultaneously tyrannized.† These two most primal of deities come together in a produc-

---

*This is part of the reason science developed so long after religion and ritual—so incredibly recently, and by no means everywhere at once.
†Furthermore, in the mythological world, unlike the objective, logical world, things can be one thing and their opposite at the same time. And this representation in the mythological world is more accurate than the objective, in the experiential manner described previously: Nature, for example, is Creator and Destroyer, just as Culture is Protector and Tyrant. It might be objected: Nature and Culture are not singular things. They can

tive, sexual union, "mingling their waters," in the ancient words. In this fashion, they produce their first progeny, the elder gods of Mesopotamia. These gods represent elements of the world more differentiated than the primordial mother and father—such as heaven and earth, mud and silt, and war and fire.* However, they are also careless, noisy, and impulsive as two-year-old children (who are, after all, primal forces in their own right). Their continual ceaseless, thoughtless activity and general unconsciousness culminates in a catastrophe: their mutual decision to wage war upon and then slay Apsu, and consequent attempt to build a stable dwelling place on his corpse.

Tiamat—chaos itself—already irritated by the brainless racket of her children, is murderously enraged by the heedless slaughter of her husband. The Terrible Goddess builds an army of eleven monsters to deal with her wayward offspring, placing a demonic figure named Kingu, whom she takes as a second husband, at their head, and delivering to him the Tablet of Destinies (indicating his authority as ultimate ruler of the universe). The relationship between this brilliant dramatic representation and how we use, or misuse, the gifts of our culture is obvious: the careless demolition of tradition is the invitation to the (re)emergence of chaos. When ignorance destroys culture, monsters will emerge.

While Tiamat busily arranges her army, the elder gods continue

---

be differentiated, so that their paradoxical components are separated, understood, and dealt with. This is all true: but the paradoxical components are often experienced simultaneously and so unified. This occurs when anyone is betrayed, for example, in a love affair. Beast and man, Medusa and beloved woman are often united experientially in the same hypothetically unitary figure. This can be a terrible discovery when made in real life.

*The same idea is expressed in Taoist cosmogony, when the yin and the yang differentiate themselves into the five elements: wood, fire, earth, metal, and water. The ancient Greeks believed, similarly, that Earth and Sky (Gaia and Uranus) gave birth to the Titans, elemental deities of great strength and power.

their activity, pairing off, producing children, and then grandchildren, of their own. One of the latter, Marduk, appears particularly talented, powerful, and promising. He is born with eyes encircling his head. He can see everywhere. He can speak magic words. He is something entirely new—and this is noted early by his progenitors. While Marduk matures, the elder gods are compelled to confront Tiamat, with whom they are now at war. One after another they attempt to defeat her. All return in abject failure. Finally, someone suggests that Marduk, though still young, should be sent to confront his terrible grandmother. Approached with this idea, he agrees, but only on the condition that he is awarded the right, henceforth—if he is victorious—to hold the Tablet of Destinies, and sit atop the dominance hierarchy of the gods.

It is in this manner that this ancient story describes the emergence of monotheism out of polytheism. The *Enuma Elish* appears to be a dramatized account of the psychological or spiritual processes comprising this transformation. The ancient Mesopotamian civilization faced the necessity of incorporating and unifying many diverse tribes and peoples, each of whom had their own gods. The god who arose out of the conflict between all those gods ("Whose god is supreme?") was, therefore, a meta-god—a god composed of what was most important about all gods. It was for such a reason, for example, that fifty different names characterized Marduk. This emergence of one from many is a very common process, described by the scholar of myth Mircea Eliade as the war of the gods in heaven, a typical mythological motif, as well as alluded to earlier.* It is the psychological counterpart, in the world of imagination, to the genuine struggle of concepts of divinity and value on earth. Tribes unite. Each has its gods. The people comprising these multitudinous groups go to war, concretely and conceptually, for

---

*E pluribus unum.*

what they believe—sometimes for generations. It is as if the gods they follow were battling for dominance over periods exceeding single human lives, using their followers as proxies. That is reflected in the ancient stories. If and when the gods come to an agreement about their relative positions—more particularly, if they arrange themselves into a hierarchy—it means that peace has genuinely been established, because peace is the establishment of a shared hierarchy of divinity, of value. Thus, an eternal question emerges whenever people of different backgrounds are required to deal with one another on a relatively permanent basis: What do all gods share that makes them gods? What is God, in essence?

That is a very difficult question. It is, on the one hand, the question of value: What is of the highest importance? It is, on the other hand, the question of sovereignty: What principle should rule? These are the questions posed by those pondering the ultimate source of divine significance itself. Their difficulty meant that they, and by extension the question of God, had to be answered over centuries, over millennia. The answer emerged first in story form. The Mesopotamians brilliantly intuited that the highest god—the highest good—involved careful attention (the multiple, head-circling eyes of Marduk) and effective language (the magic words of Marduk, capable of generating a cosmos), in addition to the courage and strength to voluntarily confront and overcome chaos, the unknown. It could be argued that these are the defining features of the great central spirit of mankind, at least insofar as that spirit is noble and admirable.

The ancient Egyptians formulated an idea similar in many important regards—which we will discuss later in detail—associating their savior-god Horus, son of Osiris, with the sharp-eyed falcon, and identifying him with the vision willing to search out, detect, understand,

and defeat evil (symbolized with the famous Egyptian image of the single eye). Representing that reality—*pay attention, above all, even to what is monstrous and malevolent, and speak wisely and truthfully*—could be the single most important accomplishment of our species.[4] It allows us to apprehend in dramatic form the fundamental necessity of coming to grips with what our senses demonstrate to us, no matter how terrifying the reality revealed. It allows for the possibility of bringing our explicit understanding closer in line with our deepest being, making possible a truer union of body and spirit through the partial comprehension and imitation of the story. Most importantly, perhaps, it allows us to realize the immense importance of words in transforming potential into actuality, and helps us understand that the role we each play in that transformation is in some vital sense akin to the divine.

After his election to the highest of places, Marduk challenges Tiamat directly, encloses her, defeated, in a giant net, and cuts her into pieces, fashioning the heavens and the earth from her remains. One of Marduk's many names is, in fact, "he who makes ingenious things as a consequence of the conflict with Tiamat."[5] It might be noted, in this regard, that tens of thousands of years ago, men literally did construct the habitable world out of the pieces of monsters, making their early dwellings from the giant bones of animals they had so courageously speared.[6] Marduk simultaneously defeats his grandmother's monstrous army, including the leader, Kingu, from whom he takes the Tablet of Destinies, confirming his place as supreme leader of the cosmos. Then he returns home, enemies in tow. His compatriots celebrate his victory and accede yet more completely to his leadership, before he assigns them their various duties. Then, after consulting Ea, the god of wisdom, Marduk determines to create man, to aid the gods most fundamentally in the eternal task of maintaining the proper balance between order and chaos—to release those very gods from their service, and to transfer their burden onto our all-too-human shoulders.*

The basic story is this: when order (Apsu) is carelessly threatened or destroyed, the terrible forces of chaos from which the world was originally derived appear once again in their most destructive, monstrous, predatory guise. Then a hero, representing the highest of values, must arise or be elected to confront this chaotic force. He does so successfully, deriving or producing something of great worth. What the hero represents is the most important of the great forces that make up the human psyche. To think of it another way: the hero is the embodied principle of action and perception that must rule over all the primordial psychological elements of lust, rage, hunger, thirst, terror, and joy. For chaos to remain effectively at bay (or, even better, tamed and therefore harnessed), this heroic principle must be regarded as the most important of all things that can organize and motivate mankind. This means, at least, that it must be continually acted out, which is what "regarded as important" actually means. It is in this way that the spirit of Marduk still possesses each individual who engages courageously in the processes of encounter and confrontation that eternally create and renew society. It is this that happens when each small child learns to regulate and unite his emotions and motivations into a coherent personality, and then goes out to challenge the unknown world.

In slightly altered form, this is the story of St. George: The inhabitants of an ancient city must obtain water from a well beside the nest of a dragon. To do so, however, they have to offer the dragon some

---

*Ea makes man from the blood of Kingu, the most terrible of Tiamat's monsters. A bright graduate student and later colleague of mine once suggested that this was because of all God's creatures, only man could deceive; only man could voluntarily bring evil and discord into the world.

sacrifice—a sheep, under most circumstances, but a maiden, if no sheep can be found. The young women of the city draw lots when the supply of sheep is exhausted. One day it is the daughter of the king herself who loses. St. George appears, confronts the dragon with the sign of the cross—symbol of the eternal Redeemer, the archetypal hero— and frees the doomed princess. The city's inhabitants then convert to Christianity. Victory over the dragon—the predator, as such, the ruler of unexplored territory—is victory over all the forces that have threatened the individual and society, over evolutionary and historical spans of time, as well as the more abstract evil we all still face, without and within. The cross, for its part, is the burden of life. It is a place of betrayal, torture, and death. It is therefore a fundamental symbol of mortal vulnerability. In the Christian drama, it is also the place where vulnerability is transcended, as a consequence of its acceptance. This voluntary acceptance is also equivalent to victory over the dragon, representation of chaos, death, and the unknown. By accepting life's suffering, therefore, evil may be overcome. The alternative is hell, at least in its psychological form: rage, resentment, and the desire for revenge and destruction.

The same story is echoed in the tales of St. Patrick, who chases the snakes out of Ireland, and St. Michael, who defeats the Christian equivalent of Kingu, "that ancient serpent called the devil" (Revelation 12:9). This is the same story recounted by J. R. R. Tolkien in *The Hobbit*, which was in turn derived from the ancient poem *Beowulf*, the tale of a hero defeating a pair of intelligent monsters—son, and then worse, mother.[7] In *The Hobbit*, the hero develops character and wisdom (as a thief, strangely enough) during his quest to help discover the ancient treasure hoarded by the dragon. The story of Perseus and Medusa, whose visage was so terrible that it turned onlookers to stone, is another variant, as is Pinocchio, who rescues his father from a sub-aquatic monster, and dies and is reborn while doing so. Something similar is portrayed in the first of the recent Avengers movies, in which Iron Man—the man who has transformed himself into a partly golden superhero—defeats the alien dragon worms of the Chitauri (allied with the satanic Loki). He then dies, is reborn, and gets the maiden (in the nonswooning guise of Ms. Pepper Potts). It must be understood: Such stories would not even be comprehensible (not least to children, as well as adults) if our evolutionary history had importantly differed, and if our entire culture had not been shaped, implicitly and explicitly, by these ancient patterns.

All these heroes act out what was perhaps the greatest discovery ever made by man's primordial ancestors: if you have the vision and the courage (and a good stout stick, when necessary), you can chase away the worst of snakes. No doubt the greatest of our ancestors were beginning to threaten snakes with sticks when we still lived in trees. No doubt it was those voluntarily snake-chasing ancestors who reaped the benefits of their bravery in the form of nearby grateful maidens (or their ancestral arboreal equivalents)—and perhaps this is why dragons hoard virgins, as well as gold. What constitutes the worst of all snakes and the stoutest of all sticks, however, might be regarded as the central religious questions of humanity. It is interesting to note that in *The Hobbit*, the worst snake is "only" a dragon, but in *The Lord of the Rings*, the worst snake, so to speak, is the much more abstract evil of the wizard Sauron. As humanity became more sophisticated in its capacity to abstract, we increasingly appreciated the fact that predatory monsters can come in many guises, only some of which are animal in their form. Literature of an arguably more sophisticated form endlessly echoes this realization.

## HERO, DRAGON, DEATH, AND REBIRTH:
## WHO YOU COULD BE (III)

In the second volume of J. K. Rowling's fantasy series, *Harry Potter and the Chamber of Secrets*, the castle of Hogwarts is threatened by strange, chaotic forces, due to the earlier and ongoing misbehavior of several powerful adult wizards (as established in volume one). Now, it is significant that Harry is orphaned: it is an integral part of the heroic pattern. He has his earthly parents, the thick and conventional Dursleys, willfully blind, shortsighted, and terribly overprotective of (and, therefore, tragically dangerous to) Dudley, their unfortunate but predictably self-centered and bullying natural son. But Harry has his heavenly parents, too, his true mother and father—symbolically, Nature and Culture (variants of chaos and order). They exist as part of his intrinsically magical potential—the magical potential of all of us, in fact, as we are all children of Nature and Culture, with the tremendous potential that implies, as well as the more mundane offspring of our particular parents.[8]

When Harry returns to Hogwarts after his summer vacation, he can detect strange and ominous noises emanating from somewhere in the building. At the same time, various students and residents of Hogwarts are found paralyzed—turned to stone—in diverse locations around the building. Turned to stone: What could that possibly mean? It certainly means to be unable to move—but it also signifies something deeper. It means to be *hunted*; to become a rabbit confronted by a wolf; to become the horrified and awestruck object of the predatory gaze. Many herbivores, comparatively defenseless, facing imminent and brutal death, freeze in place, paralyzed by fear, depending on camouflage and immobility to render them invisible to the terrible intentions

of nearby red-toothed and razor-clawed carnivores. Predatory, reptilian forms still particularly have that effect on human beings (hence our
awed fascination, for example, with dinosaurs). But to have no more
courage than a rabbit is definitely not to be everything you could be.

Eventually Harry learns that the force turning his friends into
stone is a gigantic snake, a basilisk, whose gaze exerts a paralyzing
force. He discovers that this serpent is continually slithering around
the very foundation of Hogwarts, in the immense waterworks that
serve the great castle. This basilisk is an analog to the great dragon
faced by Beowulf, hero of the thousand-year-old story that served as
pattern for Tolkien's adventures, perhaps the twentieth century's closest cousins to J. K. Rowling's extensive fantasy. It is, as well, the great
devouring shark of the movie *Jaws*, lurking in the black water of night,
ready at a moment's notice to pull the naked and unwary below; the
fragility of our homes and our institutions, which can collapse and leave
us stripped of their protective walls in a single terrible moment; and
more comprehensively, the underworld of the ancients, whose doors
gape open when everything predictable collapses. At the deepest of
levels, this is the chaos and potential that continually lurks under the
order of our familiar worlds, psychological and social.

After much searching, Harry gains entrance to this underworld
labyrinth of pipes and tunnels, and finds the central chamber. He does
this, significantly, through the sewer, acting out the ancient alchemical dictum, *in sterquilinis invenitur*: in filth it will be found.* What does

---

*It has been known for decades, explicitly (and forever, implicitly) that self-initiated
confrontation with what is frightening or unknown is frequently curative. The standard
treatment for phobias and anxiety is therefore exposure to what is feared. That treatment is effective—but the exposure must be voluntary. It is as if the anxiety systems of
the brain assume that anything that is advanced upon must not be a predator (or, if it is
a predator, it is the sort that can be easily kicked to the side and defeated). We now know
that even the emotional and bodily response to stress differs completely when that stress

this mean? That which you most need to find will be found where you least wish to look.* There, underground, Ginny (Virgin-ia), his best friend's sister and Harry's eventual serious romantic interest, lies unconscious. She is the maiden—or the *anima*, the soul—forever incarcerated by the dragon, as in the tale of St. George. It is up to Harry, orphaned hero, to wake and rescue her (just as Tolkien's Bilbo helps take the gold from the terrible Smaug; just as Disney's Prince Phillip rescues Sleeping Beauty—both rescuing what is most valuable from the clutches of a great dragon).†

---

is voluntarily faced rather than accidentally encountered. In the latter case, the threatened individual tenses up and readies him or herself defensively (see M. D. Seery, "Challenge or Threat? Cardiovascular Indexes of Resilience and Vulnerability to Potential Stress in Humans," *Neuroscience & Biobehavioral Reviews* 35 [2011]: 1603–4). That can become the chronically unhealthy posture of someone turned to stone. In the former case, the individual takes on the role of probable victor, and advances forthrightly. Such actions are indeed what has always saved humanity from the terrors of the night (and the evil lurking in the human heart). Our continual observation of that fact, over millennia, is what allowed us to represent it, abstractly, in our great religious stories, and then to imitate it, within the confines of our particular and unique life.

*This is at least in part because you are very unlikely to have already looked there, even though it would have been useful to do so.

†Something must be further clarified here. I made the case in the Overture, in Rule I, in *12 Rules for Life*, and in *Maps of Meaning* that chaos tends to find its representation in symbolic form as feminine—but here I am talking about chaos, in serpentine guise. I can explain this by elaborating on my explanation about the alchemical picture we discussed earlier—by reading it from the top down, however, this time. The more profound the threat—the deeper the chaos—the more likely that it will represent itself as mankind's most ancient enemy, the serpent. Perhaps it can be thought of like this: the unknown unknowns—those elements of being that are foreign and dangerous beyond imagination, and whose manifestation can kill or destroy psychologically—are those most likely to be represented in serpentine form. Out of this domain, which is in some important sense even more fundamental than sex itself, emerges the primordial feminine and masculine, although it seems that the feminine nonetheless retains a more primary connection with the fundamental unknowable itself. I think this has to do primarily with the absolute mystery of birth: with the relationship between the emergence of new forms from the feminine and the emergence of new forms from the absolutely unknown. It is perhaps something of this sort that accounts for the primacy of the relationship between the snake in the Garden of Eden and Eve, rather than between the snake and Adam. Perhaps, as well (and I am speculating wildly here, trying to move beyond my ignorance,

And of course, the unknown is a great predator—the basilisk Harry faces—and of course, that predator guards a great treasure, gold beyond measure or the sleeping virgin, because the individual brave enough to voluntarily beard the serpent in his lair is most likely to gain access to the untold riches that exist in potential, awaiting us in the adventure of our life, away from security and what is currently known. *Who dares wins\**—if he does not perish. And who wins also makes himself irresistibly desirable and attractive, not least because of the development of character that adventure inevitably produces. And this is what makes us forever more than rabbits.

And Harry, like Bilbo, can only manage this—can only perceive the serpent, when it is invisible to everyone else—because he has a dark side. Tolkien's Bilbo must become a thief before he can become a hero. He must incorporate his monstrousness, so that he can supersede his naive harmlessness, before he is tough enough to face the terrors that confront him. Harry is touched by evil in another manner, as part of the incomparably dark wizard Voldemort's soul is embedded within him (although neither he nor Voldemort are initially aware of this). It is for this reason that the young wizard can speak with and hear

---

trying to account for the clear and omnipresent symbolic relationship), it has forever been the case that females attract snakes (as well as other dangerous predators), most particularly when they are taking care of their young, and that the heightened danger they therefore face has burned the danger of the feminine in relationship to the serpentine forever in our imagination. This would imply that the decision to take on a relationship with a female brings with it increased exposure to the terrible unknown (something that seems clearly true in the case of all the threats that are faced by children), as perhaps does the fact of being female itself. Now the female is also a rejecting force (particularly among humans, where the females are very choosy maters [see, for example, Y. Bokek-Cohen, Y. Peres, and S. Kanazawa, "Rational Choice and Evolutionary Psychology as Explanations for Mate Selectivity," *Journal of Social, Evolutionary, and Cultural Psychology* 2 (2008): 42–55]). That holding of the power of ultimate rejection makes Nature in all its cruelty (and, it must be said, wisdom). Perhaps that is also a nontrivial contributor to the feminine-serpent relationship.

\*The motto of the British Special Air Service.

(that is, perceive) snakes. It is in keeping with this that he is disciplined and courageous, but also willing and ready to break the rules when necessary.

While in the bowels of Hogwarts, Harry comes under attack by the basilisk, which is under the control of Voldemort. Voldemort therefore bears the same relationship to the basilisk in Hogwarts as Satan does, strangely and incomprehensibly, to the vision-granting serpent in the Genesis story of the Garden of Eden. Why might this be? It could be said—and should be—that one form of serpentine chaos and danger is the threat of the reptilian predator itself. But another form, more abstract—more psychological, more spiritual—is human evil: the danger we pose to one another. At some point in our evolutionary and cultural history, we began to understand that human evil could rightly be considered the greatest of all snakes. So, the symbolic progression might be (1) snake as evil predator, then (2) external human enemy as snake/evil/predator, then (3) subjective, personal, or psychological darkness/vengefulness/deceit as snake/evil/predator. Each of these representations, which took untold centuries, perhaps millennia to conceptualize, constitute a tangible increase in the sophistication of the image of evil.[9]

All such manifestations of serpentine chaos and danger are apparently still first detected, processed, and symbolically interassociated by the ancient brain systems that evolved to protect us from predatory reptiles.[10] And freezing—prompted by those systems—solves the problem now, maybe, by hiding the individual who is currently being preyed upon, but it leaves the predator alive for tomorrow. Instead, the danger must be hunted down and destroyed—and even that is too concrete to constitute a permanent solution to the problem of evil itself (rather than a solution to any particular exemplar of evil). Most profoundly and abstractly (paralleling the idea that the greatest predator,

the greatest snake, is the evil that lurks within), evil's destruction
manifests as the life of virtue that constrains malevolence in its most
abstracted and comprehensive form. It is for this reason, for example,
that the Disney prince Phillip of *Sleeping Beauty* fame is armed for his
conflict with the great Dragon of Chaos by benevolent Nature (in the
form of the feminine fairies that accompany him and aid in his escape
from Maleficent, the Evil Queen) with the Sword of Truth and Shield
of Virtue.

Harry directly confronts the basilisk, down in the Chamber of Secrets, deep below the wizarding castle, but is cornered and in great
peril. At that propitious moment, a phoenix kept by the wise headmas-
ter of Hogwarts arrives, provides the young hero with a sword, and
then attacks the giant snake, providing Harry with time to regroup.
Harry slays the basilisk with the weapon, but is fatally bitten in the
process. This is another deep mythological echo: In the story of Genesis, for example, the encounter with the snake proves fatal to man and
woman alike, who become aware of their fragility and inevitable death
soon after they awaken and gain vision. It is also a harsh truth: predators
devour, dragons lay waste, chaos destroys. The threat is real. Even truth,
virtue, and courage are not necessarily enough, but they are our best
bet. And sometimes a little death is the medication necessary to forestall death itself. Fortunately, the phoenix has magical, revivifying tears,
which it cries into Harry's wounds. Thus, the young wizard revives,
defeats Voldemort (a much more challenging task than merely overcoming the gargantuan serpent), rescues Ginny, and saves the school.

It is with the introduction of the phoenix to the story of St. George
that Rowling reveals another element of her intuitive genius. The
phoenix is a fowl that can die and be reborn forever. It has, therefore,
throughout the ages, been a symbol of Christ, with whom the magical
bird shares many features. It is also, equally, that element of the indi-

vidual human personality that must die and regenerate, as it learns, painfully, through the oft-tragic experience that destroys previous certainty, replacing it first with doubt, and then—when successfully confronted—with new and more complete knowledge. A voluntary death-and-rebirth transformation—the change necessary to adapt when terrible things emerge—is therefore a solution to the potentially fatal rigidity of erroneous certainty, excessive order, and stultification.

## HOW TO ACT

People exchange information about how to act in many ways. They observe each other and imitate what they see. When they imitate, they use their bodies to represent the bodies of others. But this imitation is not mindless, automatized mimicry. It is instead the ability to identify regularities or patterns in the behavior of other people, and then to imitate those patterns. When a young girl plays at being a mother, for example, she does not duplicate, gesture for gesture, what she has previously observed of her mother's actions. Instead she acts "as if" she were a mother. If you ask the girl what she is doing, she will tell you that she is pretending to be a mother, but if you get her to describe what that means, particularly if she is a young child, her description will be far less complete than her actions would indicate. This means she can act out more than she can say—just as we all can. If you observed many little girls, acting out many mothers, you could derive a very good idea of what "mother" meant, in its purest form, even if you had never seen an actual mother. If you were good with words, then perhaps you could describe the essential elements of maternal behavior and transmit them. You might do that best in the form of a story.

It is easier and more direct to represent a behavioral pattern with behavior than with words. Outright mimicry does that directly, action for action. Imitation, which can produce new behaviors akin to those that motivated the mimicry, takes that one step further. Drama—formalized imitation, enacted upon a stage—is precisely behavior portraying behavior, but distilled ever closer to the essence. Literature takes that transmission one more difficult step, portraying action in the imagination of the writer and the reader, in the complete absence of both real actors and a material stage. It is only the greatest of storytellers who can manage that transformation, representing the greatest and most vitally necessary of acts in the most interesting, profound, and memorable words. Generations of great storytellers, retelling, modifying, and editing great stories, therefore end up jointly creating the greatest of stories. Once cultures become literate (something that has happened only recently, from the historical perspective), those stories can be written down. It is at this point, roughly, that myth and ritual might be said to transform themselves into religion.

The imitation and communication of the greatest, most memorable acts necessitates distillation and communication of the patterns of the deepest wisdom of mankind. If a great and memorable act is one undertaken by a particularly admirable individual, a local hero, then the greatest and most memorable acts possible would be those undertaken by the spirit (embodied in part by particular individuals) who exemplified what all local heroes everywhere have in common. That hero of heroes—that meta-hero—would have to exist, logically, in turn, *in a place that was common across all places requiring heroism.* That place might be regarded as a meta-world—even though it is real, even hyperreal (that is, more real in its abstraction across places than our direct perceptions of a given, singular time or place). It is precisely this hyperreal meta-world that consists of the continual interactions between chaos and order, which eternally serve as the battleground between good and evil characterizing the hero. The undying pattern that hero embodies, in turn—upon whose actions the individual and society both depend—is the highest of all Gods. He is both child of and mediator between those twin forces, transforming chaos into habitable order (as well as recasting order into chaos, so that it can be renewed, when it has become anachronistic and corrupt), as well as battling mightily so that good might prevail.

Everyone requires a story to structure their perceptions and actions in what would otherwise be the overwhelming chaos of being. Every story requires a starting place that is not good enough and an ending place that is better. Nothing can be judged in the absence of that end place, that higher value. Without it, everything sinks into meaninglessness and boredom or degenerates and spirals into terror, anxiety, and pain. But, as time changes all things inexorably, every specific, value-predicated story may fail, in its particular incarnation and locale, and need replacement by something newer, more complete, but different. In consequence, the actor of a given story (and, therefore, someone deeply affiliated with the plot and the characterization) still must bow to the spirit of creative transformation that originally created and may need to destroy and re-create that story. It is for this reason that spirit eternally transcends dogma, truth transcends presupposition, Marduk transcends the elder gods, creativity updates society, and Christ transcends the law (as does Harry Potter, along with his courageous but continually rule-breaking friends). But it is important to remember, as we discussed in Rule I: Those who break the rules ethically are those who have mastered them first and disciplined themselves to understand the necessity of those rules, and break them in keeping with the spirit rather than the letter of the law.

The second volume of Rowling's series proposes that predatory evil can be overcome by the soul willing to die and be reborn. The complete series ends with a creatively transformed repetition of the same message. The analogy with Christianity is obvious, and the message, in essence, the same: The soul willing to transform, as deeply as necessary, is the most effective enemy of the demonic serpents of ideology and totalitarianism, in their personal and social forms. The healthy, dynamic, and above all else truthful personality will admit to error. It will voluntarily shed—let die—outdated perceptions, thoughts, and habits, as impediments to its further success and growth. This is the soul that will let its old beliefs burn away, often painfully, so that it can live again, and move forward, renewed. This is also the soul that will transmit what it has learned during that process of death and rebirth, so that others can be reborn along with it.

Aim at something. Pick the best target you can currently conceptualize. Stumble toward it. Notice your errors and misconceptions along the way, face them, and correct them. Get your story straight. Past, present, future—they all matter. You need to map your path. You need to know where you were, so that you do not repeat the mistakes of the past. You need to know where you are, or you will not be able to draw a line from your starting point to your destination. You need to know where you are going, or you will drown in uncertainty, unpredictability, and chaos, and starve for hope and inspiration. For better or worse, you are on a journey. You are having an adventure—and your map better be accurate. Voluntarily confront what stands in your way. The way—that is the path of life, the meaningful path of life, the straight and narrow path that constitutes the very border between order and chaos, and the traversing of which brings them into balance.

Aim at something profound and noble and lofty. If you can find a better path along the way, once you have started moving forward, then switch course. Be careful, though; it is not easy to discriminate between changing paths and simply giving up. (One hint: if the new path you see forward, after learning what you needed to learn along your current way, appears more challenging, then you can be reasonably sure that you are not deluding or betraying yourself when you change your mind.) In this manner, you will zigzag forward. It is not the most efficient way to travel, but there is no real alternative, given that your goals will inevitably change while you pursue them, as you learn what you need to learn while you are disciplining yourself.

You will then find yourself turning across time, incrementally and gracefully, to aim ever more accurately at that tiny pinpoint, the X that marks the spot, the bull's-eye, and the center of the cross; to aim at the highest value of which you can conceive. You will pursue a target that is both moving and receding: moving, because you do not have the wisdom to aim in the proper direction when you first take aim; receding, because no matter how close you come to perfecting what you are currently practicing, new vistas of possible perfection will open up in front of you. Discipline and transformation will nonetheless lead you inexorably forward. With will and luck, you will find a story that is meaningful and productive, improves itself with time, and perhaps even provides you with more than a few moments of satisfaction and joy. With will and luck, you will be the hero of that story, the disciplined sojourner, the creative transformer, and the benefactor of your family and broader society.

Imagine who you could be, and then aim single-mindedly at that.

# DO NOT HIDE UNWANTED
# THINGS IN THE FOG

## THOSE DAMNED PLATES

I love my father-in-law. I respect him, too. He is extremely stable emotionally—one of those tough or fortunate people (perhaps a little of both) who can let the trials and tribulations of life roll off him and keep moving forward with little complaint and plenty of competence. He is an old guy now, Dell Roberts—eighty-eight. He has had a knee replaced, and is planning to get the remaining one done. He has had stents inserted into his coronary arteries and a heart valve replaced. He suffers from drop foot and sometimes slips and falls because of it. But he was still curling a year ago, pushing the heavy granite rock down the ice with a stick specifically designed for people who can no longer crouch down as easily as they once could.

When his wife, Beth, now deceased, developed dementia at a relatively young age, he took care of her in as uncomplaining and unresentful a manner as anyone could imagine. It was impressive. I am by no means convinced that I could have fared as well. He cared for her right to the point where it became impossible for him to lift her out of whatever chair she had settled into. This was long after she had lost the ability to speak. But it was obvious by the way her eyes lit up when he entered the room that she still loved him—and the feeling was mutual. I would not describe him as someone who is prone to avoidance when the going gets tough. Quite the contrary.

When Dell was a much younger man, he was for several decades a real estate dealer in Fairview, Alberta—the small town where I grew up (we lived right across the street from the Roberts family, in fact). During that time, he habitually went home for lunch, in accordance with the general custom. Beth typically prepared him soup (probably Campbell's, which everyone ate at that time—"M'm! M'm! Good!"), and a sandwich. One day, without warning, he snapped at his wife: "Why in the world do we always eat off these tiny plates? I hate eating off these tiny plates!"

She had been serving the sandwiches on bread-and-butter plates, which average about six or seven inches in diameter, instead of full-size dinner plates of ten to twelve inches. She related this story to her daughters, soon after, in a state of mild shock. This story has been re-told to much laughter at family gatherings many times since. After all, she had been serving him lunch on those plates for at least twenty years by the time he finally said anything. She had no idea that he was annoyed by her table settings. He had never objected. And there is something inexhaustibly amusing about that.

Now, it is possible that he was irritated by something else altogether that day and did not really care about the plates. And in one sense, it is a trivial issue. But seen another way, it is not trivial at all, for two reasons. First, if something happens every day, *it is important*, and lunch was happening every day. In consequence, if there was something about it that was chronically bothersome, even in a minor sort of way, it needed to be attended to. Second, it is very common to allow so-called minor irritations (which are not minor, as I said, if they happen constantly) to continue for years without comment or resolution.

Here is the problem: Collect a hundred, or a thousand, of those, and your life is miserable and your marriage doomed. Do not pretend you are happy with something if you are not, and if a reasonable solution might, in principle, be negotiated. Have the damn fight. Unpleasant as that might be in the moment, it is one less straw on the camel's back. And that is particularly true for those daily events that everyone is prone to regard as trivial—even the plates on which you eat your lunch. Life is what repeats, and it is worth getting what repeats right.

## JUST NOT WORTH THE FIGHT

Here is a more serious story of the same type. I had a client who had come to see me about her plans to move to private practice after many years as an accountant with a large corporation. She was well respected in her profession, and was a competent, kind, and careful person. But she was also very unhappy. I presumed initially that her unhappiness stemmed from anxiety about her career transition. But she managed that move without a hitch during the time we continued our sessions, while other issues rose to the forefront.

Her problem was not her career change. It was her marriage. She described her husband as extraordinarily self-centered and simultaneously overly concerned with how he appeared in the eyes of others. It was a contradictory combination, in some manner, although it is common enough to see this touching of opposites in a personality: If you lean too far in one direction, something else in you leans equally far in the other. So, despite the husband's narcissism (at least from his wife's perspective), he was in thrall to the opinions of everyone he met—excepting the members of his own family. He also drank too much—a habit which exaggerated his temperamental defects.

My client was not comfortable in her own home. She did not feel there was anything truly of her within the apartment she shared with her husband (the couple had no children). Her situation provided a good example of how what is outside can profoundly reflect what is inside (which is why I suggest to people who are in psychological trouble that they might begin their recovery by cleaning up—and then beautifying, if possible—their rooms). All their household furnishings, which she described as showy, ornate, and uncomfortable, had been chosen by her husband. Furthermore, he avidly collected 1960s and 70s pop art, and the walls of the house were crowded with these items, which he had spent time seeking out in galleries and otherwise gathering for many years, often while she sat waiting outside in the car.

She told me that she did not care about the furnishings and the excess of decorative objects, but that was not really true. What was true was that she did not care *for* them—not a bit. Neither the showiness nor the furnishings nor the plethora of art works that made up her husband's collection appealed to her taste. She tended toward a minimalist aesthetic (or perhaps that preference was a consequence of her husband's decorative excesses). It was never quite clear what she might have preferred, and perhaps that was part of the problem: because she did not know what she liked (and was equally vague about her dislikes), she was not in the strongest position to put forward her own opinions. It is difficult to win an argument, or even begin one, if you have not carefully articulated what you want (or do not) and need (or do not).

However, she certainly did not enjoy feeling like a stranger in her own home. For that reason, she never had friends over to visit, which was also a nontrivial problem, contributing as it did to her feelings of isolation. But the furnishings and paintings continued to accrue, one shopping expedition at a time, in Canada and abroad, and with each purchase there was less of her in the house and in the marriage, and increasingly more of her husband. Nonetheless, my client never went to war. She never had a fit of anger. She never put her fist through a particularly objectionable canvas hanging on the living room wall. In all the decades of her married life, she never had an outburst of genuine rage; she never directly and conclusively confronted the fact that she hated her home and her subordination to her husband's taste. Instead, she let him have his way, repeatedly, increment by increment, because she claimed that such trivialities were not worth fighting for. And with each defeat, the next disagreement became more necessary— although less likely, because she understood that a serious discussion, once initiated, risked expanding to include all the things that were troublesome about her marriage, and that a real, no-holds-barred battle would therefore likely ensue. Then everything wrong might spill out and have to be faced and dealt with, by one means or another. So, she kept silent. But she was chronically repressed and constantly resentful, and felt that she had wasted much of the opportunity of her life.

It is a mistake to consider the furnishings and the pop art paintings as simple material objects. They were more truly and importantly containers of information, so to speak, about the state of the marriage, and were certainly experienced as such by my client. Every single object of art was the concrete realization of a victory (Pyrrhic though it may have been) and a defeat (or, at least, a negotiation that did not occur and, therefore, a fight that was over before it started). And there were dozens or perhaps hundreds of these: each a weapon in an unspoken, destructive, and decades-long war. Unsurprisingly, given the circumstances, the couple split up—after thirty years of marriage. I believe the husband retained all the furniture and art.

Here is a thought, a terrifying and dispiriting thought, to motivate improvement in your marriage—to scare you into the appalling difficulties of true negotiation. Every little problem you have every morning, afternoon, or evening with your spouse will be repeated for each of the fifteen thousand days that will make up a forty-year marriage. Every trivial but chronic disagreement about cooking, dishes, housecleaning, responsibility for finances, or frequency of intimate contact will be duplicated, over and over, unless you successfully address it. Perhaps you think (moment to moment, at least) that it is best to avoid confrontation and drift along in apparent but false peace. Make no mistake about it, however: you age as you drift, just as rapidly as you age as you strive. But you have no direction when you drift, and the probability that you will obtain what you need and want by drifting aimlessly is very low. Things fall apart of their own accord, but the sins of men speed their deterioration: that is wisdom from the ages. It may well be that conscious apprehension of the horror of the same small hell forever repeated is precisely what is necessary to force you to confront the problems in your marriage and negotiate in good and desperate faith to solve them. However, it is the easiest of matters, particularly in the short term, to ignore the prick of conscience and let the small defeats slide, day after day. This is not a good strategy. Only careful aim and wakeful striving and commitment can eliminate the oft-incremental calamity of willful blindness, stem the entropic tide, and keep catastrophe—familial and social alike—at bay.

## CORRUPTION: COMMISSION AND OMISSION

Corruption of the form we are discussing is, in my opinion, integrally linked to deception—to lying, more bluntly—and more important, to self-deception. Now, strict logicians regard self-deception as an impossibility. They cannot understand how it is possible for a person to believe one thing and its opposite simultaneously. Logicians are not psychologists, however—and they obviously do not notice, or else fail to take into account, the fact that they themselves have family members, for example, for whom they at least occasionally feel love and hate at the same time. Furthermore, it is not obvious what "believe" means when discussing human belief, nor what is meant by "simultaneously." I can believe one thing today and another tomorrow and very often get away with it, at least in the short term. And on many occasions I have experienced what was very nearly simultaneous belief in one thing and its opposite while reading undergraduate university papers, in which the writer made a claim in one paragraph and a completely contradictory claim in the next. (Sometimes that happened within the span of a single sentence.)

There are many conditions or circumstances under which self-deception can theoretically occur. Psychoanalysts have explored many of these, with Freud leading the way. Freud believed that much of mental illness was due to repression, which is arguably and reasonably considered a form of self-deception. For him, memories of traumatically troubling events were unconsciously banished to perdition in the unconscious, where they rattled around and caused trouble, like poltergeists in a dungeon. Freud understood that the human personality was not unitary. Instead, it consists of a loose, fragmented cacophony of spirits, who do not always agree or even communicate. The truth of this claim is self-evident, at least in one simple manner: we can think about things—we can simulate potential or alternative actions or events—without immediately having to act them out. Dissociation of thought and action is necessary for abstract thought even to exist. Thus, we can clearly think or say one thing and do another. This is fine when merely thinking, prior to acting, but perhaps not so good when we promise or claim to believe something and then act in a manner indicating that we truly have faith in something else. This is a form of deception, a disjunction in character, a contradiction between modes of being. It has even been named: to claim one belief and then to act (or speak) in a different or even opposite manner constitutes a *performative contradiction*, according to certain modern philosophers:[1] an implicit lie, in my opinion. The holding of contradictory beliefs also becomes a problem when the holder attempts to act out both simultaneously and discovers, often to his or her great chagrin, the paradox that makes such an attempt impossible.

Freud catalogued an extensive list of phenomena akin to repression—the active rejection of potentially conscious psychological material from awareness—which he termed "defense mechanisms." These include denial ("the truth is not so bad"), reaction formation ("I really, really, really love my mother"), displacement ("the boss yells at me, I yell at my wife, my wife yells at the baby, the baby bites the cat"), identification ("I am bullied, so I am motivated to be a bully"), rationalization (a self-serving explanation for a low-quality action), intellectualization (a favorite of the early, funny, neurotic Woody Allen), sublimation ("I can always *paint* nude women"), and projection ("I am not touchy; you are just annoying"). Freud was an outstanding philosopher of deceit. He was not afraid to point out the relationship between dishonesty and psychopathology. Nonetheless, his ideas of self-deception suffer, in my opinion, from two major errors.

First error: Freud failed to notice that sins of omission contributed to mental illness as much as, or more than, the sins of commission, listed above, that constitute repression. In doing so, he merely thought in the typical manner. People generally believe that actively doing something bad (that is the sin of commission) is, on average, worse than passively not doing something good (that is the sin of omission). Perhaps this is because there are always good things we are not doing; some sins of omission are therefore inevitable. In any case, there are still times when willful blindness nonetheless produces more serious catastrophes, more easily rationalized away, than the active or the unconscious repression of something terrible but understood (the latter being a sin of commission, because it is known). The former problem—willful blindness—occurs when you *could* come to know something but cease exploring so that you fail to discover something that might cause you substantial discomfort. Spin doctors call this self-imposed ignorance "plausible deniability," which is a phrase that indicates intellectualized rationalization of the most pathological order. It should be noted that such blindness is often regarded as an outright crime. If you are a CEO, for example, and you suspect that your treasurer is cooking the books, and you do not investigate because you do not want to know, you may still be liable for your inaction—as is appropriate. Failing to look under the bed when you strongly suspect a monster is lurking there is not an advisable strategy.

Second error: Freud assumed that things experienced are things understood. In accordance with that assumption, he believed that a memory trace existed, somewhere in the mind, that accurately represented the past, like an objective video recording. These would be reasonable presumptions, if our experience was simply a series of objectively real and self-evident events transmitted through our senses, thought about, evaluated, and then acted upon. If this was all true, traumatic experience would be accurately represented in memory, even when pushed out of awareness by unconscious mechanisms (or conscious—but Freud presumed the former) because of its understood but terrible nature. However, neither reality nor our processing of reality is as objective or articulated as Freud presupposed.

Imagine, for example, that you have been ignored, romantically— more than you can tolerate—for several months by your wife or husband. Then you encounter him or her leaning over the fence, talking in a friendly manner (and perhaps no more than that) to an attractive neighbor. How we process such anomalous, novel, troublesome, or even traumatic experience is very rarely a matter of perception, followed by conscious understanding and thought, then emotion or motivation derived from that thought, then action. What happens instead is akin to what we discussed at length in Rule I and Rule II: We process the unknown world from the bottom up. We encounter containers of information, so to speak, whose full import is by no means self-evident. Upon witnessing your spouse talking to the neighbor, therefore, it is not as if you think, in an altogether articulated and fully developed philosophical form: "I have been lonesome and deprived physically for months by my spouse. Although I have not said anything in detail, this has caused me constant frustration and pain. Now he (or she) is rubbing it in, as far as I am concerned, by being so outgoing with a comparative stranger when I have experienced so little attention." It is much more likely that anger, grief, and loneliness have accumulated within you with each rejection, bit by bit, until you are filled to the brim—and, now, overflowing.

That sudden appearance of negative emotion does not necessarily mean that you are even now fully conscious of its accumulation. You may well (as in the case of my father-in-law, or my client) have experienced the frustration build up gradually enough so that you found yourself more irritable and unhappy, but that does not necessarily mean that you noticed the cause. And what *is* the cause? The range of possibilities is uncomfortably broad. Perhaps you are not being ignored at all. Instead, you have been having trouble at work, and that has produced a decrease in your overall confidence. In consequence, you have become sensitized to any signs of rejection, even imaginary, within your marriage. So, what you must determine is not so much why your wife or husband is no longer attentive to you, but what it is about your boss, colleagues, or career that is destabilizing you. That puts the true cause of your discomfort a long distance away from the symptoms (the feelings of rejection) that are making you irritable, sensitive, and hurt. There is nothing obvious about the relationship between cause and effect in such cases. Perhaps you really are being ignored, just as you suspect. Perhaps it is a sign of an impending affair and a manifestation of the trajectory that leads to divorce. Both of those, if true, are serious problems. It is no wonder you are upset. But you may remain stubbornly unwilling to consider that your career or marriage is in trouble. And that is no surprise. But it is not helpful.

On top of all that is the general complexity of life, complicating the search for clarity. Consider the question "What really happened?" say, in a failed marriage, divorce, and child-custody battle. The answer to that query is so complex that settling the disagreements frequently requires court evaluation and multi-party assessment. Even then, one or even both of the protagonists is unlikely to believe that the truth has been served. This is partly because events in general and interpersonal events specifically do not exist as simple, objective facts, independent of one another. Everything depends for its meaning—for the information it truly represents—on the context in which it is embedded, much of which is not available for perception or consideration when the event in question occurs. The meaning of what someone's wife says to him today is dependent on everything both have ever said to each other, everything they have ever done together, and the contents of their mutual imaginations—and that does not exhaust the complexity. Such meaning may even be importantly dependent on how, for example, the wife's mother treated her father (or her grandmother treated her grandfather), as well as the relationship between men and women in the broader culture. That is why domestic arguments so often spiral out of control, particularly when a pattern of continual and effective communication has never been established. One thing leads to a deeper thing, and that leads deeper yet, until an argument that started over what size plates are best used at lunchtime turns into a no-holds-barred war about whether the marriage in question would be better dissolved. And there is certainly fear of falling down a hole of that size (again, particularly when much has remained unspoken) that motivates the proclivity to keep things to yourself when they would be better, but dangerously, said.

## WHAT IS THE FOG?

Imagine that you are afraid. You have reason to be. You are afraid of yourself. You are afraid of other people. You are afraid of the world. You are nostalgic for the innocence of the past; for the time before you learned the terrible things that shattered the trust characterizing your childhood. The knowledge you have gained of yourself, other people, and the world has embittered more than enlightened. You have been betrayed, hurt, and disappointed. You have become distrustful even of hope itself, as your hope has been repeatedly shattered (and that is the very definition of hopelessness). The last thing you want is to know more. Better to leave *what is* enshrouded in mystery. Better, as well, to avoid thinking too much (or at all) about *what could be*. When ignorance is bliss, after all, 'tis folly to be wise.

Imagine, more precisely, that you are so afraid that you will not allow yourself even to know what you want. Knowing would simultaneously mean hoping, and your hopes have been dashed. You have your reasons for maintaining your ignorance. You are afraid, perhaps, that there is nothing worth wanting; you are afraid that if you specify what you want precisely you will simultaneously discover (and all too clearly) what constitutes failure; you are afraid that failure is the most likely outcome; and, finally, you are afraid that if you define failure and then fail, you will know beyond a shadow of a doubt that it was you that failed, and that it was your fault.

So, you do not allow yourself to know what you want. You manage this by refusing to think it through. You are happy, satisfied, and engaged sometimes and unhappy, frustrated, and nihilistic other times, but you will not enquire deeply into why, because then you would know, and then you would encounter yet-again shattered hope and confirmed disappointment. You are also afraid, but for different reasons, to allow others to know what you want. First, if they were to find out just what you wanted, then they might tell you, and then you would know, even if you were fighting against gathering that very knowledge. Second, if they knew, they could then deny you what you truly wanted, even needed, and hurt you much more efficiently than they might if your deepest desires (and, therefore, your vulnerabilities) remained secret.

The fog that hides is the refusal to notice—to attend to—emotions and motivational states as they arise, and the refusal to communicate them both to yourself and to the people who are close to you. A bad mood signifies something. A state of anxiety or sadness signifies

something, and not likely something that will please you to discover.
The most probable outcome of successfully articulating an emotion
that has accrued without expression over time is tears—an admission
of vulnerability and pain (which are also feelings that people do not
like to allow, particularly when they are feeling distrustful and angry).
Who wants to dig down into the depths of pain and grief and guilt
until the tears emerge? And voluntary refusal to take notice of our
emotional states is not the only impediment to dealing with them.
If your wife or husband (or whomever else you are tangled up with,
unhappily, at the moment) says something that comes too close to
the painful truth, for example, then a sharp and insulting remark will
often shut them up—and is therefore very likely to be offered. This is
partly a test: does the person being insulted care enough about you
and your suffering to dig past a few obstacles and unearth the bitter
truth? It is also partly, and more obviously, defensive: if you can chase
someone away from something you yourself do not want to discover,
that makes your life easier in the present. Sadly, it is also very disappointing if that defense succeeds, and is typically accompanied by a
sense of abandonment, loneliness, and self-betrayal. You must nonetheless still live among other people, and they with you. And you have
desires, wants, and needs, however unstated and unclear. And you are
still motivated to pursue them, not least because it is impossible to live
without desire, want, and need. Your strategy, under such conditions?
Show your disappointment whenever someone close to you makes you
unhappy; allow yourself the luxury and pleasure of resentment when
something does not go your way; ensure that the person who has transgressed against you is frozen out by your disapproval; force them to
discover with as much difficulty as possible exactly what they have
done to disappoint you; and, finally, let them grope around blindly in
the fog that you have generated around yourself until they stumble

into and injure themselves on the sharp hidden edges of your unre-
vealed preferences and dreams. And maybe these responses are tests,
too—tests deeply associated with the lack of courage to trust: "If you
really loved me, you would brave the terrible landscape that I have
arrayed around myself to discover the real me." And perhaps there is
even something to such claims, implicit though they may be. A certain
testing of commitment might have its utility. Everything does not have
to be given away for free. But even a little unnecessary mystery goes a
long way.

And you still must live with yourself. In the short term, perhaps
you are protected from the revelation of your insufficiency by your
refusal to make yourself clear. Every ideal is a judge, after all: the judge
who says, "You are not manifesting your true potential." No ideals?
No judge. But the price paid for that is purposelessness. This is a high
price. No purpose? Then, no positive emotion, as most of what drives
us forward with hope intact is the experience of approaching something we deeply need and want. And worse, when we are without purpose: chronic, overwhelming anxiety, as focused purpose constrains
what is otherwise likely to be the intolerable chaos of unexploited possibility and too much choice.

If you make what you want clear and commit yourself to its pursuit,
you may fail. But if you do not make what you want clear, then you
will certainly fail. You cannot hit a target that you refuse to see. You
cannot hit a target if you do not take aim. And, equally dangerously, in
both cases: you will not accrue the advantage of aiming, but missing.
You will not benefit from the learning that inevitably takes place when
things do not go your way. Success at a given endeavor often means
trying, falling short, recalibrating (with the new knowledge generated
painfully by the failure), and then trying again and falling short—
often repeated, *ad nauseam*. Sometimes all that learning, impossible

without the failure, leads you to see that aiming your ambition in a different direction would be better (not because it is easier; not because you have given up; not because you are avoiding—but because you have learned through the vicissitudes of your experience that what you seek is not to be found where you were looking, or is simply not attainable in the manner by which you chose to pursue it).

So, what might you do—what should you do—as an alternative to hiding things in the fog? *Admit to your feelings.* This is a very tricky matter (and it does not simply mean "give in" to them). First, noting, much less communicating, feelings of (petty) anger or pain due to lonesomeness, or anxiety about something that might be trivial, or jealousy that is likely unwarranted is embarrassing. The admission of such feelings is a revelation of ignorance, insufficiency, and vulnerability. Second, it is unsettling to allow for the possibility that your feelings, however overwhelming and convincing, might be misplaced and, in your ignorance, pointing you in the wrong direction. It is possible that you have misinterpreted the situation entirely, for reasons of which you remain fundamentally unconscious. It is for such reasons that trust is vital: but trust of the mature and tragic sort. A naive person trusts because he or she believes that people are essentially or even universally trustworthy. But any person who has truly lived has been—or has—betrayed.

Someone with experience knows that people are capable of deception and willing to deceive. That knowledge brings with it an arguably justified pessimism about human nature, personal and otherwise, but it also opens the door to another kind of faith in humanity: one based on courage, rather than naivete. I will trust you—I will extend my hand to you—despite the risk of betrayal, because it is possible, through trust, to bring out the best in you, and perhaps in me. So, I will accept substantial risk to open the door to cooperation and negotiation. And even if you do betray me, in a not-too unforgivable manner (assuming a certain degree, shall we say, of genuine apology and contrition on your part), I will continue to extend my hand. And part of the way I will do that is by telling you what I am feeling.

A certain necessary humility must accompany such raw revelations. I should not say—at least not ideally—"You have been ignoring me lately." I should say, instead, "I feel isolated and lonely and hurt, and cannot help but feel that you have not been as attentive to me over the last few months as I would have liked or that might have been best for us as a couple. But I am unsure if I am just imagining all this because I am upset or if I am genuinely seeing what is going on." The latter statement gets the point across, but avoids the accusatory stance that so often serves as the first defense against a serious, get-to-the-bottom-of-things conversation. And it is very possible that you are wrong about just what is causing you to feel the way you do. If you are, you need to know it, because there is no point in propagating errors that are causing you and others pain and interfering with your future. Best to find out what is true—best to disperse the fog—and find out if the sharp objects you feared were lurking there are real or fantastical. And there is always the danger that some of them are real. But it is better to see them than to keep them occluded by the fog, because you can at least sometimes avoid the danger that you are willing to see.

## EVENTS AND MEMORIES

Events, as they lay themselves out in front of us, do not simply inform us of why they occur, and we do not remember the past in order to objectively record bounded, well-defined events and situations. The latter act is impossible, in any case. The information in our experience is latent, like gold in ore—the case we made in Rule II. It must be extracted and refined with great effort, and often in collaboration with other people, before it can be employed to improve the present and the future. We use our past effectively when it helps us repeat desirable—and avoid repeating undesirable—experiences. We want to know what happened but, more importantly, we want to know *why*. *Why* is wisdom. *Why* enables us to avoid making the same mistake again and again, and if we are fortunate helps us repeat our successes.

Extracting useful information from experience is difficult. It requires the purest of motivations ("things should be made better, not worse") to perform it properly. It requires the willingness to confront error, forthrightly, and to determine at what point and why departure from the proper path occurred. It requires the willingness to change, which is almost always indistinguishable from the decision to leave something (or someone, or some idea) behind. Therefore, the simplest response imaginable is to look away and refuse to think, while simultaneously erecting unsurmountable impediments to genuine communication.

Unfortunately, in the longer term, this willful blindness leaves life murky and foggy; leaves it void, unseen, without form, confused—and leaves you bewildered and astonished.[2] This is all a strange concatenation of the psychological and the real, the subjective and the objective. Is something frightening, or am I afraid? Is something beautiful, or am I imposing the idea of beauty upon it? When I become angry with someone, is it because of something they have done, or my lack of control? Such questions define the state of confusion you occupy chronically when the bottom has fallen out of your world. That state can have an objective element, because a fall is often caused by something real, such as a death, a serious illness, or a bout of unemployment; but it is also subjective, associated with a state composed of pain, doubt, confusion, and the inability to choose—or even perceive—a path forward.

The ground of Being is subject and object simultaneously—
motivation, emotion, and material thing all at once—before perception
is clarified, before the world is articulated. The wife remains uncom-
prehended. The context of her speech remains unexplored, for fear of
what that exploration might reveal. The situation cannot be described
because the word is left vague and unformed. Our own personal motivations begin in hidden form, and remain that way, because we do not
want to know what we are up to. The wheat remains unseparated from
the chaff. The gold remains in the clutches of the dragon, as does the
virgin. The philosopher's stone remains undiscovered in the gutter;
and the information hidden in the round chaos, beckoning, remains
unexplored. Such omission is the voluntary refusal of expanded consciousness. After all, the pathway to the Holy Grail has its beginnings
in the darkest part of the forest, and what you need remains hidden
where you least want to look.

If you pile up enough junk in your closet, one day, when you are
least prepared, the door will spring open, and all of what has been
packed inside, growing inexorably in the darkness, will bury you, and
you may not have enough time or energy left in your life to confront
it, sort through it, keep what you need, and discard the rest. This is
what it means to be crushed under excess baggage. This is the return
of Tiamat, the great Mesopotamian Goddess of Chaos, destroyer of
those who act improperly.

The world is full of hidden dangers and obstacles—and opportunities. Leaving everything hidden in the fog because you are afraid of
the danger you may find there will be of little help when fate forces
you to run headlong toward what you have refused to see. Impaling
yourself on sharp branches, stumbling over boulders, and rushing by
places of sanctuary, you will finally refuse to admit you could have
burned away the haze with the bright light of your consciousness, had

you not hidden it under a bushel. Then you will come to curse man, reality, and God himself for producing such an impenetrable maze of impediments and barriers. Corruption will beckon to you, led as you increasingly will be by dark, unexamined motivations—bred by failure, amplified by frustration—viciously culminating in the resentful belief that those who have transgressed against you are getting from you exactly what they deserve. This attitude and the actions and inactions it will inevitably produce will impoverish your life, your community, your nation, and the world. This will in turn impoverish Being itself (and that will be exactly what your darkest unexamined motivations desire).

With careful searching, with careful attention, you might tip the balance toward opportunity and against obstacle sufficiently so that life is clearly worth living, despite its fragility and suffering. If you truly wanted, perhaps you would receive, if you asked. If you truly sought, perhaps you would find what you seek. If you knocked, truly wanting to enter, perhaps the door would open. But there will be times in your life when it will take everything you have to face what is in front of you, instead of hiding away from a truth so terrible that the only thing worse is the falsehood you long to replace it with.

Do not hide unwanted things in the fog.

---

# NOTICE THAT OPPORTUNITY
# LURKS WHERE RESPONSIBILITY
# HAS BEEN ABDICATED

## MAKE YOURSELF INVALUABLE

In my dual role as clinical psychologist and professor, I have coached many people in the development of their careers. Sometimes those I am coaching consult me because their coworkers, subordinates, or bosses will not do their jobs properly. They are supervised by, working alongside, or managing people who are narcissistic, incompetent, malevolent, or tyrannical. Such things happen and must be dealt with in whatever reasonable manner will bring them to a halt. I do not encourage people to martyr themselves. It is a bad idea to sacrifice yourself uncomplainingly so that someone else can take the credit. Nonetheless, under such circumstances—if you are a wise and attentive person— you might still notice that your unproductive coworkers are leaving a plethora of valuable tasks undone. You might then ask yourself, "What would happen if I took responsibility for doing them?" It is a daunting question. What is left undone is often risky, difficult, and necessary. But that also means—does it not?—that it is worthwhile and significant. And you may have the eyes to see that there is a problem, despite your all-too-frequent blindness. How do you know that it is not, therefore, *your* problem? Why do you notice this issue and not some other? This is a question worth considering in depth.

If you want to become invaluable in a workplace—in any community—just do the useful things no one else is doing. Arrive earlier and leave later than your compatriots (but do not deny yourself your life).[1] Organize what you can see is dangerously disorganized. Work, when you are working, instead of looking like you are working. And finally, learn more about the business—or your competitors—than you already know. Doing so will make you invaluable—a veritable lynchpin. People will notice that and begin to appreciate your hard-earned merits.

You might object, "Well, I just could not manage to take on something that important." What if you began to build yourself into a person who could? You could start by trying to solve a small problem—something that is bothering you, that you think you could fix. You could start by confronting a dragon of just the size that you are likely to defeat. A tiny serpent might not have had the time to hoard a lot of gold, but there might still be some treasure to be won, along with a reasonable probability of succeeding in such a quest (and not too much chance of a fiery or toothsome death). Under reasonable circumstances, picking up the excess responsibility is an opportunity to become truly invaluable. And then, if you want to negotiate for a raise, or more autonomy—or more free time, for that matter—you can go to your boss and say, "Here are ten things that were crying out to be done, each of them vital, and I am now doing all of them. If you help me out a bit, I will continue. I might even improve. And everything, including your life, will improve along with me." And then, if your boss has any sense—

and sometimes bosses do—then your negotiation will be successful. That is how such things work. And do not forget that there is no shortage of genuinely good people who are thrilled if they can give someone useful and trustworthy a hand up. It is one of the truly altruistic pleasures of life, and its depth is not to be underestimated, or to be disregarded with the cheap cynicism that masks itself as world-weary wisdom.

It appears that the meaning that most effectively sustains life is to be found in the adoption of responsibility. When people look back on what they have accomplished, they think, if they are fortunate: "Well, I did that, and it was valuable. It was not easy. But it was worth it." It is a strange and paradoxical fact that there is a reciprocal relationship between the worth of something and the difficulty of accomplishing it. Imagine the following conversation: "Do you want difficulty?" "No, I want ease." "In your experience, has doing something easy been worthwhile?" "Well, no, not very often." "Then perhaps you really want something difficult." I think that is the secret to the reason for Being itself: *difficult is necessary.*

It is for this reason that we voluntarily and happily place limitations on ourselves. Every time we play a game, for example, we accept a set of arbitrary restrictions. We narrow and limit ourselves, and explore the possibilities thereby revealed. That is what makes the game. But it does not work without the arbitrary rules. You take them on voluntarily, absurdly, as in chess: "I can only move this knight in an L. How ridiculous. But how fun!" Because it is not fun, oddly enough, if you can move any piece anywhere. It is not a game anymore if you can make any old move at all. Accept some limitations, however, and the game begins. Accept them, more broadly speaking, as a necessary part of Being and a desirable part of life. Assume you can transcend them by accepting them. And then you can play the limited game properly.

And this is all not merely of psychological import, and it is by no means just a game. People need meaning, but problems also need solving. It is very salutary, from the psychological perspective, to find something of significance—something worth sacrificing for (or to), something worth confronting and taking on. But the suffering and malevolence that characterize life are real, with the terrible consequences of the real—and our ability to solve problems, by confronting them and taking them on, is also real. By taking responsibility, we can find a meaningful path, improve our personal lot psychologically, and make what is intolerably wrong genuinely better. Thus, we can have our cake and eat it, too.

## RESPONSIBILITY AND MEANING

The idea that life is suffering is a relatively universal truism of religious thinking. This is the first of the Four Noble Truths of Buddhism as well as a key Hindu concept. There is a tradition that the ancient Indian word for suffering—*dukkha* (from the Pali language) or *duhka* (from Sanskrit)—is derived from *dus* (bad) and *kha* (hole)—particularly the hole in a horse-drawn cart wheel, through which the axle passes. The proper place for such a hole is dead center, right on target. The ride is likely to be very bumpy, otherwise—with the bumps directly proportional in magnitude to the degree of offset. This is quite reminiscent, to me, of the Greek term *hamartia*, which is frequently translated as "sin," in the context of Christian thought.

*Hamartia* was originally an archery term, and it meant to miss the mark or target. There are many ways that a target can be missed. Frequently, in my clinical practice—and in my personal life—I observed that people did not get what they needed (or, equally importantly perhaps, what they wanted) because they never made it clear to themselves or others what that was. It is impossible to hit a target, after all, unless you aim at it. In keeping with this: People are more commonly upset by what they did not even try to do than by the errors they actively committed while engaging with the world.[2] At least if you misstep while doing something, you can learn from doing it wrong. But to remain passive in the face of life, even if you excuse your inaction as a means of avoiding error—that is a major mistake. As the great blues musician Tom Waits insists (in his song "A Little Rain"): "You must risk something that matters."

This is the colossal blunder made, for example, by the fictional Peter Pan. "Pan"—a name echoing the Greek god of the wilds—means "encompassing everything." Peter Pan, the magical boy, is capable of everything. He is potential itself, like every child, and that makes him magical, in the same way that every child is magical. But time whittles that magic away, transforming the fascinating potentiality of childhood into the oft-apparently more mundane but genuine actuality of adulthood. The trick, so to speak, is to trade that early possibility for something meaningful, productive, long term, and sustainable. Peter Pan refuses to do so. This is at least in part because his major role model is Captain Hook. Captain Hook is the archetypal Tyrannical King, the pathology of order—a parasite and a tyrant, terrified of death. He has his reasons. Death stalks Hook in the form of a crocodile with a clock in his stomach. That is time: ticktock, ticktock. That is life vanishing, as the seconds march by. The crocodile has had a taste of Hook, too, and liked it. That is life, as well. It is not only cowards who are terrified by what lurks down in the chaotic depths. It is a rare person who has not suffered through disappointment, disease, and the death of a loved one by the time childhood ends. Such experiences can leave those who have had them bitter, resentful, predatory, and tyrannical—just like Hook. With a role model like the captain, it is no wonder Peter Pan does not want to grow up. Better to remain king of the Lost Boys. Better to remain lost in fantasy with Tinkerbell, who provides everything a female partner can provide—except that she does not exist.

Wendy, the great love of Pan's life, chooses to grow up, despite her admiration for her friend Peter. She takes a husband, facing—even welcoming—her maturation, and its lurking hints of mortality and death. She consciously chooses to sacrifice her childhood for the realities of adulthood, but gains real life in return. Peter remains a child: magical, to be sure, but still a child—and life, limited, finite, and unique, passes him by. In the J. M. Barrie play *Peter Pan or The Boy Who Would Not Grow Up*, Pan is portrayed as unafraid of death, which he faces on Marooners' Rock. His attitude might be misunderstood by inattentive viewers as courage. After all, Pan says, "To die will be an awfully big adventure."* But the psychologically insightful unseen narrator objects: "To live would be an awfully big adventure" (truly, a statement about what might have happened had the Boy King chosen Wendy), noting, immediately afterward, "but he can never quite get the hang of it."† Pan's hypothetical lack of fear of death is not courage, but the manifestation of his basically suicidal nature, the sickness of life (which he is constantly manifesting by his very refusal to mature).

It is by no means a good thing to be the oldest person at the frat party. It is desperation, masquerading as cool rebelliousness—and there is a touchy despondence and arrogance that goes along with it. It smacks of Neverland. In the same manner, the attractive potential of a directionless but talented twenty-five-year-old starts to look hopeless and pathetic at thirty, and downright past its expiration date at forty.

---

*Peter Pan, Act III, gutenberg.net.au/ebooks03/0300081h.html.
†Peter Pan, Act V, scene 2 (closing paragraph), gutenberg.net.au/ebooks03/0300081h .html.

You must sacrifice something of your manifold potential in exchange for something real in life. Aim at something. Discipline yourself. Or suffer the consequence. And what is that consequence? All the suffering of life, with none of the meaning. Is there a better description of hell?

Life is *duhka* for the Buddhists—equally, perhaps, although less explicitly, for the Hindus. The Hebrew Scriptures, for their part, chronicle the history of the suffering of the Jewish people, individually and as a nation, although the triumphs are not ignored. Even those who are called on by YHWH Himself to move into the adventure of life by no means escape catastrophe. Perhaps Abraham, the archetypal Patriarch, had an intuition of this. He was clearly something of a Peter Pan himself. The biblical account insists that Abraham stayed safely ensconced within his father's tent until he was seventy-five years old (a late start, even by today's standards). Then, called by God—inspired by the voice within, let us say, to leave family and country—he journeys forward into life. And what does he encounter, after heeding the divine call to adventure? First, famine. Then tyranny in Egypt; the potential loss of his beautiful wife to more powerful men; exile from his adopted country; conflicts over territory with his kinsmen; war, and the kidnapping of his nephew; extended childlessness (despite God's promise to make him the progenitor of a great nation); and finally, terrible conflict between his spouses.

The Abrahamic story made a great impact on me when I began to study and appreciate it more deeply. It has at its core a strange combination of pessimism and realistic, genuine encouragement. The pessimism? Even if you are called by God Himself to venture out into the world, as Abraham was, life is going to be exceptionally difficult. Even under the best of all conceivable circumstances, almost insuperable obstacles will emerge and obstruct your path. The encouragement? You will have the opportunity to reveal yourself as much stronger and more competent than you might imagine. There is a potential within you (some of that magic so evident in childhood) that will emerge when circumstances demand and transform you—God willing—into someone who can prevail.

There is a very old idea, which I have only recently come to comprehend, at least in part. It is something you see manifested in many literary, imagistic, and dramatic forms, ancient and modern. It has to do with responsibility and meaning, but its true significance appears hidden, in precisely the same way that the wisdom dreams can bring forth is so often hidden. It is associated with the labyrinthine myth of the hero: He who speaks magic words, sees what others cannot (or refuse to see), overcomes the giant, leads his people, slays the dragon, finds the treasure hard to attain, and rescues the virgin. These are all variants of the same perceptual and behavioral pattern, which is an outline of the universally adaptive pattern of being. The hero is also he who rescues his father from the belly of the beast. What could this idea, expressed so commonly in narrative form, possibly mean?

## RESCUE YOUR FATHER: OSIRIS AND HORUS

Consider the ancient Egyptian story of Osiris, Set, Isis, and Horus.* The Egyptians regarded Osiris as the founding deity of the state. You can profitably consider him to be an amalgam of all the personality characteristics of all the people who established the astonishing civilization on the Nile River. Osiris was worshipped as the culture-establishing hero, whose world-creating exploits as a young,

---

*I provided an extensive analysis in my first book, *Maps of Meaning*, as well as mentioning it in *12 Rules for Life*, Rule 7: Pursue what is meaningful (not what is expedient).

vibrant god produced one of the first great and enduring civilizations. But he aged, as all things do, and became willfully blind. The Egyptians insisted that this crucially important figure in their mythology possessed both of these attributes—and that insistence constituted a great truth. The great founder-god became anachronistic but, more importantly, he began to close his eyes when he knew full well he should have kept them open. Osiris stopped paying attention to how his kingdom was being run. That was willful blindness, and there is no blaming that on mere age. It is a terrible temptation, as it allows for the sequestration into the future the trouble we could face today. That would be fine if trouble did not compound, like interest—but we all know that it does.

Osiris's decision to close his eyes when he should have kept them open exacted a brutally heavy price: subjugation to his evil brother, Set. The idea that the state had a malevolent brother was an axiom, we might say, of the Egyptian worldview—no doubt the consequence of a complex, long-standing civilization observing its own flaws—and something that has retained its relevance to the current day. Once a properly functional hierarchy has been established, an opportunity opens for its positions of authority to be usurped, not by people who have the competence demanded by the task at hand, but by those willing to use manipulation, deceit, and compulsion to gain status and control. It was all those counterproductive forces that the Egyptians were attempting to conceptualize in the figure of Set, the enemy of illumination, enlightenment, vision, and consciousness.[3] It was Set's greatest ambition to rule Egypt, to take the place of the rightful Pharaoh. By turning a blind eye to his evil brother's machinations—by refusing to see—Osiris allowed Set to gain strength. This proved fatal (or as fatal as an error can be to an immortal). Set bided his time, until he caught Osiris in a moment of weakness. Then he dismembered him and scattered the pieces over the Egyptian countryside. It was not (is not) possible to finally kill Osiris, the eternal human impulse toward social organization. That is a force that will not die. But it is possible to break him into pieces—to make it difficult for him to get his act together—and that is exactly what Set managed.

Osiris, god of order, falls apart. This happens all the time, in people's individual lives, and equally in the history of families, cities, and states. Things fall apart when love affairs collapse, careers deteriorate, or cherished dreams die; when despair, anxiety, uncertainty, and hopelessness manifest themselves in the place of habitable order; and when nihilism and the abyss make their dread appearance, destroying the desirable and stable values of current life. Under such circumstances, chaos emerges. And that is why the goddess Isis, Queen of the Underworld and consort of Osiris, makes her appearance when Osiris is destroyed by Set. Isis scours the countryside, searching for the vital essence of Osiris. She finds it in the form of his dismembered phallus—vessel of the seminal idea, the spermatic word, the fructifying principle—and makes herself pregnant. What does this mean? The queen of the underworld, the goddess of chaos, is also the force that eternally renews. All the potential constrained by the previous system of apprehension, of category, of assumption—all the invisible limitation imposed upon the inhabitants of that orderly state—is released, for better and worse, when that system breaks into pieces. Thus, when the center will no longer hold—even at the darkest hour—new possibility makes itself manifest. It is for this reason that the archetypal Hero is born when things are at their worst.

The now pregnant Isis returns to her home in the underworld and gives birth, in due time, to Horus, rightful son of the long-lost king, alienated as he matures from his now corrupted kingdom (something we all experience during our maturation). His primary attribute is the eye—the famous Egyptian single eye—while his avatar is the falcon, a bird that takes precise aim at its prey, strikes the target with deadly accuracy, and possesses an acuity of vision unparalleled in the kingdom of living things. More importantly, however, Horus has the *will* to see, along with the ability. This is courage itself: the refusal to shrink from what makes itself known, no matter how terrible it seems. Horus is the great god of attention, and the Egyptians determined, in their strange narrative manner—in a form of imaginative thinking that stretched over thousands of years—that the faculty of attention should rule over all others. Horus differs from Osiris, his father, in his willingness to see. He sees his uncle Set, for example, precisely for what he is. Set is pure malevolence; evil itself. Nonetheless, upon his maturity, Horus returns to the kingdom usurped from his father and confronts his uncle. They engage in an epic battle. The young god and rightful heir to the throne sees the opportunity lurking where responsibility has been abdicated, and is unwilling to look away. This is no feat for the faint of heart—not when it is taken all the way to its logical conclusion; not when the corruption and the willful blindness is exposed, all the way to the bottom. To look upon evil with eyes unshielded is dangerous beyond belief, regardless of how necessary it is to look. This is represented by Horus's initial partial defeat: During their confrontation, Set tears out one of his courageous nephew's eyes.

Despite the damage he sustains, Horus emerges victorious. It is of vital importance to reiterate, in light of this victory, the fact that he enters the battle voluntarily. It is a maxim of clinical intervention—a consequence of observation of improvement in mental health across many schools of practical psychological thought—that voluntary confrontation with a feared, hated, or despised obstacle is curative. We become stronger by voluntarily facing what impedes our necessary progress. This does not mean "bite off more than you can chew" (any more than "voluntarily enter battle" means "seek conflict carelessly"). We are well advised to take on challenges at precisely the rate that engages and compels alertness, and forces the development of courage, skill, and talent, and to avoid foolhardy confrontation with that which lies beyond current comprehension.

How is it possible to gauge the rate at which challenges should be sought? It is the instinct for meaning—something far deeper and older than mere thought—that holds the answer. Does what you are attempting compel you forward, without being too frightening? Does it grip your interest, without crushing you? Does it eliminate the burden of time passing? Does it serve those you love and, perhaps, even bring some good to your enemies? That is responsibility. Constrain evil. Reduce suffering. Confront the possibility that manifests in front of you every second of your life with the desire to make things better, regardless of the burden you bear, regardless of life's often apparently arbitrary unfairness and cruelty. All other approaches merely deepen the pit, increase its heat, and doom those who inhabit it to continual worsening of their already serious problems. Everyone knows it. Everyone's conscience proclaims it. Everyone's true friend or loved one observes it and despairs when they see someone for whom they care failing to do what needs to be done.

Horus takes his eye back from the defeated Set and banishes him beyond the borders of the kingdom. There is no killing Set. He is eternal as Osiris, eternal as Isis and Horus. The evil that threatens at all levels of experience is something—or someone—that everyone has to contend with always, psychologically and socially. But for a time evil can be overcome, banished, and defeated. Then peace and harmony can prevail for as long as people do not forget what brought them both about.

Horus recovers his eye. A sensible person, in such a situation, would thank his lucky stars, place his eye back into its empty socket, and get on with his life. But that is not what Horus does. He returns, instead, to the underworld, to the belly of the beast, to the kingdom of the dead, where he knows he will find the spirit of Osiris. Dismembered though he may be, near death—even dead, in a sense—Osiris inhabits the underworld domain of chaos itself. That is the dead father in the belly of the beast. Horus finds the once-great king and grants to him the eye torn out by Set. Once again—because of the sacrifice and vision of his son—the ancient of days can see. Horus then takes his father, vision restored, and returns with him to the kingdom, so they can rule in tandem. The Egyptians insisted that it was this combination of vision, courage, and regenerated tradition that constituted the proper sovereign of the kingdom. It was this juxtaposition of wisdom and youth that comprised the essence of the power of the Pharaoh, his immortal soul, the source of his authority.

When you face a challenge, you grapple with the world and inform yourself. This makes you more than you are. It makes you increasingly into who you could be. Who could you be? You could be all that a man or woman might be. You could be the newest avatar, in your own unique manner, of the great ancestral heroes of the past. What is the upper limit to that? We do not know. Our religious structures hint at it. What would a human being who was completely turned on, so to speak, be like? How would someone who determined to take full responsibility for the tragedy and malevolence of the world manifest himself? The ultimate question of Man is not who we are, but who we could be.

When you peer into an abyss, you see a monster. If it is a small abyss, then it is a small monster. But if it is the ultimate abyss, then it is the ultimate monster. That is certainly a dragon—perhaps even the dragon of evil itself. The conceptualization of the monster in the abyss is the eternal predator lurking in the night, ready and able to devour its unsuspecting prey. That is an image that is tens of millions of years old, something coded as deeply in the recesses of our biological structure as anything conceptual can be coded. And it is not just the monsters of nature, but the tyrants of culture and the malevolence of individuals. It is all of that, with the latter dominant, terrible as that is to consider. And it is in the nature of mankind not to cower and freeze as helpless prey animals, nor to become a turncoat and serve evil itself, but to confront the lions in their lairs. That is the nature of our ancestors: immensely courageous hunters, defenders, shepherds, voyagers, inventors, warriors, and founders of cities and states. That is the father you could rescue; the ancestor you could become. And he is to be discovered in the deepest possible place, as that is where you must go if you wish to take full responsibility and become who you could be.

## AND WHO MIGHT THAT BE?

Let us agree, to begin with, that you have a minimum moral obligation to take care of yourself. Maybe you are just selfishly interested in taking care of yourself. But then the questions arise: What do you mean by "care"? Which "yourself" are you talking about? We will just consider pure selfishness to begin with, uncontaminated self-interest. That keeps it simple. That means, for starters, that you are free do anything you want—because you do not have to care about anyone else. But then something in you might well object: "Wait just a moment. That will not work." Why not? Well, which self are you taking care of? Are you taking care of the you that specifically exists this minute? What will happen, then, in the next? Because the future is coming, as certainly, for all intents and purposes, as the sun rises in the morning. And you are best advised to be ready for it.

You know the risks if you choose to maximize now at the expense of later. Imagine that you are about to utter something thoughtless and angry. You think, "Take no prisoners," and say whatever comes to mind, no matter how unjust and cruel. You experience a release of positive emotion and enthusiasm along with that, as well as the satisfying venting of resentment. Immediately thereafter, however, you are in trouble, and that trouble might stick around for a very long time. You have clearly not acted in your best interests, even though you did just what you selfishly wanted to. And no one with any sense tells their beloved son or daughter, "Look, kid, just do exactly what feels good in the moment, and to hell with everything else. It does not matter." You do not say that, because you know full well that the future is coming for your child as surely as it comes for you. The mere fact that something makes you happy in the moment does not mean that it is in your best interest, everything considered. Life would be simple if that were the case. But there is the you now, and the you tomorrow, and the you next week, and next year, and in five years, and in a decade—and you are required by harsh necessity to take all of those "yous" into account. That is the curse associated with the human discovery of the future and, with it, the necessity of work—because to work means to sacrifice the hypothetical delights of the present for the potential improvement of what lies ahead.

Now, there is some utility in discounting the importance of the "yous" who exist far enough into the future, because the future is uncertain. It is not the case that you should be as concerned about the effects of your current actions twenty years down the road as you are now, because there is a very high probability that you are here right now (if you are reading this) and somewhat less of a chance that you will be around then. And then there are the errors of prediction you will make when looking so far ahead. But the mounting uncertainty of distance in time does not stop sensible people from preparing for their later years. Here is what the future means: If you are going to take care of yourself, you are already burdened (or privileged) with a social responsibility. The you for whom you are caring is a community that exists across time. The necessity for considering this society of the individual, so to speak, is a burden and an opportunity that seems uniquely characteristic of human beings.

Animals do not seem to consider the future in the same manner as we do. If you visit the African veldt, and you observe a herd of zebras, you will often see lions lazing about around them. And as long as the lions are lying around relaxing, the zebras really do not mind. This attitude seems a little thoughtless, from the human perspective. The zebras should instead be biding their time until the lions go to sleep. Then they should run off to a corner of the field in a herd and conspire a bit. And then several dozen of them should rush the sleeping lions and stomp them to death. That would be the end of the lion problem. But that is not what zebras do. They think, "Ah, look at those relaxed lions! Relaxed lions are never a problem!" Zebras do not seem to have any real sense of time. They cannot conceptualize themselves across the temporal expanse. But human beings not only manage such conceptualization, they cannot shake it. We discovered the future, some long time ago—and now the future is where we each live, in potential. We treat that as *reality*. It is a reality that only *might be*—but it is one with a high probability of becoming *now*, eventually, and we are driven to take that into account.

You are stuck with yourself. You are burdened with who you are right now and who you are going to be in the future. That means that if you are treating yourself properly, you must consider your repetition across time. You are destined to play a game with yourself today that must not interfere with the game you play tomorrow, next month, next year, and so on. Thus, narrow selfishness is destined to be non-productive. It is for this reason, among others, that a strictly individualist ethic is a contradiction in terms. There is in fact little difference between how you should treat yourself—once you realize that you are a community that extends across time—and how you should treat other people.

In a marriage, for example, you face the same problem with your marital partner as you do with yourself: You are stuck with the consequences of an iterating game. You can treat your husband or wife any old way right now, this moment, no matter how horrid and thoughtless that way might be, but you are going to wake up with him or her tomorrow, and next month, and a decade from now (and, if not that person, then someone else equally unfortunate). If you treat the person you are committed to in a manner that does not work when it is repeated across time, then you are playing a degenerating game, and you are both going to suffer terribly for it. This problem is not materially different from failing to make peace with your future self. The consequences are identical.

## HAPPINESS AND RESPONSIBILITY

People want to be happy, and no wonder. I have longed deeply, many times, for the return of happiness—hoping for its current presence—and I am certainly not alone in that. However, I do not believe you should *pursue* happiness. If you do so, you will run right into the iteration problem, because "happy" is a right-now thing. If you place people in situations where they are feeling a lot of positive emotion, they get present-focused and impulsive.[4] This means "make hay while the sun shines"—take your opportunities while things are good and act now. But *now* is by no means everything, and unfortunately, everything must be considered, at least insofar as you are able. In consequence, it is unlikely that whatever optimizes your life across time is happiness. I am not denying its desirability, by the way. If happiness comes to you, welcome it with gratitude and open arms (but be careful, because it does make you impetuous).

What might serve as a more sophisticated alternative to happiness? Imagine it is living in accordance with the sense of responsibility, because that sets things right in the future. Imagine, as well, that you must act reliably, honestly, nobly, and in relationship to a higher good, in order to manifest the sense of responsibility properly. The higher good would be the simultaneous optimization of your function and the function of the people around you, across time, as we have discussed previously. That is the highest good. Imagine that you make that aim conscious, that you articulate that aim as an explicit goal. Then a question arises: "What is the consequence of that psychologically?"

First, consider that most of the positive emotion people experience does not come from attaining something. There is the simple pleasure (more accurately, the satisfaction) that comes from having a good meal when hungry, and there is the more complex but similar satisfaction that is associated with accomplishing something difficult and worthwhile. Imagine, for example, that you graduate from grade 12. Graduation Day marks the event. It is a celebration. But the next day that is over, and you immediately face a new set of problems (just as you are hungry again only a few hours after a satisfying meal). You are no longer king of the high school: you are bottom dog in the work force, or a freshman at a postsecondary institution. You are in the position of Sisyphus. You strove and struggled to push your boulder to the pinnacle, and you find yourself, instead, at the foot of the mountain.

There is a near-instantaneous transformation that comes as a consequence of attainment. Like impulsive pleasure, attainment will produce positive emotion. But, also like pleasure, attainment is unreliable. Another question thus emerges: "What is a truly reliable source of positive emotion?" The answer is that people experience positive emotion in relationship to the *pursuit* of a valuable goal. Imagine you have a goal. You aim at something. You develop a strategy in relationship to that aim, and then you implement it. And then, as you implement the strategy, you observe that it is working. *That is* what produces the most reliable positive emotion.[5] Imagine over time that the attitudes and actions that manage this most effectively (in a competition that is very Darwinian) come, eventually, to dominate over all others.[6] Imagine that is true psychologically and socially, simultaneously. Imagine that this occurs in your own life, but also across the centuries, as everyone interacts and talks and raises a particular mode of being to primary status.

This implies something crucial: no happiness in the absence of responsibility. No valuable and valued goal, no positive emotion. You might object, "Well, what exactly constitutes a valid goal?" Imagine that you are pursuing something pleasurable, but short term and trivial. The wise part of you will be comparing that pursuit to the possible goal of acting in the best interest of your community of future selves and your community of other people. Perhaps you are unwilling to allow yourself to realize that wisdom: You do not wish to bear the responsibility—not in place of an immediate, impulsive focus on pleasure. You are fooling yourself, however, especially at the deeper levels of your being, if you believe such avoidance will prove successful. The wise and ancient parts of you, seriously concerned with your survival, are neither easy to deceive nor to set aside. But you take aim at a trivial goal anyway, and develop a rather shallow strategy to attain it, only to find it is not satisfying because you do not care enough. It does not matter to you—not deeply. Furthermore, the fact that you are not pursuing the goal you should rightly be pursuing means that you are feeling guilty, ashamed, and lesser at the same time.

This is not a helpful strategy. It is not going to work. I have never met anyone who was satisfied when they knew they were not doing everything they should be doing. We are temporally aware creatures: We know that we are continually and inescapably playing an iterated game from which we cannot easily hide. No matter how much we wish to discount the future completely, it is part of the price we paid for being acutely self-conscious and able to conceptualize ourselves across the entire span of our lives. We are stuck with it. There is no escaping from the future—and when you are stuck with something and there is no escaping from it, the right attitude is to turn around voluntarily and confront it. That works. And so, instead of your short-term impulsive goal, you lay out a much larger-scale goal, which is to act properly in relationship to the long term for everyone.

## PICK UP THE EXTRA WEIGHT

There is a proper way to behave—an ethic—and you are destined to contend with it. You cannot help but calculate yourself across time, and everyone else across time, and you are reporting back to yourself, inevitably, on your own behavior and misbehavior. What works across multiple time frames and multiple places for multiple people (including yourself)—that is the goal. It is an emergent ethic, hard to formulate explicitly, but inescapable in its existence and its consequences, and an ineradicably deep part of the game of Being. Great players are attractive. Attractive people attract mates. The closer we match the pattern—the emergent pattern—the more likely we are to survive and protect our families. The playing field selects the players on the basis of their ethical behavior. And we are therefore biologically prepared to respond positively to and to imitate the Great Player—and to disapprove, even violently, of the deceiver, the cheat, and the fraud. And it is your conscience—your instinct for moral virtue—that indicates deviation from the path. When your child purposefully trips an opponent during a soccer game, or fails to pass to an open teammate with a great opportunity to score, you frown. You feel shame, as you should, because you are witnessing the betrayal of someone you love, by someone you love—and that is your child's self-betrayal. Something similar occurs when you violate your own sense of propriety. It is the same instinct, and it is best attended to. If you do not follow the right path, you will wander off a cliff and suffer miserably—and there is simply no way that the most profound parts of yourself are going to allow that without protest.

You might rationalize: "There is no cliff here now. There is no cliff I can see nearby. And a cliff I will not tumble off for ten years is a long way away." But the part of your psyche that is most profound invariably objects: "Such thinking is not appropriate. It will not do. What is ten years away is still real, despite its distance (allowing for unavoidable errors of prediction). If there is a catastrophe waiting there, we are not going to aim at it now. Not without objection." If your behavior suggests that you are tilting in that direction, then you are going to feel guilty and horrible about it, if you are lucky and even minimally awake. And thank God for that. If the cost of betraying yourself, in the deepest sense, is guilt, shame, and anxiety, the benefit of not betraying yourself is meaning—the meaning that sustains. That is the most valuable of opportunities that lurks where responsibility has been abdicated.

If you attend to your conscience, you will begin to determine that some of the things you are doing are wrong. More precisely: if you are alerted to the possibility of your own wrongdoing by your conscience, and you then begin to engage in a true dialogue with that same agent, you will begin to develop a clear picture of what is wrong—and, by implication, of what is right. Right is not least the opposite of wrong—and wrong is in some clear sense more blatant and obvious. A sense of right can therefore be developed and honed through careful attention to what is wrong. You act and betray yourself, and you feel bad about that. You do not know exactly why. You try to avoid thinking about it, because it is less painful and easier in the short term not to think about it. You try with all your might to ignore it, but all that does is increase your sense of self-betrayal and further divide you against yourself.

So, you reconsider, perhaps, and you confront your discomfort. You note your disunity and the chaos that comes with it. You ask yourself—you pray to discover—what you did wrong. And the answer arrives. And it is not what you want. And part of you must therefore die, so that you can change. And the part that must die struggles for its existence, puts forward its rationale, and pleads its case. And it will do so with every trick in its possession—employing the most egregious lies, the bitterest, most resentment-eliciting memories of the past, and the most hopelessly cynical attitudes about the future (indeed, about the value of life itself). But you persevere, and discriminate, judge, and decide exactly why what you did was wrong, and you start to understand, by contrast, what might have been right. And then you determine to start acting in accordance with your conscience. You decide that it is a partner, despite its adversarial form. You put all that you have discovered to be right into action, and you begin your ascent. You start to monitor yourself, ever more careful to ensure you are doing the right thing—listening to what you say, watching yourself act, trying not to deviate from the straight and narrow path. That becomes your goal.

An idea begins to take shape: "I am going to live my life properly. I am going to aim at the good. I am going to aim at the highest good I can possible manage." Now, all the parts of you taking care of your future self are on board. You are all aimed in one direction. You are no longer a house divided against itself. You are standing solidly on a firm foundation. You are no longer so easy to dissuade or discourage. Your resolution trumps your nihilism and despair. The struggle you have had with your own tendency to doubt and dissimulate protects you against the unwarranted and cynical criticisms of others. There is a high goal, a mountain peak, a star that shines in the darkness, beckoning above the horizon. Its mere existence gives you hope—and that is the meaning without which you cannot live.

Remember Pinocchio? When Geppetto wants to transform the wooden-headed puppet he created into something real, he first raises his eyes above the horizon and wishes on a star. It is the same star that announces Pinocchio's birth at the beginning of the movie and whose light is reflected in the golden badge granted to Jiminy Cricket at the close. It is the same star, symbolically speaking, that announces the birth of Christ in the depths of the darkness. Geppetto focuses on the star and makes a wish. The wish is that his marionette with strings controlled by someone or something else will become real. The story of the puppet and his temptations and trials is a psychological drama. We all understand it, even though we cannot necessarily articulate that understanding. It is necessary to lift your eyes above the horizon, to establish a transcendent goal, if you wish to cease being a puppet, under the control of things you do not understand and perhaps do not want to understand. Then all the subsystems or subpersonalities that might otherwise be pursing their own limited fulfillment will join together under the aegis of the truly ideal, and the consequence of that will be an engagement that approximates the ultimate or total. Under such conditions, all the parts of you are going to be on board. That is the psychological equivalent of monotheism. That is the emergence of the higher self that might be the true servant of God, in whatever metaphysical reality potentially underlies what is obvious to our blind and limited mortal selves.

What is the antidote to the suffering and malevolence of life? The highest possible goal. What is the prerequisite to pursuit of the highest possible goal? Willingness to adopt the maximum degree of responsibility—and this includes the responsibilities that others disregard or neglect. You might object: "Why should I shoulder all that burden? It is nothing but sacrifice, hardship, and trouble." But what makes you so sure you do not want something heavy to carry? You positively need to be occupied with something weighty, deep, profound, and difficult. Then, when you wake up in the middle of the night and the doubts crowd in, you have some defense: "For all my flaws, which are manifold, at least I am doing *this*. At least I am taking care of myself. At least I am of use to my family, and to the other people around me. At least I am moving, stumbling upward, under the load I have determined to carry." You can attain some genuine self-respect that way—but it is not a mere shallow psychological construct that has to do with how you are construing yourself in the moment. It is far deeper than that—and it is not only psychological. It is *real*, as well as psychological.

Your life becomes meaningful in precise proportion to the depths of the responsibility you are willing to shoulder. That is because you are now genuinely involved in making things better. You are minimizing the unnecessary suffering. You are encouraging those around you, by example and word. You are constraining the malevolence in your own heart and the hearts of others. A bricklayer may question the utility of laying his bricks, monotonously, one after another. But perhaps he is not merely laying bricks. Maybe he is building a wall. And the wall is part of a building. And the building is a cathedral. And the purpose of the cathedral is the glorification of the Highest Good. And under such circumstances, every brick laid is an act that partakes of the divine. And if what you are doing in your day-to-day activity is not enough, then you are not aiming at the construction of a proper cathedral. And that is because you are not aiming high enough. Because if you were, then you would experience the sense of meaning in relationship to your sufficiently high goal, and it would justify the misery and limitations of your life. If you have something meaningful to pursue, then you are engrossed in life. You are on a meaningful path. The most profound and reliable instinct for meaning—if not perverted by self-deceit and sin (there is no other way to state it)—manifests itself when you are on the path of maximum virtue.

The sense of meaning is an indicator that you are on that path. It is an indication that all the complexity that composes you is lined up within you, and aimed at something worth pursuing—something that balances the world, something that produces harmony. It is something you hear made manifest in music, and the profound sense of meaning that music intrinsically produces. Maybe you are a nihilistic death-metal punk. You are deeply skeptical and pessimistic. You find meaning nowhere. You hate everything, just on principle. But then your favorite nihilistic death-metal punk band lead guitarist and his bandmates start to blast out their patterned harmonies—each in alignment with the other—and you are caught! "Ah, I do not believe in anything—but, God, that music!" And the lyrics are destructive and nihilistic and cynical and bitter and hopeless but it does not matter, because the music beckons and calls to your spirit, and fills it with the intimation of meaning, and moves you, so that you align yourself with the patterns, and you nod your head and tap your feet to the beat, participating despite yourself. It is those patterns of sound, layered one on top of another, harmoniously, moving in the same direction, predictably and unpredictably, in perfect balance: order and chaos, in their eternal dance. And you dance with it, no matter how scornful you are. You align yourself with that patterned, directional harmony. And in that you find the meaning that sustains.

You are possessed of an instinct—a spirit—that orients you toward the highest good. It calls your soul away from hell and toward heaven. And because it is there, you find yourself frequently disillusioned. People disappoint you. You betray yourself; you lose a meaningful connection to your workplace, boss, or partner. You think, "The world is not set right. It is deeply troubling to me." That very disenchantment, however, can serve as the indicator of destiny. It speaks of abdicated responsibility—of things left undone, of things that still *need to be done*. You are irritated about that need. You are annoyed with the government, you are embittered and resentful about your job, you are unhappy with your parents, and you are frustrated with all these people around you who will not take on responsibility. There are, after all, things that are crying out to be accomplished. You are outraged that what needs to be done *is not being done*. That anger—that outrage—is, however, a *doorway*. That observation of abdicated responsibility is the indication of destiny and meaning. The part of you that is oriented toward the highest good is pointing out the disjunction between the ideal you can imagine—the ideal that is possessing you—and the reality you are experiencing. There is a gap there, and it is communicating its need to be filled. You can give way to fury, in consequence, and blame it on someone else—and it is not as if other people are not contributing to the problems. Or you can come to understand that your very disappointment is an indication to you from the most fundamental levels of your being that there is something wrong that needs to be set right—and, perhaps, *by you*. What is it, that concern, that care, that irritation, that distraction? It is not the call to happiness. It is the call to the action and adventure that make up a real life. Consider, once again, the biblical story of Abraham. God comes to Abraham, and says,

> Go from your country, your people and your father's household to the land I will show you.
>
> I will make you into a great nation, and I will bless you; I will make your name great, and you will be a blessing.
>
> I will bless those who bless you, and whoever curses you I will curse; and all peoples on earth will be blessed through you. (Genesis 12:1–3)

That late bloomer Abraham has been hanging around his father's tent for far too many years, to put it mildly. But if God's call comes, it is better to heed it, no matter how late (and in that, there is real hope, for those who believe that they have delayed too long). Abraham leaves his country, and his people, and his father's household, and journeys out into the world, following the still small voice; following God's call. And it is no call to happiness. It is the complete bloody catastrophe we previously described: famine, war, and domestic strife. All this might make the reasonable individual (not to mention Abraham himself) doubt the wisdom of listening to God and conscience, and of adopting the responsibility of autonomy and the burden of adventure. Better to be lying in a hammock, devouring peeled grapes in the security of Dad's tent. What calls you out into the world, however—to your destiny—is not ease. It is struggle and strife. It is bitter contention and the deadly play of the opposites. It is probable—inevitable—that the adventure of your life will frustrate and disappoint and unsettle you, as you heed the call of conscience and shoulder your responsibility and endeavor to set yourself and the world right. But that is where the deep meaning that orients you and shelters you is to be found. That is where things will line up for you; where things that have been scattered apart and broken will come together; where purpose will manifest itself; where what is proper and good will be supported and what is weak and resentful and arrogant and destructive will be defeated. That is where the life that is worth living is to be eternally found— and where you can find it, personally, if only you are willing.

Notice that opportunity lurks where responsibility has been abdicated.

_____

# DO NOT DO WHAT YOU HATE

## PATHOLOGICAL ORDER IN ITS DAY-TO-DAY GUISE

I once had a client who was subject to a barrage of constant idiocy as part of her work in a giant corporation. She was a sensible, honest person who had withstood and managed a difficult life and who genuinely wished to contribute and work in a manner commensurate with her good sense and honesty. She became subject while employed in the corporate environment to a long, in-person and email-mediated dispute about whether the term "flip chart" (a common phrase, referring to a large pad of paper sheets, typically supported by a tripod) was in fact a term of abuse. For those of you who still find it difficult to believe that conversations such as this occupy the hours of corporate workers, try a quick Google search. "Flip chart derogatory" will suffice. You will see immediately that concern about this issue genuinely and rather widely exists. Many meetings were held by her superiors at work to discuss this issue.

"Flip" was apparently at one time a derogatory term for Filipino (I could find little evidence for its use now). Even though the former slur has nothing whatsoever to do with "flip chart," the administrators of her firm felt that their time was well spent discussing the hypothetically prejudicial nature of the phrase and formulating a replacement term, the use of which eventually became mandatory among employees. This was all despite the fact that no employee of Filipino nationality or descent had ever complained about the corporation's use of the term. According to the Global Language Monitor (languagemonitor .com), which monitors but does not approve politically correct word usage, the proper term is now "writing block," despite the fact that a flip chart is in no way a "block."

In any case, the corporation in question settled on "easel pad," which seems somewhat more descriptively accurate—not that this comparatively elegant solution detracts from the foolishness in question. After all, we are still left with "flip-flopped," "flippant," "flip-flops," "flippers," and so on, and at least the first two of those sound more derogatory on first exposure than "flip chart," if we are going to concern ourselves with such things. Now, you might wonder: "What difference does this minor change in terminology really make? It is a trivial problem. Why would someone become concerned about the fact that such change is being discussed? Why not ignore it, as it is best to ignore so much folly, and concentrate on something of more importance?" Because, of course, you could claim that paying attention to someone attending to such issues is as much a waste of time as attending to the discussion in the first place. And I would say that is precisely the conundrum Rule V is trying to address. When do you stop participating in a worrisome process that you see, or think you see, unfolding in front of you?

My client first wrote me about the fact that not only was the string of communication discussing the use of "flip chart" well received by her coworkers, but that a contest of sorts immediately emerged to identify and communicate additional words that might also be offensive.* "Blackboard" was mentioned, as was "master key" (the former perhaps because referring to anything as "black"—even if it is black—is somehow racist in our hypersensitive times; the latter because of its hypothetical relationship to terminology historically associated with slavery). My client tried to make sense of what she was witnessing: "Such discussions give people the superficial sense of being good, noble, compassionate, openhearted, and wise. So, if for the sake of argument anyone disagrees, how could that person join the discussion without being considered anticompassionate, narrow minded, racist and wicked?"

She was also perturbed because no one at her workplace was apparently bothered that any given group of people might endow themselves with the authority to ban words (and to disdain or even discipline those who continued to use them) without perceiving any ethical overreach on their part, and without perceiving the danger of such censorship, which could easily extend, say, to personal opinions, topics of conversation—or, for that matter, books. Finally, she believed that the entire discussion constituted a prime example of "diversity," "inclusivity," and "equity"—terms that had become veritable mantras for the departments of Human Resources or Learning and Development (the latter of which she worked for). She regarded them as "engines of corporate indoctrination and ideological propaganda" and as part of the manner in which the political correctness that characterizes, above all, many university programs extends its reach into the broader culture. More importantly, however, she asked me in one of her letters, "Is this a case where enough is enough?" When and where do we stop?

---

*I have obtained direct express permission from my client to communicate all this information in this manner.

If a tiny minority of people even hypothetically finds some words offensive, then what? Do we continue to ban words endlessly?"

What my client was perceiving—at least as far as she was concerned—was *not* a single event, hypothetically capable of heading those involved in it down a dangerous path, but a clearly identifiable and causally related variety or sequence of events, all heading in the same direction. Those events seemed to form a coherent pattern, associated with an ideology that was directional in its intent, explicitly and implicitly. Furthermore, the effect of that directionality had been manifesting itself, by all appearances, for a reasonable amount of time, not only in the corporate world my client inhabited, but in the broader world of social and political institutions surrounding the corporation for which she worked. Although rather isolated in the department she happened to work in (the very epicenter of the ideological blitz of the corporation in question), she could see around her evidence that the processes disturbing her were also having a detrimental effect on other people. And then there was the effect on her conscience. It is important to understand that these issues were not minor philosophical concepts to her. They were bothering her deeply and upsetting her life.

It is, of course, the case that being required to do stupid, hateful things is demoralizing. Someone assigned a pointless or even counterproductive task will deflate, if they have any sense, and find within themselves very little motivation to carry out the assignment. Why? Because every fiber of their genuine being fights against that necessity. We do the things we do because we think those things important, compared to all the other things that could be important. We regard what we value as worthy of sacrifice and pursuit. That worthiness motivates us to act, despite the fact that action is difficult and dangerous. When we are called upon to do things that we find hateful and stupid, we are simultaneously forced to act contrary to the structure of values motivating us to move forward stalwartly and protecting us from dissolution into confusion and terror. "To thine own self be true,"[1] as Polonius has it, in Shakespeare's *Hamlet*. That "self"—that integrated psyche—is in truth the ark that shelters us when the storms gather and the water rises. To act in violation of its precepts—its fundamental beliefs—is to run our own ship onto the shoals of destruction. To act in violation of the precepts of that fundamental self is to cheat in the game we play with ourselves, to suffer the emptiness of betrayal, and to perceive abstractly and then experience in embodied form the loss that is inevitably to come.

What price did my client pay for her initial subjugation to the arbitrary dictates of her managers? She was an immigrant from a former Soviet bloc country and had experienced more than a sufficient taste of authoritarian ideology. In consequence, her inability to determine how she might object to what was happening left her feeling both weak and complicit. Furthermore, no sensible person could possibly remain motivated to put forth effort anywhere such as her workplace had become, where absurdities of a conceptual sort were not only continually occurring but encouraged or, even worse, required. Such "action" makes a mockery of productive work itself—even the very idea of productive work (and that is in fact part of the true motivation for such behavior: those jealous of genuine competence and productivity have every reason to undermine and denigrate even the concept of both). So, what did she do about the demoralizing state in which she found herself?

My client did not feel sufficiently confident in her position or in the ability of her managers to engage in a genuine conversation with them about her objections, although it was clear from my conversations with her that she wished very much to escape from the situation.

In consequence, she began to develop what might be considered a rear-guard action. She was already involved in developing in-house educa-tion projects for the company, as we mentioned. It was possible for her, therefore, to begin to branch out, offering her services as a speaker at a variety of corporate conferences. Although she never directly con-fronted the flip chart issue (and may have been wise to avoid doing so), she began to speak out against the kind of pseudoscience that char-acterizes many of the ideas that corporate managers, particularly in Human Resources departments, regard as valid. She presented a num-ber of talks, for example, criticizing the widespread fad of "learning styles"—a theory predicated on the idea that there are between four and eight different modalities that individuals prefer and that aid them if used when they are trying to master new ideas. These include, for example, visual, auditory, verbal, physical, and logical, among others.

The problem with the learning styles theory? Most basically: there is simply no evidence whatsoever for its validity. First, although stu-dents may express a preference for information being delivered in one form over another, practically delivering it in that form does not im-prove their academic performance.[2] Second (and this makes sense, given the first problem), there is no evidence that teachers can accu-rately assess the "learning style" of their students.[3] So, although it was not possible for my client to directly confront the particular foolish-ness that was disturbing her, after long strategizing and much work she did manage to push back very effectively against the ignorance that characterized what passed for psychological knowledge among a substantial subset of her coworkers (as well as those who worked in other companies, where the same things were taking place). She had also done some work as a journalist for one of the major newspapers in Albania, her country of origin, and began to make continuing to do so a higher priority. This did not pay well, but she developed a stellar professional reputation there, and fought hard in print for what she believed in, warning the citizens of her once-Communist-dominated state of the move toward totalitarian opinion beginning to make itself attractive to people in the West.

What price did she pay for her decision to stand up and fight? To begin with, she had to face her fear of reprisal, as well as the fact that such fear—in combination with the profound distaste she felt for the ideological maneuvers characterizing her workplace—was destroying her interest in her office profession, as well as making her feel inadequate and cowardly. Then, she had to broaden her professional activities: first, taking the risk of offering herself as a speaker at corporate conventions (and people are generally very loath to talk publicly—it is a common fear, often severe enough to interfere with career progression[4]); second, mastering the literature, enabling her to speak in a credible and informed manner; and third, presenting material that, given its critical nature, was bound to offend a reasonable proportion of those in the audience (precisely those who had accepted and who were propagating the theories that she was now discrediting). This all meant the facing of her fear—of inaction, as well as action. These moves challenged her deeply—but the consequence was an expansion of personality and competence, as well as the knowledge that she was making a genuine social contribution.

I believe that the good that people do, small though it may appear, has more to do with the good that manifests broadly in the world than people think, and I believe the same about evil. We are each more responsible for the state of the world than we believe, or would feel comfortable believing. Without careful attention, culture itself tilts toward corruption. Tyranny grows slowly, and asks us to retreat in comparatively tiny steps. But each retreat increases the possibility of the next retreat. Each betrayal of conscience, each act of silence (despite the resentment we feel when silenced), and each rationalization weakens resistance and increases the probability of the next restrictive move forward. This is particularly the case when those pushing forward delight in the power they have now acquired—and such people are always to be found. Better to stand forward, awake, when the costs are relatively low—and, perhaps, when the potential rewards have not yet vanished. Better to stand forward before the ability to do so has been irretrievably compromised. Unfortunately, people often act in spite of their conscience—even if they know it—and hell tends to arrive step by step, one betrayal after another. And it should be remembered that it is rare for people to stand up against what they know to be wrong even when the consequences for doing so are comparatively slight. And this is something to deeply consider, if you are concerned with leading a moral and careful life: if you do not object when the transgressions against your conscience are minor, why presume that you will not willfully participate when the transgressions get truly out of hand?

Part of moving Beyond Order is knowing when you have such a reason. Part of moving Beyond Order is understanding that your conscience has a primary claim on your action, which supersedes your conventional social duty. If you decide to stand up and refuse a command, if you do something of which others disapprove but you firmly believe to be correct, you must be in a position to trust yourself. This means that you must have attempted to live an honest, meaningful, productive life (of precisely the sort that might characterize someone else you would tend to trust). If you have acted honorably, so that you are a trustworthy person, it will be your decision to refuse to comply or to act in a manner contrary to public expectation that will help society itself maintain its footing. By doing so you can be part of the force of truth that brings corruption and tyranny to a halt. The sovereign individual, awake and attending to his or her conscience, is the force that prevents the group, as the necessary structure guiding normative social relations, from becoming blind and deadly.

I do not want to end this section on a falsely optimistic note. I know from further correspondence with my client that she shifted her employment from one large organization to another several times in the years that followed. In one case, she found a good position, where it was possible to engage in productive, sensible, meaningful work. However, although successful there, she was laid off during a corporate reorganization, and has since found the other companies she has worked for as thoroughly possessed by the current linguistic and identity-politics fads as her original place of employment. Some dragons are everywhere, and they are not easy to defeat. But her attempts to fight back—her work debunking pseudoscientific theories; her work as a journalist—helped buttress her against depression and bolster her self-regard.

## FORTIFY YOUR POSITION

When culture disintegrates—because it refuses to be aware of its own pathology; because the visionary hero is absent—it descends into the chaos that underlies everything. Under such conditions, the individual can dive voluntarily as deeply as he or she dares into the depths and rediscover the eternal principles renewing vision and life. The alternative is despair, corruption, and nihilism—thoughtless subjugation to the false words of totalitarian utopianism and life as a miserable, lying, and resentful slave.

If you wish instead to be engaged in a great enterprise—even if you regard yourself as a mere cog—you are required not to do things you hate. You must fortify your position, regardless of its meanness and littleness, confront the organizational mendacity undermining your spirit, face the chaos that ensues, rescue your near-dead father from the depths, and live a genuine and truthful life. Otherwise, nature hides her face, society stultifies, and you remain a marionette, with your strings pulled by demonic forces operating behind the scenes—and one more thing: it is your fault. No one is destined in the deterministic sense to remain a puppet.

We are not helpless. Even in the rubble of the most broken-down lives, useful weapons might still be found. Likewise, even the giant most formidable in appearance may not be as omnipotent as it proclaims or appears. Allow for the possibility that you may be able to fight back; that you may be able to resist and maintain your soul—and perhaps even your job. (But a better job may also beckon if you can tolerate the idea of the transformation.) If you are willing to conceptualize yourself as someone who could—and, perhaps more importantly, should—stand fast, you may begin to perceive the weapons at your disposal. If what you are doing is causing you to lash out at others impulsively; if what you are doing is destroying your motivation to move forward; if your actions and inactions are making you contemptuous of yourself and, worse, of the world; if the manner in which you conduct your life is making it difficult for you to wake happily in the morning; if you are plagued by a deep sense of self-betrayal—perhaps you are choosing to ignore that still small voice, inclined as you may be to consider it something only attended to by the weak and naive.

If you are at work, and called upon to do what makes you contemptuous of yourself—weak and ashamed, likely to lash out at those you love, unwilling to perform productively, and sick of your life—it is possible that it is time to meditate, consider, strategize, and place yourself in a position where you are capable of saying no.* Perhaps you will garner additional respect from the people you are opposing on moral grounds, even though you may still pay a high price for your actions. Perhaps they will even come to rethink their stance—if not now, with time (as their own consciences might be plaguing them in that same still small manner).

## PRACTICALITIES

Perhaps you should also be positioning yourself for a lateral move—into another job, for example, noting as you may, "This occupation is deadening my soul, and that is truly not for me. It is time to take the painstaking steps necessary to organize my CV, and to engage in the difficult, demanding, and often unrewarding search for a new job" (but you have to be successful only once). Maybe you can find something that pays better and is more interesting, and where you are working with people who not only fail to kill your spirit, but positively rejuvenate it. Maybe following the dictates of conscience is in fact the best possible plan that you have—at minimum, otherwise you have to live with your sense of self-betrayal and the knowledge that you put up with what you truly could not tolerate. Nothing about that is good.

*I might get fired.* Well, prepare now to seek out and ready yourself for another job, hopefully better (or prepare yourself to go over your manager's head with a well-prepared and articulate argument). And do not begin by presuming that leaving your job, even involuntarily, is necessarily for the worst.

---

*Perhaps not just once, because that makes your reaction too impulsive; perhaps not just twice, because that still may not constitute sufficient evidence to risk undertaking what might be a genuine war; but definitely three times, when a pattern has been clearly established.

*I am afraid to move.* Well, of course you are, but afraid compared to what? Afraid in comparison to continuing in a job where the center of your being is at stake; where you become weaker, more contemptible, more bitter, and more prone to pressure and tyranny over the years? There are few choices in life where there is no risk on either side, and it is often necessary to contemplate the risks of staying as thoroughly as the risks of moving. I have seen many people move, sometimes after several years of strategizing, and end up in better shape, psychologically and pragmatically, after their time in the desert.

*Perhaps no one else would want me.* Well, the rejection rate for new job applications is extraordinarily high. I tell my clients to assume 50:1, so their expectations are set properly. You are going to be passed over, in many cases, for many positions for which you are qualified. But that is rarely *personal*. It is, instead, a condition of existence, an inevitable consequence of somewhat arbitrary subjection to the ambivalent conditions of worth characterizing society. It is the consequence of the fact that CVs are easy to disseminate and difficult to process; that many jobs have unannounced internal candidates (and so are just going through the motions); and that some companies keep a rolling stock of applicants, in case they need to hire quickly. That is an actuarial problem, a statistical problem, a baseline problem—and not necessarily an indication that there is something specifically flawed about you. You must incorporate all that sustainingly pessimistic realism into your expectations, so that you do not become unreasonably downhearted. One hundred and fifty applications, carefully chosen; three to five interviews thereby acquired. That could be a mission of a year or more. That is much less than a lifetime of misery and downward trajectory. But it is not nothing. You need to fortify yourself for it, plan, and garner support from people who understand what you are up to and are realistically appraised of the difficulty and the options.

Now it may also be that you are lagging in the development of your skills and could improve your performance at work so that your chances of being hired elsewhere are heightened. But there is no loss in that. You cannot effectively pronounce "no" in the presence of corrupt power when your options to move are nonexistent. In consequence, you have a moral obligation to place yourself in a position of comparative strength, and to do then what is necessary to capitalize on that strength. You may also have to think through worst-case situations and to discuss them with those who will be affected by your decisions. But it is once again worth realizing that staying where you should not be may be the true worst-case situation: one that drags you out and kills you slowly over decades. That is not a good death, even though it is slow, and there is very little in it that does not speak of the hopelessness that makes people age quickly and long for the cessation of career and, worse, life. That is no improvement. As the old and cruel cliché goes: If you must cut off a cat's tail, do not do it half an inch at a time. You may well be in for a few painful years of belated recognition of insufficiency, and required to send out four or five or ten job applications a week, knowing full well that the majority will be rejected with less than a second look. But you need to win the lottery only once, and a few years of difficulty with hope beat an entire dejected lifetime of a degenerating and oppressed career.

And let us be clear: It is not a simple matter of hating your job because it requires you to wake up too early in the morning, or to drag yourself to work when it is too hot or cold or windy or dry or when you are feeling low and want to curl up in bed. It is not a matter of frustration generated when you are called on to do things that are menial or necessary such as emptying garbage cans, sweeping floors, cleaning bathrooms, or in any other manner taking your lowly but well-deserved place at the bottom of the hierarchy of competence—even of seniority. Resentment generated by such necessary work is most often merely ingratitude, inability to accept a lowly place at the beginning, unwillingness to adopt the position of the fool, or arrogance and lack of discipline. Refusal of the call of conscience is by no means the same thing as irritation about undesirably low status.

That rejection—that betrayal of soul—is truly the requirement to perform demonstrably counterproductive, absurd, or pointless work; to treat others unjustly and to lie about it; to engage in deceit, to betray your future self; to put up with unnecessary torture and abuse (and to silently watch others suffer the same treatment). That rejection is the turning of a blind eye, and the agreement to say and do things that betray your deepest values and make you a cheat at your own game. And there is no doubt that the road to hell, personally and socially, is paved not so much with good intentions as with the adoption of attitudes and undertaking of actions that inescapably disturb your conscience.

Do not do what you hate.

RULE VI

# ABANDON IDEOLOGY

## THE WRONG PLACES

After I published my last book, my wife, Tammy, and I embarked on a lengthy speaking tour throughout the English-speaking world and a good part of Europe, particularly in the north. Most of the theaters I spoke at were old and beautiful, and it was a delight to be in buildings with such rich architectural and cultural histories, where so many of the bands we loved had played, and where other performing artists had had their great moments. We booked 160 theaters—generally with a capacity of about 2,500 to 3,000 people (although there were smaller venues in Europe, and larger in Australia). I was—and am—struck to the core by the fact that there was such an extensive audience for my lectures—and that we found that audience seemingly everywhere. The same surprise extends to my YouTube and podcast appearances—on my own channels, in interviews on others, and in the innumerable clips that people have voluntarily cut from my longer talks and discussions with journalists. These have been watched or listened to hundreds of millions of times. And finally, there is the afore-mentioned book, which will have sold something like four million copies in English by the time the present volume is published, and which will be translated into fifty additional languages, assuming matters continue as they are now. It is not at all easy to know what to think about finding myself with an audience like that.

What is going on? Any sensible person would be taken aback—to put it mildly—by all of this. It seems that my work must be addressing something that is missing in many people's lives. Now, as I mentioned previously, I am relying for much of my content on the ideas of great psychologists and other thinkers, and that should count for something. But I have also been continually considering what else more specific (if anything) might be attracting people's attention, and have been relying on two sources of information to try to determine exactly that. The first is the response I get directly from individuals themselves, when I meet them in the immediate aftermath of one of my lectures or when they stop me on the street, in airports, cafés, or other public places.

In one midwestern American city (I think it might have been Louis-ville), a young man met me after my lecture and said, "Quick story. Two years ago, I was released from prison. Homeless. Broke. I started listening to your lectures. Now I have a full-time job, and I own my apartment, and my wife and I just had our first child—a daughter. Thank you." And the "thank you" was accompanied with direct eye contact and a firm handshake, and the story was told in the voice of conviction. And people tell me very similar stories on the street, often in tears, although the one I just related was perhaps a bit more extreme than the average tale. They share very private good news (the kind you share only with people to whom you can safely tell such things). And I feel greatly privileged to be one of those people, although it is emo-

tionally demanding to be the recipient of continual personal revelations, regardless (or maybe even because) of the fact that they are so
positive. I find it heart-wrenching to see how little encouragement
and guidance so many people have received, and how much good can
emerge when just a little more is provided. "I knew you could do it" is
a good start, and goes a long way toward ameliorating some of the unnecessary pain in the world.

So, that is one form of story that I hear, continually, in many variants. When we meet, one on one, people also tell me that they enjoy
my lectures and what I have written because what I say and write provides them with the words they need to express things they already
know, but are unable to articulate. It is helpful for everyone to be able
to represent explicitly what they already implicitly understand. I am
frequently plagued with doubts about the role that I am playing, so the
fact that people find my words exist in accordance with their deep but
heretofore unrealized or unexpressed beliefs is reassuring, helping me
maintain faith in what I have learned and thought about and have now
shared so publicly. Helping people bridge the gap between what they
profoundly intuit but cannot articulate seems to be a reasonable and
valuable function for a public intellectual. And then there is the final
piece of information bearing on whatever it is that I am accomplishing.
I have garnered it as a direct consequence of the live lectures that I
have had so many opportunities to deliver. It is a privilege and a gift to
be able to talk repeatedly to large groups of people. It provides a real-
time opportunity to judge the zeitgeist, the spirit of the times. It also
allows me to formulate and immediately test new ideas for their com-
municability and their ability to grip attention and, thereby, to judge
their quality—at least in part. This occurs during the talk when I attend to how the audience responds.

In *12 Rules for Life*, Rule 9: Assume that the person you are listening to might know something you do not, I suggest that when speaking to a large group you should nonetheless always be attending to specific individuals—the crowd is somewhat of an illusion. However, you can augment your individual-focused visual attention by simultaneously listening to the entire group, so that you hear them rustling around, laughing, coughing, or whatever they happen to be doing, while you concentrate on perceiving specific individuals. What you want to see from the person you are facing is rapt attention. What you want to hear from the crowd is dead silence. You want to hear *nothing*. Achieving that means your listeners are not distracted by everything they could be thinking about while in attendance. If you are an audience member at a performance, and you are not completely enthralled by the content, you become preoccupied by some slight physical discomforts, and shift from place to place. You become aware of your own thoughts. You begin to think about what you need to do tomorrow. You whisper something to the person beside you. That all adds up to discontent in the audience, and audible noise. But if you, as speaker, are positioned properly on stage, physically and spiritually, then everybody's attention will be focused with laser-like intensity on whatever you are saying, and no one will make a sound. In this manner, you can tell what ideas have power.

While watching and listening in the way I just described to all the gatherings I have spoken to, I became increasingly aware that the mention of one topic in particular brought every audience (and I mean that without exception) to a dead-quiet halt: responsibility—the very topic we made central in this book in Rule IV: Notice that opportunity lurks where responsibility has been abdicated. That response was fascinating—and not at all predictable. Responsibility is not an easy sell. Parents have been striving forever to make their kids responsible.

Society attempts the same thing, with its educational institutions, apprenticeships, volunteer organizations, and clubs. You might even consider the inculcation of responsibility the fundamental purpose of society. But something has gone wrong. We have committed an error, or a series of errors. We have spent too much time, for example (much of the last fifty years), clamoring about rights, and we are no longer asking enough of the young people we are socializing. We have been telling them for decades to demand what they are owed by society. We have been implying that the important meanings of their lives will be given to them because of such demands, when we should have been doing the opposite: letting them know that the meaning that sustains life in all its tragedy and disappointment is to be found in shouldering a noble burden. Because we have not been doing this, they have grown up looking in the wrong places. And this has left them vulnerable: vulnerable to easy answers and susceptible to the deadening force of resentment. What about the unfolding of history has left us in this position? How has this vulnerability, this susceptibility, come about?

## PERHAPS HE IS ONLY SLEEPING

In the last quarter of the nineteenth century, the German philosopher Friedrich Nietzsche famously announced "God is dead." This utterance has become so famous that you can even see it scribbled on the walls of public bathrooms, where it often takes the following form: "God is dead" —Nietzsche. "Nietzsche is dead" —God. Nietzsche did not make this claim in a narcissistic or triumphant manner. The great thinker's opinion stemmed from his fear that all the Judeo-Christian values serving as the foundation of Western civilization had been made dangerously subject to casual rational criticism, and that the most important axiom upon which they were predicated—the existence of a transcendent, all-powerful deity—had been fatally challenged. Nietzsche concluded from this that everything would soon fall apart, in a manner catastrophic both psychologically and socially.

It does not require a particularly careful reader to note that Nietzsche described God, in *The Gay Science*, as the "holiest and mightiest of all that the world has yet owned," and modern human beings as "the murderers of all murderers."[1] These are not the sorts of descriptions you might expect from a triumphant rationalist celebrating the demise of superstition. It was instead a statement of absolute despair. In his other works, particularly in *The Will to Power*, Nietzsche describes what would occur in the next century and beyond because of this murderous act.[2] He prophesied (and that is the correct word for it) that two major consequences would arise—apparent opposites, although each linked inextricably and causally together—and both associated with the death of traditional ritual, story, and belief.

As the purpose of human life became uncertain outside the purposeful structure of monotheistic thought and the meaningful world it proposed, we would experience an existentially devastating rise in nihilism, Nietzsche believed. Alternatively, he suggested, people would turn to identification with rigid, totalitarian ideology: the substitute of human ideas for the transcendent Father of All Creation. The doubt that undermines and the certainty that crushes: Nietzsche's prognostication for the two alternatives that would arise in the aftermath of the death of God.

The incomparable Russian novelist Fyodor Dostoyevsky addressed the same question as Nietzsche—at about the same time—in his masterwork *The Possessed* (alternatively known as *Demons* or *The Devils*).[3] The protagonist in that novel, Nikolai Stavrogin, is wed to the same ideals that eventually birthed revolutionary communism, although he lives his fictional life decades before the full-fledged turmoil began in what became the Soviet Union. The appearance of these ideals was not a positive development, in Dostoevsky's view. He could see that the adoption of a rigid, comprehensive utopian ideology, predicated on a few apparently self-evident axioms, presented a political and spiritual danger with the potential to far exceed in brutality all that had occurred in the religious, monarchical, or even pagan past. Dostoyevsky, like Nietzsche, foresaw that all of this was coming almost fifty years (!) before the Leninist Revolution in Russia. That incomprehensible level of prophetic capacity remains a stellar example of how the artist and his intuition brings to light the future far before others see it.

Nietzsche and Dostoevsky both foresaw that communism would appear dreadfully attractive—an apparently rational, coherent, and moral alternative to religion or nihilism—and that the consequences would be lethal. The former wrote, in his inimitably harsh, ironic, and brilliant manner, "In fact, I even wish a few experiments might be made to show that in socialistic society life denies itself, and itself cuts away its own roots. The earth is big enough and man is still unexhausted enough for a practical lesson of this sort and *demonstratio ad absurdum*—even if it were accomplished only by a vast expenditure of lives—to seem worthwhile to me."[4] The socialism Nietzsche referred to was not the relatively mild version later popular in Britain, Scandinavia, and Canada, with its sometimes genuine emphasis on the improvement of working-class life, but the full-blown collectivism of Russia, China, and a host of smaller countries. Whether we have truly learned the "practical lesson"—the demonstration of the absurdity of the doctrine—as a consequence of Nietzsche's predicted "vast expenditure of lives" remains to be seen.

Nietzsche appears to have unquestioningly adopted the idea that the world was both objective and valueless in the manner posited by the emergent physical sciences. This left him with a single remaining escape from nihilism and totalitarianism: the emergence of the individual strong enough to create his own values, project them onto valueless reality, and then abide by them. He posited that a new kind of man—the Übermensch (the higher person or superman)—would be necessary in the aftermath of the death of God, so that society would not drift toward the opposing rocky shoals of despair and oversystematized political theorizing. Individuals who take this route, this alternative to nihilism and totalitarianism, must therefore produce their own cosmology of values.

However, the psychoanalysts Freud and Jung put paid to that notion, demonstrating that we are not sufficiently in possession of ourselves to create values by conscious choice. Furthermore, there is little evidence that any of us have the genius to create ourselves *ex nihilo*— from nothing—particularly given the extreme limitations of our experience, the biases of our perceptions, and the short span of our lives. We have a nature—or, too often, it has us—and only a fool would now dare to claim that we have sufficient mastery of ourselves to create, rather than discover, what we value. We have the capacity for spontaneous revelatory experience—artistic, inventive, and religious. We discover new things about ourselves constantly, to our delight—and also to our dismay, as we are so often overcome by our emotions and motivations. We contend with our nature. We negotiate with it. But it is not at all obvious that the individual will ever be capable of bringing the new values that Nietzsche so fervently longed for into being.

There are other problems with Nietzsche's argument, as well. If each of us lives by our own created and projected values, what remains to unite us? This is a philosophical problem of central importance. How could a society of Übermenschen possibly avoid being at constant odds with one another, unless there was something comparable about their created values? Finally, it is by no means obvious that any such supermen have ever come into existence. Instead, over the last century and a half, with the modern crisis of meaning and the rise of totalitarian states such as Nazi Germany, the USSR, and Communist China, we appear to have found ourselves in exactly the nihilistic or ideologically possessed state that Nietzsche and Dostoevsky feared, accompanied by precisely the catastrophic sociological and psychological consequences they foretold.

It is also by no means self-evident that value, subjective though it appears to be, is not an integral part of reality, despite the undeniable utility of the scientific method. The central scientific axiom left to us by the Enlightenment—that reality is the exclusive domain of the objective—poses a fatal challenge to the reality of religious experience, if the latter experience is fundamentally subjective (and it appears to be exactly that). But there is something complicating the situation that seems to lie between the subjective and the objective: What if there are experiences that typically manifest themselves to one person at a time (as seems to be the case with much of revelation), but appear to form a meaningful pattern when considered collectively? That indicates something is occurring that is not merely subjective, even though it cannot be easily pinned down with the existing methods of science. It could be, instead, that the value of something is sufficiently idiosyncratic—sufficiently dependent on the particularities of time, place, and the individual experiencing that thing—that it cannot be fixed and replicated in the manner required for it to exist as a scientific object. This does not mean, however, that value is not *real*: It means only that it is so complex that it cannot yet and may never fit itself within the scientific worldview. The world is a very strange place, and there are times when the metaphorical or narrative description characteristic of culture and the material representation so integral to science appear to touch, when everything comes together—when life and art reflect each other equally.

The psyche—the soul—that produces or is the recipient of such experiences appears incontrovertibly real: the proof lying not least in our actions. We all axiomatically assume the reality of our individual existences and conscious experiences, and we extend the same courtesy to others (or else). It is by no means unreasonable to suggest that such existence and experience has a deep underlying biological and physical structure. Those with a psychoanalytic bent certainly assume so, as do many who study biological psychology, particularly if they focus on motivation and emotion.[5] That structure, accepted as a given by scientists and by the general population in equal measure, appears to manifest religious experience as part of its basic function—and that religious function has enough commonality across people to make us at least understand what "religious experience" means—particularly if we have had a taste of it at some point in life.

What does that imply? It might be that the true meaning of life is available for discovery, if it can be discovered at all, by each individual, alone—although in communication with others, past and present. It may well be, therefore, that the true meaning of life is not to be found in what is objective, but in what is subjective (but still universal). The existence of conscience, for example, provides some evidence for that, as does the fact that religious experiences can reliably be induced chemically, as well as through practices such as dancing, chanting, fasting, and meditating. Additionally, the fact that religious ideas are capable of uniting vast numbers of people under a single moral umbrella (although such ideas can divide across sects, as well) also indicates something universal calling from within. Why do we so easily assume that nothing about that is real, given its apparent commonality and necessity—given, as well, the near certainty that the capacity for valuing is an ancient evolved function, selected for by the very reality we are attempting to define and understand?

We have seen the consequences of the totalitarian alternatives in which the collective is supposed to bear the burdens of life, lay out the proper pathway, and transform the terrible world into the promised utopia. The communists produced a worldview that was attractive to fair-minded people, as well as those who were envious and cruel. Perhaps communism may even have been a viable solution to the problems of the unequal distribution of wealth that characterized the industrial age, if all of the hypothetically oppressed were good people and all of the evil was to be found, as hypothesized, in their bourgeoisie overlords. Unfortunately for the communists, a substantial proportion of the oppressed were incapable, unconscientious, unintelligent, licentious, power mad, violent, resentful, and jealous, while a substantial proportion of the oppressors were educated, able, creative, intelligent, honest, and caring. When the frenzy of dekulakization swept through the newly established Soviet Union, it was vengeful and jealous murderers who were redistributing property, while it was competent and reliable farmers, for the most part, from whom it was violently taken. One unintended consequence of that "redistribution" of good fortune was the starvation of six million Ukrainians in the 1930s, in the midst of some of the most fertile land in the world.

The other major villains of the twentieth century, Germany's National Socialists, were, of course, also powerful and dangerous ideologues. It has been suggested that Hitler's acolytes were inspired by Nietzsche's philosophy. This claim may hold some truth in a perverse manner, as they were certainly trying to create their own values, although not as the individuals whose development the philosopher promoted. It is more reasonable to say that Nietzsche identified the cultural and historical conditions that made the rise to influence of ideas akin to those promoted by the Nazis extremely likely. The Nazis were trying to create a post-Christian, postreligious perfect man, the ideal Aryan, and certainly formulated that ideal in a manner not in accordance with the dictates of either Judaism or Christianity. Thus, the perfect Aryan could be and certainly was conceptualized by the Nazis as a "higher man." This does not mean that the Nazi ideal as postulated bore any resemblance to the Nietzschean ideal. Quite the contrary: Nietzsche was a fervent admirer of individuality and would have considered the idea of the higher man as state creation both absurd and abhorrent.

## THE FATAL ATTRACTION OF THE FALSE IDOL

Consider those who have not gone so far as to adopt the discredited ideologies of the Marxist-Leninists and the Nazis, but who still maintain faith in the commonplace isms characterizing the modern world: conservatism, socialism, feminism (and all manner of ethnic- and gender-study isms), postmodernism, and environmentalism, among others. They are all monotheists, practically speaking—or polytheistic worshippers of a very small number of gods. These gods are the axioms and foundational beliefs that must be accepted, a priori, rather than proven, before the belief system can be adopted, and when accepted and applied to the world allow the illusion to prevail that knowledge has been produced.

The process by which an ism system can be generated is simple in its initial stages but baroque enough in its application to mimic (and replace) actual productive theorizing. The ideologue begins by selecting a few abstractions in whose low-resolution representations hide large, undifferentiated chunks of the world. Some examples include "the economy," "the nation," "the environment," "the patriarchy," "the people," "the rich," "the poor," "the oppressed," and "the oppressors." The use of single terms implicitly hypersimplifies what are in fact extraordinarily diverse and complex phenomena (that masked complexity is part of the reason that the terms come to carry so much emotional weight). There are many reasons, for example, why people are poor. Lack of money is the obvious cause—but that hypothetical obviousness is part of the problem with ideology. Lack of education, broken families, crime-ridden neighborhoods, alcoholism, drug abuse, criminality and corruption (and the political and economic exploitation that accompanies it), mental illness, lack of a life plan (or even failure to realize that formulating such a plan is possible or necessary), low conscientiousness, unfortunate geographical locale, shift in the economic landscape and the consequent disappearance of entire fields of endeavor, the marked proclivity for those who are rich to get richer still and the poor to get poorer, low creativity/entrepreneurial interest, lack of encouragement—these are but a few of the manifold problems that generate poverty, and the solution to each (assuming that a solution exists) is by no means obviously the same. Nor are the villains hiding behind each putative and differentiable cause the same villains (assuming that there are even villains to be found).

All such problems require careful, particularized analysis, followed by the generation of multiple potential solutions, followed by the careful assessment of those solutions to ensure that they are having their desired effect. It is uncommon to see any serious social problem addressed so methodically. It is also rare that the solutions generated, even by methodical process, produce the intended outcome. The great difficulty of assessing problems in sufficient detail to understand what is causing them, followed by the equally great difficulty of generating and testing particularized solutions, is sufficient to deter even the stouthearted, let us say, from daring to tackle a true plague of mankind. Since the ideologue can place him or herself on the morally correct side of the equation without the genuine effort necessary to do so validly, it is much easier and more immediately gratifying to reduce the problem to something simple and accompany it with an evildoer, who can then be morally opposed.

After breaking the world into large, undifferentiated pieces, describing the problem(s) that characterize each division, and identifying the appropriate villains, the ism theorist then generates a small number of explanatory principles or forces (which may indeed contribute in some part to the understanding or existence of those abstracted entities). Then he or she grants to that small number primary causal power, while ignoring others of equal or greater importance. It is most effective to utilize a major motivational system or large-scale sociological fact or conjecture for such purposes. It is also good to select those explanatory principles for an unstated negative, resentful, and destructive reason, and then make discussion of the latter and the reason for their existence taboo for the ideologue and his or her followers (to say nothing of the critics). Next, the faux theorist spins a post-hoc theory about how every phenomenon, no matter how complex, can be considered a secondary consequence of the new, totalizing system. Finally, a school of thought emerges to propagate the methods of this algorithmic reduction (particularly when the thinker is hoping to attain dominance in the conceptual and the real worlds), and those who refuse to adopt the algorithm or who criticize its use are tacitly or explicitly demonized.

Incompetent and corrupt intellectuals thrive on such activity, such games. The first players of a given game of this sort are generally the brightest of the participants. They weave a story around their causal principle of choice, demonstrating how that hypothetically primary motivational force profoundly contributed to any given domain of human activity. Sometimes this is even helpful, as such activity may shed light on how a motivation heretofore taboo to discuss or consider might play a larger role in affecting human behavior and perception than was previously deemed acceptable (this is what happened, for example, with Freud, and his emphasis on sex). Their followers, desperate to join a potentially masterable new dominance hierarchy (the old one being cluttered by its current occupants), become enamored of that story. While doing so, being less bright than those they follow, they subtly shift "contributed to" or "affected" to "caused." The originator(s), gratified by the emergence of followers, start to shift their story in that direction as well. Or they object, but it does not matter. The cult has already begun.

This kind of theorizing is particularly attractive to people who are smart but lazy. Cynicism serves as an aid, too, as does arrogance. The new adherents will be taught that mastering such a game constitutes education, and will learn to criticize alternative theories, different methods, and increasingly, even the idea of fact itself. If an impenetrable vocabulary accompanies the theory, so much the better. It will then take potential critics some valuable time even to learn to decode the arguments. And there is a conspiratorial aspect that rapidly comes to pervade the school where such "education" occurs, and where such activity is increasingly all that is permitted: Do not criticize the theory—and do not get singled out. Do not become unpopular. Even: Do not receive a bad grade, or a poor review, for expressing a taboo opinion (and even when this does not occur in practice, the fear that it might keeps many students and professors, or employees and employers, in check).

Freud, as we noted, attempted to reduce motivation to sexuality, to libido. The same can be done quite effectively by anyone sufficiently literate, intelligent, and verbally fluent. This is because "sexuality" (like any multifaceted single term) can be defined as tightly or as loosely as necessary by those who use it for comprehensively explanatory purposes. No matter how defined, sex is a crucially important biological phenomenon—key to complex life itself—and its influence may therefore be genuinely detected or plausibly invented in any important field of endeavor and then exaggerated (while other factors of significant import are diminished in importance). In this manner, the single explanatory principle can be expanded indefinitely, in keeping with the demands placed upon it.

Marx did the same thing when he described man in a fundamentally economic, class-based manner, and history as the eternal battleground of bourgeoisie and proletariat. Everything can be explained by running it through a Marxist algorithm. The wealthy are wealthy because they exploit the poor. The poor are poor because they are exploited by the wealthy. All economic inequality is undesirable, unproductive, and a consequence of fundamental unfairness and corruption. There is, of course—as in the case of Freud—some value in Marx's observations. Class is an important element of social hierarchies, and tends to maintain itself with a certain stability across time. Economic well-being, or the lack thereof, is of crucial significance. And the damnable fact of the Pareto distribution[6]—the tendency of those who have more to get more (which seems to apply in any economic system)—does mean that wealth accumulates in the hands of a minority of people. The people who make up that minority do change substantively, regardless of the aforementioned class stability,[7] and that is a crucial point, but the fact that the comparatively rich are always a minority—and a small one, at that—seems dismally immutable.

Regardless of its hypothetical virtues, however, the implementation of Marxism was a disaster everywhere it was attempted—and that has motivated attempts by its unrepentant would-be present-day adherents to clothe its ideas in new garb and continue forward, as if nothing of significance has changed. Thinkers powerfully influenced by Marx and overwhelmingly influential in much of the academy today (such as Michel Foucault and Jacques Derrida) modified the Marxist simplification essentially by replacing "economics" with "power"—as if power were the single motivating force behind all human behavior (as opposed, say, to competent authority, or reciprocity of attitude and action).

Ideological reduction of that form is the hallmark of the most dangerous of pseudo-intellectuals. Ideologues are the intellectual equivalent of fundamentalists, unyielding and rigid. Their self-righteousness and moral claim to social engineering is every bit as deep and dangerous. It might even be worse: ideologues lay claim to rationality itself. So, they try to justify their claims as logical and thoughtful. At least the fundamentalists admit devotion to something they just believe arbitrarily. They are a lot more honest. Furthermore, fundamentalists are bound by a relationship with the transcendent. What this means is that God, the center of their moral universe, remains outside and above complete understanding, according to the fundamentalist's own creed. Right-wing Jews, Islamic hard-liners, and ultra-conservative Christians must admit, if pushed, that God is essentially mysterious. This concession provides at least some boundary for their claims, as individuals, to righteousness and power (as the genuine fundamentalist at least remains subordinate to Something he cannot claim to totally understand, let alone master). For the ideologue, however, nothing remains outside understanding or mastery. An ideological theory explains everything: all the past, all the present, and all the future. This means that an ideologue can consider him or herself in possession of the complete truth (something forbidden to the self-consistent fundamentalist). There is no claim more totalitarian and no situation in which the worst excesses of pride are more likely to manifest themselves (and not only pride, but then deceit, once the ideology has failed to explain the world or predict its future).

The moral of the story? Beware of intellectuals who make a monotheism out of their theories of motivation. Beware, in more technical terms, of blanket univariate (single variable) causes for diverse, complex problems. Of course, power plays a role in history, as does economics. But the same can be said of jealousy, love, hunger, sex, cooperation, revelation, anger, disgust, sadness, anxiety, religion, compassion, disease, technology, hatred, and chance—none of which can definitively be reduced to another. The attraction of doing so is, however, obvious: simplicity, ease, and the illusion of mastery (which can have exceptionally useful psychological and social consequences, particularly in the short term)—and, let us not forget, the frequent discovery of a villain, or set of villains, upon which the hidden motivations for the ideology can be vented.

## RESSENTIMENT

Ressentiment[8]—hostile resentment—occurs when individual failure or insufficient status is blamed both on the system within which that failure or lowly status occurs and then, most particularly, on the people who have achieved success and high status within that system. The former, the system, is deemed by fiat to be unjust. The successful are deemed exploitative and corrupt, as they can be logically read as undeserving beneficiaries, as well as the voluntary, conscious, self-serving, and immoral supporters, if the system is unjust. Once this causal chain of thought has been accepted, all attacks on the successful can be construed as morally justified attempts at establishing justice—rather than, say, manifestations of envy and covetousness that might have traditionally been defined as shameful.

There is another typical feature of ideological pursuit: the victims supported by ideologues are always innocent (and it is sometimes true that victims *are* innocent), and the perpetrators are always evil (evil perpetrators are also not in short supply). But the fact that there exist genuine victims and perpetrators provides no excuse to make low-resolution, blanket statements about the global locale of blameless victimization and evil perpetration—particularly of the type that does not take the presumed innocence of the accused firmly into account. *No group guilt should be assumed*—and certainly not of the multigenerational kind.[9] It is a certain sign of the accuser's evil intent, and a harbinger of social catastrophe. But the advantage is that the ideologue, at little practical costs, can construe him or herself both as nemesis of the oppressor and defender of the oppressed. Who needs the fine distinctions that determination of individual guilt or innocence demands when a prize such as that beckons?

To take the path of ressentiment is to risk tremendous bitterness. This is in no small part a consequence of identifying the enemy without rather than within. If wealth is the problem at issue, for example, and the wealthy perceived as the reason for poverty and all the other problems of the world, then the wealthy become the enemy—indistinguishable, in some profound sense, from a degree of evil positively demonic in its psychological and social significance. If power is the problem, then those who have established any authority at all are the singular cause of the world's suffering. If masculinity is the problem, then all males (or even the concept of male) must be attacked and vilified.* Such division of the world into the devil without and the saint within justifies self-righteous hatred—necessitated by the morality of the ideological system itself. This is a terrible trap: Once the source of evil has been identified, it becomes the duty of the righteous to eradicate it. This is an invitation to both paranoia and persecution. A world where only you and people who think like you are good is also a world where you are surrounded by enemies bent on your destruction, who must be fought.

It is much safer morally to look to yourself for the errors of the world, at least to the degree to which someone honest and free of willful blindness might consider. You are likely to be much more clear minded about what is what and who is who and where blame lies once you contemplate the log in your own eye, rather than the speck in your brother's. It is probable that your own imperfections are evident and plentiful, and could profitably be addressed, as step one in your Redeemer's quest to improve the world. To take the world's sins onto yourself—to assume responsibility for the fact that things have not been set right in your own life and elsewhere—is part of the messianic

---

*And don't think the game can't be played (isn't played) in the opposite manner. The same applies for femininity, for example, in too many places in the world: in Arabic, for example, the word *awrah* denotes the body's intimate parts, which must be clothed. The term's root *awr* means something approximating "weakness," "imperfection," or "defectiveness." "Nakedness" is the most common English translation. Other meanings include "falseness," "artificiality," or "blindness." According to the dictionary compiled by Mohammad Moin, a well-known Iranian scholar of Persian literature and Iranian studies, *awrah* means both "nakedness" or "shame" and "young woman." In keeping with this network of ideas, the word *awrat*, derived from *awrah*, has been used widely in various Arabic-influenced cultures to signify "woman." It is for such reasons that women are viewed by those who follow the Wahhabi strand of Islam, for example—ultraconservative, austere, and puritanical—as sufficiently responsible for the evil and temptation of the world that their movements must be drastically and severely restricted, even that they are not allowed to show themselves in any important manner in the public sphere.

path: part of the imitation of the hero, in the most profound of senses. This is a psychological or spiritual rather than a sociological or political issue. Consider the characters fabricated by second-rate crafters of fiction: they are simply divided into those who are good and those who are evil. By contrast, sophisticated writers put the divide inside the characters they create, so that each person becomes the locus of the eternal struggle between light and darkness. It is much more psychologically appropriate (and much less dangerous socially) to assume that you are the enemy—that it is your weaknesses and insufficiencies that are damaging the world—than to assume saintlike goodness on the part of you and your party, and to pursue the enemy you will then be inclined to see everywhere.

It is impossible to fight patriarchy, reduce oppression, promote equality, transform capitalism, save the environment, eliminate competitiveness, reduce government, or to run every organization like a business. Such concepts are simply too low-resolution. The Monty Python comedy crew once offered satirical lessons for playing the flute: blow over one end and move your fingers up and down on the holes.[10] True. But useless. The necessary detail is simply not there. Similarly, sophisticated large-scale processes and systems do not exist in a manner sufficiently real to render their comprehensive unitary transformation possible. The idea that they do is the product of twentieth-century cults. The beliefs of these cults are simultaneously naive and narcissistic, and the activism they promote is the resentful and lazy person's substitute for actual accomplishment. The single axioms of the ideologically possessed are gods, served blindly by their proselytizers.

Like God, however, ideology is dead. The bloody excesses of the twentieth century killed it. We should let it go, and begin to address and consider smaller, more precisely defined problems. We should conceptualize them at the scale at which we might begin to solve them, not by blaming others, but by trying to address them personally while simultaneously taking responsibility for the outcome.

Have some humility. Clean up your bedroom. Take care of your family. Follow your conscience. Straighten up your life. Find something productive and interesting to do and commit to it. When you can do all that, find a bigger problem and try to solve that if you dare. If that works, too, move on to even more ambitious projects. And, as the necessary beginning to that process . . . abandon ideology.

## RULE VII

---

# WORK AS HARD AS YOU POSSIBLY
# CAN ON AT LEAST ONE THING AND
# SEE WHAT HAPPENS

## THE VALUE OF HEAT AND PRESSURE

When coal is subjected to intense heat and pressure, far below the Earth's surface, its atoms rearrange themselves into the perfect repeating crystalline alignment characterizing a diamond. The carbon that makes up coal also becomes maximally durable in its diamond form (as diamond is the hardest of all substances). Finally, it becomes capable of reflecting light. This combination of durability and glitter gives a diamond the qualities that justify its use as a symbol of value. That which is valuable is pure, properly aligned, and glitters with light— and this is true for the person just as it is for the gem. Light, of course, signifies the shining brilliance of heightened and focused consciousness. Human beings are conscious during the day, when it is light. Much of that consciousness is visual and therefore dependent on light. To be illumined or enlightened is to be exceptionally awake and aware—to attain a state of being commonly associated with divinity. To wear a

diamond is to become associated with the radiance of the Sun, like the
king or queen whose profile is stamped on the sunlike disc of the gold
coin, a near-universal standard of worth.

Heat and pressure transform the base matter of common coal into
the crystalline perfection and rare value of the diamond. The same
can be said of a person. We know that the multiple forces operating in
the human soul are often not aligned with one another. We do the
things we wish we would not do and do not do the things we know we
should do. We want to be thin, but we sit on the couch eating Cheetos
and despairing. We are directionless, confused, and paralyzed by indecision. We are pulled in all directions by temptations, despite our
stated will, and we waste time, procrastinate, and feel terrible about it,
but we do not change.

It was for such reasons that archaic people found it easy to believe
that the human soul was haunted by ghosts—possessed by ancestral
spirits, demons, and gods—none of whom necessarily had the best
interests of the person at heart. Since the time of the psychoanalysts,
these contrary forces, these obsessive and sometimes malevolent spirits, have been conceptualized psychologically as impulses, emotions, or
motivational states—or as complexes, which act like partial personalities united within the person by memory but not by intent. Our
neurological structure is indeed hierarchical. The powerful instinctual servants at the bottom, governing thirst, hunger, rage, sadness,
elation, and lust, can easily ascend and become our masters, and just
as easily wage war with one another. The resilience and strength of a
united spirit is not easy to attain.

A house divided against itself, proverbially, cannot stand. Likewise,
a poorly integrated person cannot hold himself together when challenged. He loses union at the highest level of psychological organization. He loses the properly balanced admixture of properties that is

another feature of the well-tempered soul, and cannot hold his self together. We know this when we say "He lost it" or "He just fell apart." Before he picks up the pieces and rearranges them, such a person is likely to fall prey to domination by one or more partial personalities. This might be a spirit of rage, or anxiety, or pain, leaping in to occupy the person when his temper is lost. You can see this occurring most clearly in the case of a two-year-old having a tantrum. He has lost himself temporarily, and is for the moment pure emotion. This is an occurrence that is often deeply upsetting to the two-year-old himself, and one of an intensity that would be terrifying to beholders if manifested by an adult. The archaic motivational systems governing anger merely push the toddler's developing personality aside, and have their way with his mind and actions. This is a true and unfortunate defeat for the still-fragile centralizing ego, struggling against powerful forces toward psychological and social integration.

Lack of internal union also makes itself known in the increased suffering, magnification of anxiety, absence of motivation, and lack of pleasure that accompany indecision and uncertainty. The inability to decide among ten things, even when they are desirable, is equivalent to torment by all of them. Without clear, well-defined, and non-contradictory goals, the sense of positive engagement that makes life worthwhile is very difficult to obtain. Clear goals limit and simplify the world, as well, reducing uncertainty, anxiety, shame, and the self-devouring physiological forces unleashed by stress. The poorly integrated person is thus volatile and directionless—and this is only the beginning. Sufficient volatility and lack of direction can rapidly conspire to produce the helplessness and depression characteristic of prolonged futility. This is not merely a psychological state. The physical consequences of depression, often preceded by excess secretion of the stress hormone cortisol, are essentially indistinguishable from rapid aging (weight gain, cardiovascular problems, diabetes, cancer, and Alzheimer's).[1]

The social consequences are just as serious as the biological. A person who is not well put together overreacts to the slightest hint of frustration or failure. He cannot enter into productive negotiations, even with himself, because he cannot tolerate the uncertainty of discussing potential alternative futures. He cannot be pleased, because he cannot get what he wants, and he cannot get what he wants because he will not choose one thing instead of another. He can also be brought to a halt by the weakest of arguments. One of his multiple, warring subpersonalities will latch on to such arguments, often contrary to his best interest, and use them, in the form of doubts, to buttress its contrarian position. A deeply conflicted person can therefore be stopped, metaphorically, with the pressure of a single finger exerted on his chest (even though he may lash out against such an obstacle). To move forward with resolve, it is necessary to be organized—to be directed toward something singular and identifiable.

Aim. Point. All this is part of maturation and discipline, and something to be properly valued. If you aim at nothing, you become plagued by everything. If you aim at nothing, you have nowhere to go, nothing to do, and nothing of high value in your life, as value requires the ranking of options and sacrifice of the lower to the higher. Do you really want to be anything you could be? Is that not too much? Might it not be better to be something specific (and then, perhaps, to add to that)? Would that not come as a relief—even though it is also a sacrifice?

## THE WORST DECISION OF ALL

When I was in graduate school at McGill University in Montreal studying for my clinical PhD, I noticed a pronounced improvement

in character in everyone who continued in the progressively more difficult five- to six-year program. Their social skills improved. They
became more articulate. They found a profound sense of personal purpose. They served a useful function in relation to others. They became more disciplined and organized. They had more fun. This was
all despite the facts that the graduate courses were often of lower quality than they might have been, the clinical placements unpaid and difficult to come by, and the relationships with graduate supervisors
sometimes (but by no means always) subpar. Those beginning graduate work were often still immature and confused. But the discipline
imposed upon them by the necessity of research—and more particularly, thesis preparation—soon improved their characters. To write
something long, sophisticated, and coherent means, at least in part, to
become more complex, articulate, and deeper in personality.

When I became a professor and started mentoring undergraduate
and graduate students, I observed the same thing. The undergrad psychology students who allied themselves with a lab (and therefore took
on additional work) obtained better grades than those who burdened
themselves less. Taking on the functions of junior researchers helped
them establish a place and a community, while requiring them to discipline themselves, not least by necessitating more efficient use of
their time. I observed a similar process when working as a clinical
psychologist. I typically encouraged my clients to choose the best path
currently available to them, even if it was far from their ideal. This
sometimes meant tolerating at least a temporary decrease in ambition,
or in pride, but had the advantage of substituting something real for
something available only in fantasy. Improvements in mental health
almost invariably followed.

Is there anything worth committing to? I am now old enough to have
seen what happens when the various manners in which this question

might be answered manifest themselves. In my career as undergraduate, graduate student, professor, clinical psychologist, researcher, and in my various additional forays, I have seen the same twin paths of development manifest themselves repeatedly. Both are available, in principle, to everyone—to each of the half-developed, wandering, prematurely cynical, questioning, doubtful, and hopeful fools that we all are to varying degrees when young and on the brink of adulthood. It has become self-evident to me that many commitments have enduring value: those of character, love, family, friendship, and career foremost among them (and perhaps in that order). Those who remain unable or unwilling to establish a well-tended garden, so to speak, in any or all those domains inevitably suffer because of it. However, commitment requires its pound of flesh. To pursue an undergraduate degree means sacrifice and study, and the choice of a given discipline means forgoing the possibility of other pathways of study. The same goes for selecting a partner or group of friends. Cynicism about such things, or mere indecision or doubt, finds an easy but truly adversarial ally in the mindlessly nihilistic rationality that undermines everything: Why bother? What difference is it going to make in a thousand years? What makes one pathway preferable to another—or to none—anyway?

It is possible to be content, or even happy, with one partner or another, or with one group of friends or another, or with one career or another. In some sense, the satisfaction that these arrangements bring could have been generated by different choices. They are also each deeply flawed: romantic partners can be fickle and complex, as can friends, and every career or job is characterized by frustration, disappointment, corruption, arbitrary hierarchy, internal politics, and sheer idiocy of decision making. We could conclude from that lack of spe-

cific or ideal value that nothing matters more than anything else—or
to draw the even more hopeless allied conclusion that nothing therefore matters at all. But those who draw such conclusions, no matter
how well armed they are with rationally coherent arguments, pay a
high price. People suffer for it if they quit before completing an undergraduate degree or the study of a trade. And this means "quit," not fail,
although the two can be difficult to distinguish. Sometimes people fail
because they just cannot manage the job, despite good intentions and
necessary discipline. It takes a certain verbal capacity to operate effectively as a lawyer, and a certain degree of facility with mechanical
objects, for example, to become a carpenter. Sometimes the match between person and choice is so poor that even commitment will not
suffice to bring about the desired end. But very often failure is a consequence of insufficient single-mindedness, elaborate but pointless
rationalization, and rejection of responsibility. And little good comes
of that.

People who do not choose a job or a career commonly become un-
moored and drift. They may attempt to justify that drifting with a
facade of romantic rebelliousness or prematurely world-weary cynicism. They may turn to casual identification with avant-garde artistic
exploration or treat the attendant despair and aimlessness with the
pursuit of hard-core alcohol and drug use and their instant gratifica-
tions. But none of that makes for a successful thirty-year-old (let alone
someone a decade older). The same holds true for people who cannot
choose and then commit to a single romantic partner, or are unable or
unwilling to be loyal to their friends. They become lonely, isolated,
and miserable, and all that merely adds the additional depth of bitterness to the cynicism that spurred the isolation in the first place. That
is not the sort of vicious circle that you want to characterize your life.

The people I knew who finished their undergraduate degrees or trade programs were better for it. Not "good," necessarily. Not functioning optimally. Not necessarily thrilled with their choices, or devoid of doubt and misgiving. Not even certain to continue in pursuit of what they had studied. But far better than those who withdrew and drifted. The commitments and the sacrifices thereby entailed matured those who endured and made them better people. So, what is the conclusion? There are many things to which we might commit ourselves. A case can be made for the arbitrary and even meaningless nature of any given commitment, given the plethora of alternatives, given the corruption of the systems demanding that commitment. But the same case cannot be made for the fact of commitment itself: Those who do not choose a direction are lost. It is far better to become something than to remain anything but become nothing. This is despite all the genuine limitations and disappointments that becoming something entails. Everywhere, the cynic despairs, are bad decisions. But someone who has transcended that cynicism (or more accurately, replaced it with an even more profound doubt—that is, the doubt that doubt itself is an ultimately reliable guide) objects: the worst decision of all is none.

## DISCIPLINE AND UNITY

The discipline that enables concentration on one thing begins young. At a very early age, children begin to order the multiplicity of emotions and motivations that constitute their basic instincts of survival into the strategies of cooperation and competition that involve others, voluntarily—and children who are well constituted and fortunate manage this in a manner that is simultaneously socially desirable and psychologically healthy. When a child's self-directed experience is interrupted by the emergence of an instinctual system (when the child is hungry, angry, tired, or cold), the good parent steps in, solving the problem disrupting the child's fragile unity or, better yet, teaching the child to solve the problem himself. When the latter process has been completed with sufficient thoroughness, the child is ready to join the social world. This must happen by the age of four, or it may never happen.[2] A child must be sufficiently self-organizing to be desirable to his or her peers by the age of four or risk permanent social ostracism. A child who is still having temper tantrums by that age runs precisely that risk.

The process of integration is furthered by peers—friends—for the child well trained or fortunate enough to be accepted. When a child plays a game with others, she is disciplining herself. She is learning to subordinate all her competing impulses to the dictates of that game—one thing, despite the potential multiplicity of rules; learning to subjugate herself voluntarily to its rules and well-defined goals. To play in such a manner, she must transform herself into a functional subunit of a larger social machine. This can be interpreted as a sacrifice of individuality, if individuality is defined as limitless choice of impulsive gratification. But it is much more accurately *development* of individuality, considered at a higher level: the properly functioning and integrated individual tempers the desires of the present with the necessities of the future (including the necessity of playing well with others). It is in this manner that the multifarious games of childhood temper the screaming cacophony of late infancy. The payoff for such development is, of course, the security of social inclusion, and the pleasure of the game.

This, it should be noted, is not *repression*. This point must be made clear, as people believe that the things discipline imposed by choice prevents us from doing will somehow be lost forever. It is this belief, in large part—often expressed with regard to creativity—that makes so many parents afraid of damaging their children by disciplining them. But proper discipline organizes rather than destroys. A child terrified into obedience or shielded from every possible chance of misbehavior is not disciplined, but abused. A child who has been disciplined properly, by contrast—by parents, other adults, and most significantly, by other children—does not battle with, defeat, and then permanently *inhibit* her aggression. Such a child does not even sublimate that aggression, or transform it into something different. Instead, she integrates it into her increasingly sophisticated game-playing ability, allowing it to feed her competitiveness and heighten her attention, and making it serve the higher purposes of her developing psyche. A well-socialized child does not therefore lack aggression. *She just becomes extremely good at being aggressive*, transmuting what might otherwise be a disruptive drive into the focused perseverance and controlled competitiveness that make for a successful player. By the dawn of adolescence, such a child can organize herself into ever more complex games—joint, goal-directed activities that everyone plays voluntarily, and that everyone enjoys and benefits from, even if only one person or one team can win at a time. This ability is civilization itself in its nascent form, at the level of the individual player and group. This is where both cooperation and the opportunity to compete and win make themselves simultaneously manifest. This is all necessary preparation for the more permanent choices that must be made for a successful adulthood.

It is certainly possible—and reasonable—to have some doubt and to argue about which game might best be played here and now; but it is not reasonable to state that all games are therefore unnecessary.

Likewise, although it may be possible to argue about which morality is the *necessary* morality, it is not possible to argue that morality itself is thus unnecessary. Doubt about which game is appropriate right now is not relativism. It is the intelligent consideration of context. The fact that happiness is not appropriate, for example, at a funeral, does not mean that happiness itself lacks value. Likewise, the claim that morality is both necessary and inevitable is not totalitarian. It is merely the observation that basic, primitive unidimensional values must be subsumed under socially organized structures for peace and harmony to exist and be maintained. It was the bringing together of a warring multiplicity under the unifying doctrines of Christianity that civilized Europe. It could, perhaps, have been Buddhism, Confucianism, or Hinduism, insofar as the East is also both broadly civilized and unified. But it could not have been the absence of any doctrine whatsoever. Without a game, there is no peace, only chaos. Furthermore, the game that exists must be playable (as we discussed in Rule IV: Notice that opportunity lurks where responsibility has been abdicated). This means that it must be structured by a communally acceptable set of rules—by only those constraints that many people are willing to abide by, for a long time. It is possible that many such games exist, theoretically, but it is at least equally possible that there are only a few. In any case, the rules of Christianity and the rules of Buddhism are by no means arbitrary, by no means nonsensical superstition, any more than the rules of a playable game are merely arbitrary or nonsensically superstitious. To think that peace can exist without the overarching and voluntarily accepted game is to misunderstand the ever-present danger of the fragmented tribalism to which we can so easily and devastatingly regress.

Once the social world has forced the child to integrate his multiple subpersonalities, he can play with others. After that, he should be ready to engage in the more serious games that make up jobs or professions, with their highly structured expectations, skills, and rules. He must learn those, as well as—when older—the dance of the sexes. He must integrate his socialized personality with that of another, so that the couple he makes with that other can exist together peacefully, productively, within society, over the long term—while maintaining voluntary willingness to do so. This is the dual process of psychological and social integration that accompanies apprenticeship, all associated with the outsourcing of sanity. Adherence to this process will make him a socially sophisticated, productive, and psychologically healthy adult, capable of true reciprocity (and, perhaps, the temporary suspension of the demand of reciprocity necessary to raise children).

But the story of integration and socialization does not end here. This is because two things are happening at once, during an apprenticeship worthy of the name (just as learning to play a game and learning to be a good sport happen at the same time, while playing). Initially, the apprentice must become a servant of tradition, of structure, and of dogma, just as the child who wants to play must follow the rules of the game. At its best, this servitude means grateful alliance, in one form or another, with the institutions typically considered patriarchal. Apprenticeship means heat and pressure (as new workmen are tried by their peers, as articling law students are tried by their employers, as medical residents are tried by physicians, nurses, and patients). The goal of this heat and pressure is subordination of an undeveloped personality (by no means "individual" at this point) to a single path, for the purposes of transformation from undisciplined beginner to accomplished master.

The master, who is the rightful product of apprenticeship, is, however, no longer the servant of dogma. Instead, he is now himself served by dogma, which he has the responsibility to maintain as well as the right to change, when change is necessary. This makes the master, who once allowed himself to be enslaved, an emergent follower of spirit—the wind (spirit) that bloweth where it listeth (John 3:8). The master can allow himself his intuitions, as the knowledge obtained by the discipline he has acquired will enable him to criticize his own ideas and assess their true value. He may therefore more clearly perceive the fundamental patterns or principles that underlie the dogmas of his discipline, and draw inspiration from those, instead of blindly adhering to the rules as currently articulated or embodied. He may even rely on the integrated union of his personality and his training to modify or transform even those more fundamental, deeply intuited principles, in the service of an even higher union.

## DOGMA AND SPIRIT

The limiting disciplines that serve both as precondition for a game and for the development of a unity of being can usefully be considered Thou Shalt Nots—rules that highlight what is definitely not to be done, while whatever is supposed to be done is taking place. Abiding by these rules produces a development of character—character with a particular nature or essence (we have already discussed this as, say, the development of personal desirability as a player of many games, or sequences of games). As is the case in many other situations, it appears that this idea is already implicit in the stories that make up the bedrock of our culture. This is particularly evident in the Gospel of Mark, which is a commentary on what are among the most influential Rules of the Game ever formulated—the Mosaic Ten Commandments (and,

even more broadly, a commentary on rules themselves). The commandments follow:

1. Though shalt have no other gods before me.
2. Though shalt not make unto thee any graven image.
3. Thou shalt not take the name of the Lord thy God
   in vain.
4. Remember the sabbath day, to keep it holy.
5. Honor thy father and thy mother.
6. Thou shalt not kill.
7. Thou shalt not commit adultery.
8. Thou shalt not steal.
9. Thou shalt not bear false witness against thy neighbor.
10. Thou shalt not covet.

The first speaks to the necessity of aiming at the highest possible
unity; the second to the danger of worshipping false idols (by confusing the representation, or the image, with the ineffable it is supposed
to represent); the third means that it is wrong to claim moral inspiration from God while knowingly committing sinful acts; the fourth
means that it is necessary to leave time to regularly consider what is
truly valuable or sacred; the fifth keeps families together, mandating
honor, respect, and gratitude from children as just reward for the sacrifices made by parents; the sixth prevents murder (obviously) but, by
doing so, also protects the community from potential descent into constant and potentially multigenerational feuding; the seventh mandates
the sacredness of the marriage vow, predicated on the assumption
(like the fifth) that the stability and value of the family is of para-
mount importance; the eighth allows for honest, hardworking people

to reap the benefits of their efforts without fear that what they have produced will be taken from them arbitrarily (and, thereby, makes civilized society a possibility); the ninth maintains the integrity of the law, reducing or eliminating its use as a weapon; and the tenth is a reminder that envy and the resentment it breeds is a destructive force of the highest power.

It is worthwhile thinking of these Commandments as a minimum set of rules for a stable society—an iterable social game. The Commandments are rules established in the book of Exodus, and part of that unforgettable story. But they are also pointers to something else—something that simultaneously emerges from and transcends the rules and constitutes their essence. The core idea is this: subjugate yourself voluntarily to a set of socially determined rules—those with some tradition in their formulation—and a unity that transcends the rules will emerge. That unity constitutes what you could be, if you concentrate on a particular goal and see it through.

There is a story relevant to this idea in the Gospel of Mark. The pertinent section begins with Christ journeying to the temple of Jerusalem, where He casts out the moneychangers and merchants and addresses the crowd with an irresistible charisma. And, as the tale goes, "the scribes and chief priests heard it, and sought how they might destroy him: for they feared him, because all the people was astonished at his doctrine" (Mark 11:18). In consequence, they begin to conspire, questioning this strange prophet, hoping to entice Him into a heretical and therefore potentially fatal statement, sending to Him "certain of the Pharisees and of the Herodians, to catch him in his words" (Mark 12:13). Christ deals masterfully, to say the least, with the questioners, reducing them to an aggrieved and resentful silence. The section ends with what is arguably the most difficult and treacherous of questions, posed by a particularly cunning but also perhaps begrudgingly admiring interlocutor (Mark 12:28–34):

> And one of the scribes came, and having heard them reasoning together, and perceiving that he had answered them well, asked him, Which is the first commandment of all?
>
> And Jesus answered him, The first of all the commandments is, Hear, O Israel; The Lord our God is one Lord:
>
> And thou shalt love the Lord thy God with all thy heart, and with all thy soul, and with all thy mind, and with all thy strength: this is the first commandment.
>
> And the second is like, namely this, Thou shalt love thy neighbor as thyself. There is none other commandment greater than these.
>
> And the scribe said unto him, Well, Master, thou hast said the truth: for there is one God; and there is none other but he:
>
> And to love him with all the heart, and with all the understanding, and with all the soul, and with all the strength, and to love his neighbor as himself, is more than all whole burnt offerings and sacrifices.
>
> And when Jesus saw that he answered discreetly, he said unto him, Thou art not far from the kingdom of God. And no man after that durst ask him any question.

What does this all mean? The personality integrated by disciplined adherence to a set of appropriate rules is simultaneously (although perhaps unknowingly) guided by or imitating the highest possible ideal—precisely that ideal that constitutes whatever common element of "moral" makes all the rules good, just, and necessary. That ideal, according to Christ's answer, is something singular (the "one Lord"), thoroughly embodied (loved with "all thy heart," "soul," "understand-ing," and "strength"), and then manifested as a love that is identical for self and all mankind.

Western culture is "unconsciously" underpinned by a very profound drama, reflecting all this, because of its origin in Judeo-Christian con-ceptualization. Psychologically speaking, Christ is a representation, or an embodiment, of the mastery of dogma and the (consequent) emer-gence of spirit. Spirit is the creative force that gives rise to what be-comes dogma, with time. Spirit is also that which constantly transcends such time-honored tradition, when possible. It is for this reason that an apprenticeship ends with a masterpiece, the creation of which signi-fies not only the acquisition of the requisite skill, but the acquisition of the ability to create new skills.

Although Christ commits many acts that might be considered revo-lutionary, as we discussed in Rule I, He is nonetheless explicitly por-trayed in the Gospels as the master of tradition, and says of Himself, "Think not that I am come to destroy the law, or the prophets: I am not come to destroy, but to fulfill" (Matthew 5:17, KJV). The New Inter-national Version of the Bible perhaps puts it more comprehensibly: "Do not think that I have come to abolish the Law or the Prophets; I have not come to abolish them but to fulfill them." Christ therefore presents Himself as both the product of tradition, and the very thing that creates and transforms it. The same pattern of creative conflict pervades the Old Testament, which is in large part a series of stories about the spirit in prophetic opposition to the inevitable corruption of dogma harnessed to serve power. It is the personality who mimics that model who might be regarded as truly Western, in the deepest of psy-chological senses.

If you work as hard as you can on one thing, you will change. You will start to also become one thing, instead of the clamoring multitude you once were. That one thing, developed properly, is not only the disciplined entity formed by sacrifice, commitment, and concentration. It is that which creates, destroys, and transforms discipline itself—civilization itself—by expressing its unity of personality and society. It is the very Word of truth, upon whose function all habitable order, wrenched out of chaos, eternally depends.

Work as hard as you possibly can on at least one thing and see what happens.

---

# TRY TO MAKE ONE ROOM IN YOUR HOME AS BEAUTIFUL AS POSSIBLE

## CLEANING YOUR ROOM IS NOT ENOUGH

I have become known for encouraging people to clean up their rooms. Perhaps that is because I am serious about that prosaic piece of advice, and because I know that it is a much more difficult task than it appears. I have been unsuccessfully cleaning up my room, by the way—my home office (which I generally keep in relatively pristine condition)—for about three years now. My life was thrown into such chaos over that period by the multitude of changes I experienced—political controversies, transformation of career, endless travel, mountains of mail, the sequence of illnesses—that I simply became overwhelmed. The disorganization was heightened by the fact that my wife and I had just finished having much of our house renovated, and everything we could not find a proper place for ended up in my office.

There is a meme floating around the internet, accusing me of hypocrisy on account of this: a still taken from a video I shot in my office, with a fair bit of mess in the background (and I cannot say that I look much better myself). Who am I to tell people to clean up their rooms before attempting to fix the rest of the world when, apparently, I cannot do it myself? And there is something directly synchronistic and meaningful about that objection, because I am not in proper order at that moment myself, and my condition undoubtedly found its reflection in the state of my office. More piled up every day, as I traveled, and everything collected around me. I plead exceptional circumstances, and I put many other things in order during the time my office was degenerating, but I still have a moral obligation to get back in there and put it right. And the problem is not just that I want to clean up the mess. I also want to make it beautiful: my room, my house, and then, perhaps, in whatever way I can manage, the community. God knows it is crying out for it.

Making something beautiful is difficult, but it is amazingly worthwhile. If you learn to make something in your life truly beautiful— even one thing—then you have established a relationship with beauty. From there you can begin to expand that relationship out into other elements of your life and the world. That is an invitation to the divine. That is the reconnection with the immortality of childhood, and the true beauty and majesty of the Being you can no longer see. You must be daring to try that.

If you study art (and literature and the humanities), you do it so that you can familiarize yourself with the collected wisdom of our civilization. This is a very good idea—a veritable necessity—because people have been working out how to live for a long time. What they have produced is strange but also rich beyond comparison, so why not use it as a guide? Your vision will be grander and your plans more comprehensive. You will consider other people more intelligently and completely. You will take care of yourself more effectively. You will understand the present more profoundly, rooted as it is in the past, and you will come to conclusions much more carefully. You will come to treat the future, as well, as a more concrete reality (because you will have developed some true sense of time) and be less likely to sacrifice it to impulsive pleasure. You will develop some depth, gravitas, and true thoughtfulness. You will speak more precisely, and other people will become more likely to listen to and cooperate productively with you, as you will with them. You will become more your own person, and less a dull and hapless tool of peer pressure, vogue, fad, and ideology.

Buy a piece of art. Find one that speaks to you and make the purchase. If it is a genuine artistic production, it will invade your life and change it. A real piece of art is a window into the transcendent, and you need that in your life, because you are finite and limited and bounded by your ignorance. Unless you can make a connection to the transcendent, you will not have the strength to prevail when the challenges of life become daunting. You need to establish a link with what is beyond you, like a man overboard in high seas requires a life preserver, and the invitation of beauty into your life is one means by which that may be accomplished.

It is for such reasons that we need to understand the role of art, and stop thinking about it as an option, or a luxury, or worse, an affectation. Art is the bedrock of culture itself. It is the foundation of the process by which we unite ourselves psychologically, and come to establish productive peace with others. As it is said, "Man shall not live by bread alone" (Matthew 4:4). That is exactly right. We live by beauty. We live by literature. We live by art. We cannot live without some connection to the divine—and beauty is divine—because in its absence life is too short, too dismal, and too tragic. And we must be sharp and awake and prepared so that we can survive properly, and orient the world properly, and not destroy things, including ourselves—and beauty can help us appreciate the wonder of Being and motivate us to seek gratitude when we might otherwise be prone to destructive resentment.

## MEMORY AND VISION

> The pride of the peacock is the glory of God.
> The lust of the goat is the bounty of God.
> The wrath of the lion is the wisdom of God.
> The nakedness of woman is the work of God.
> Excess of sorrow laughs. Excess of joy weeps.
> The roaring of lions, the howling of wolves, the raging of the
>     stormy sea, and the destructive sword, are portions of
>     eternity too great for the eye of man.
>
> —WILLIAM BLAKE, FROM "PROVERBS OF HELL,"
> *The Marriage of Heaven and Hell*

When I was a child, I knew the contours and details of all the houses in my immediate neighborhood. I knew the back alleys, the places behind the fences, the location of each crack in the pavement, and the shortcuts that could be taken from one place to another. My geographical locale was not large, but I had explored it thoroughly and my knowledge of it was very detailed. Now that I am an adult, the same is not true. I lived in Fairview, the town I grew up in for most of my childhood and adolescence, for only nine years, but I am still able to picture in high resolution the street I lived on. I have lived in Toronto, on the same street, for more than twice as long, but I still have only a vague sense of the houses that surround mine.

I do not think that is a good thing. I feel far less at home because of it.

It is as if when I walk down the street and glance at a local house, I think of "house" as an icon (because, really, what practical difference does it make to me what particularities characterize each house?), and then my attention is turned to something else. I do not see the house, with its specific shingles, colors, flowers, and architectural details, despite the interest that might have been elicited in me had I paid careful attention. By this point in my life, I have seen so many houses in so many places that I know what a house is likely to do when I walk by it—which is very little. Thus, I ignore the engaging idiosyncrasies and beauties of its details—its unique character, for better or worse—and see just enough to stay oriented as I walk past and continue to think and be elsewhere as I do so. There is real loss in that. I am simply *not there* in my adult neighborhood the same way I was as a child in my home-town. I am separated from the reality of the world. And a very deep feeling of belonging is missing in some important way because of that.

Perception has been replaced for me with functional, pragmatic memory. This has made me more efficient, in some ways, but the cost is an impoverished experience of the richness of the world. I remember when I started working as a junior professor in Boston, when my kids were about two and three years old. I was very preoccupied with my work, trying to keep up, trying to advance my career, trying to make enough money to support my family on a single income. I would come home and take a walk with Tammy and our children, Mikhaila and Julian. I found it very difficult to remain patient with them. I had too much work to do, always—or believed I did—and had disciplined myself through years of effort to focus continually on that. If we went for a walk, I wanted to know exactly where we were going, just how long it would take to get there, and precisely when we were going back. This is no attitude to adopt when trying to have a pleasant and reasonable time with toddlers. Not if you want to immerse yourself in

the experience. Not if you want to watch and participate in the pleasure they take in their timeless discovery. Not unless you want to risk
missing something of crucial import.

It was very difficult for me to relax and focus on the present and
watch my little kids pursue their meandering route through the neighborhood, with no particular destination, purpose, or schedule in mind,
engaging themselves deeply in an encounter with a local dog, bug, or
earthworm, or in some game they invented on the way. Now and then,
however, I could snap briefly into that same frame of reference (that is
one of the wonderful gifts provided by young children) and see the
pristine world they inhabited, still untrammeled by practiced and efficient memory, capable of producing pure joy in the newness of everything. But I was still possessed enough by my future concerns to be
involuntarily pulled back into intense preoccupation with getting the
next thing done.

I knew perfectly well that I was missing out on beauty and meaning
and engagement, regardless of whatever advantages in efficiency my
impatience brought. I was narrow, sharp, and focused, and did not
waste time, but the price I paid for that was the blindness demanded
by efficiency, accomplishment, and order. I was no longer seeing the
world. I was seeing only the little I needed to navigate it with maximum speed and lowest cost. None of that was surprising. I had the
responsibilities of an adult. I had a demanding job. I had to take care of
my family, and that meant sacrificing the present and attending to the
future. But having little children around and noticing their intense
preoccupation with the present, and their fascination with what was
directly around them, made me very conscious of the loss that accompanied maturity. Great poets are expressly aware of this, and they do
what they can to remind the rest of us:

There was a time when meadow, grove, and stream,

The earth, and every common sight,

To me did seem

Apparelled in celestial light,

The glory and the freshness of a dream.

It is not now as it hath been of yore;—

Turn wheresoe'er I may,

By night or day.

The things which I have seen I now can see no more. . . .

Ye blessèd creatures, I have heard the call

Ye to each other make; I see

The heavens laugh with you in your jubilee;

My heart is at your festival,

My head hath its coronal,

The fulness of your bliss, I feel—I feel it all.

Oh evil day! if I were sullen

While Earth herself is adorning,

This sweet May-morning,

And the Children are culling

On every side,

In a thousand valleys far and wide,

Fresh flowers; while the sun shines warm,

And the Babe leaps up on his Mother's arm:—

I hear, I hear, with joy I hear!

—But there's a Tree, of many, one,

A single field which I have looked upon,

Both of them speak of something that is gone;

The Pansy at my feet

Doth the same tale repeat:

Whither is fled the visionary gleam?
Where is it now, the glory and the dream?

—WILLIAM WORDSWORTH, "ODE: INTIMATIONS OF IMMORTALITY
FROM RECOLLECTIONS OF EARLY CHILDHOOD"

Some, in fact, never lose the glorious vision of childhood. This is particularly true of artists (and, indeed, seems a vital part of what makes them artists). William Blake, the English painter, printmaker, and poet, appears to have been one such person. He inhabited a uniquely visionary world. Blake perceived something closer to what the philosopher Immanuel Kant termed "the thing in itself"[1] than do most mortals, left as we are with the pale reflection of our surroundings that our increasingly restricted mature perceptions deliver to us. Blake was also exquisitely sensitive to the metaphoric or dramatic significance of each apparently isolated event—the manner in which each event is rife with endless poetically echoing connotations:

Every Farmer Understands
Every Tear from Every Eye
Becomes a Babe in Eternity
This is caught by Females bright
And returnd to its own delight
The Bleat the Bark Bellow & Roar
Are Waves that Beat on Heavens Shore
The Babe that weeps the Rod beneath
Writes Revenge in realms of Death
The Beggars Rags fluttering in Air
Does to Rags the Heavens tear
The Soldier armd with Sword & Gun

Palsied strikes the Summers Sun
The poor Mans Farthing is worth more
Than all the Gold on Africs Shore
One Mite wrung from the Labrers hands
Shall buy & sell the Misers Lands
Or if protected from on high
Does that whole Nation sell & buy
He who mocks the Infants Faith
Shall be mockd in Age & Death
He who shall teach the Child to Doubt
The rotting Grave shall neer get out
He who respects the Infants faith
Triumphs over Hell & Death

—William Blake, "Auguries of Innocence" (lines 67–90)

The vision of a true artist such as Blake is truly too much, because what is beyond our memory-restricted perceptions is too much. It is the unfathomable totality of the world, past, present, and future bound up together: every level connected to every other level, nothing existing in isolation, everything implying something vital but beyond our comprehension, and all of it speaking of the overwhelming mystery of Being. The visionary concentrates on something we all see, hypothetically: a vase of flowers, perhaps, in all its complexity and beauty, each bloom springing forth out of nothingness, before its dissolution and return; a haystack in the spring, and its appearance in the summer, autumn, and winter, observing and portraying the absolute mystery of its existence, with its different shades of light and color, as well as the underlying commonality of form, which we can easily confuse with the full and incomprehensible actuality of what is there.

How do you know but ev'ry Bird that cuts the airy way, Is an
immense world of delight, clos'd by your senses five?

—WILLIAM BLAKE, FROM "A MEMORABLE FANCY,"
*The Marriage of Heaven and Hell*

To perceive Van Gogh's painting *Irises*—from which the illustration
that begins this chapter is derived—is, for example, to gaze through a
window back into the eternity that our perceptions once revealed, so
that we can remember how awe inspiring and miraculous the world
really is, under the mundane familiarity to which we have reduced it.
To share in the artist's perception reunites us with the source of inspiration that can rekindle our delight in the world, even if the drudgery
and repetition of daily life has reduced what we see to the narrowest
and most pragmatic of visions.

But for those first affections,
Those shadowy recollections,
Which, be they what they may
Are yet the fountain-light of all our day,
Are yet a master-light of all our seeing;
Uphold us, cherish, and have power to make
Our noisy years seem moments in the being
Of the eternal Silence: truths that wake,
To perish never;
Which neither listlessness, nor mad endeavour,
Nor Man nor Boy,
Nor all that is at enmity with joy,
Can utterly abolish or destroy!

—WILLIAM WORDSWORTH, "ODE: INTIMATIONS OF IMMORTALITY
FROM RECOLLECTIONS OF EARLY CHILDHOOD"

All of this is very frightening. It is frightening to perceive the shells of ourselves that we have become. It is frightening to glimpse, even for a moment, the transcendent reality that exists beyond. We think we border our great paintings with luxurious, elaborate frames to glorify them, but we do it at least as much to insist to ourselves that the glory of the painting itself ends at the frame. That bounding, that bordering, leaves the world we are familiar with comfortably intact and unchanged. We do not want that beauty reaching out past the limitations imposed on it and disturbing everything that is familiar.

We do the same with museums, those asylums for genius: we isolate everything that is great—everything that could in principle be distributed throughout the world. Why cannot every small town have a shrine devoted to one great piece of art, instead of having every piece collected in a manner impossible for anyone ever to take in at once? Is not one masterpiece enough for a room, or even for a building? Ten great works of art, or a hundred, in a single room is absurd, given that each is a world in and of itself. Such mass collection is a degrading of the unique singular particularity and worth of what is priceless and irreplaceable. It is fear that entices us to imprison art. And no wonder.

> Have you reckon'd a thousand acres much? have you reckon'd
>     the earth much?
> Have you practis'd so long to learn to read?
> Have you felt so proud to get at the meaning of poems?
> Stop this day and night with me and you shall possess the
>     origin of all poems,
> You shall possess the good of the earth and sun, (there are
>     millions of suns left,)
> You shall no longer take things at second or third hand, nor

look through the eyes of the dead, nor feed on the
spectres in books,
You shall not look through my eyes either, nor take things
from me,
You shall listen to all sides and filter them from your self.

—WALT WHITMAN, "SONG OF MYSELF"

It can be overwhelming to open ourselves up to the beauty in
the world that we as adults have painted over with simplicity. In not
doing so, however—in not taking a proper walk with a young child, for
example—we lose track of the grandeur and the awe the untrammeled
world is constantly capable of producing, and reduce our lives to bleak
necessity.

## THE LAND YOU KNOW, THE LAND YOU DO NOT KNOW, AND THE LAND YOU CANNOT EVEN IMAGINE

You inhabit the land you know, pragmatically and conceptually. But
imagine what lies just outside of that. There exists an immense space
of things you do not know, but which other people might comprehend, at least in part. Then, outside of what anyone knows, there is the
space of things that no one at all knows. Your world is known territory, surrounded by the relatively unknown, surrounded by the absolutely unknown—surrounded, even more distantly, by the absolutely
unknowable. Together, that is the canonical, archetypal landscape.
The unknown manifests itself to you in the midst of the known. That
revelation—sometimes exciting, but often quite painful—is the source
of new knowledge. But a fundamental question remains: How is that
knowledge generated? What is comprehended and understandable

does not just leap in one fell swoop from the absolutely unknown to the thoroughly and self-evidently articulated. Knowledge must pass through many stages of analysis—a multitude of transformations—before it becomes, let us say, commonplace.

The first stage is that of pure action—reflex action, at the most basic of levels.[2] If something surprises you, you react to it first with your body. You crouch defensively, or freeze, or run away in panic. Those are all forms of representation and categorization, in nascent form. Crouch means predatory attack. Freeze means predatory threat. Panic means terror necessitating escape. The world of possibility begins to actualize itself with such instinctual, embodied action, unconscious and uncontrollable. The first realization of possibility, of potential, is not conceptual. It is embodied, but it is still representational. (It is no longer the thing in itself we referred to earlier, but the transmutation of that thing into a commensurate physical response. That is a *representation*.)

Maybe you are at home, at night. Assume you are alone. It is dark and late. An unexpected noise startles you, and you freeze. That is the first transmutation: unknown noise (a pattern) to frozen position. Then your heart rate rises, in preparation for (unspecified) action.[3] That is the second transmutation. You are preparing to move. Next, your imagination populates the darkness with whatever might be making the noise.[4] That is the third transmutation, part of a complete and practical sequence: embodied responses (freezing and heart-rate increase) and then imagistic, imaginative representation. The latter is part of exploration, which you might extend by overcoming your terror and the freezing associated with it (assuming nothing else too unexpected happens) and investigating the locale, once a part of your friendly house, from where the noise appeared to emanate. You have now engaged in active exploration—a precursor to direct perception (hopefully nothing too dramatic); then to explicit knowledge of the source; and then back to routine and complacent peace, if the noise proves to be nothing of significance. That is how information moves from the unknown to the known. (Except that sometimes the noise does not prove insignificant. Then there is trouble.)

Artists are the people who stand on the frontier of the transformation of the unknown into knowledge. They make their voluntary foray out into the unknown, and they take a piece of it and transform it into an image. Maybe they do it through choreography and dance—by representing the manifestation of the world in physical display, communicable, although not in words, to others. Maybe they do it by acting, which is a sophisticated form of embodiment and imitation, or by painting or sculpting. Perhaps they manage it through screenwriting, or by penning a novel. After all that come the intellectuals, with philosophy and criticism, abstracting and articulating the work's representations and rules.

Consider the role that creative people play in cities. They are typically starving a bit, because it is virtually impossible to be commercially successful as an artist, and that hunger is partly what motivates them (do not underestimate the utility of necessity). In their poverty, they explore the city, and they discover some ratty, quasi-criminal area that has seen better days. They visit, look, and poke about, and they think, "You know, with a little work, this area could be cool." Then they move in, piece together some galleries, and put up some art. They do not make any money, but they civilize the space a bit. In doing so, they elevate and transform what is too dangerous into something cutting edge. Then a coffee shop pops up, and maybe an unconventional clothing store. The next thing you know, the gentrifiers move in. They are creative types, too, but more conservative (less desperate, perhaps; more risk averse, at least—so they are not the first ones on the edge of the frontier). Then the developers show up. And then the chain stores appear, and the middle or upper class establishes itself. Then the artists have to move, because they can no longer afford the rent. That is a loss for the avant-garde, but it is okay, even though it is harsh, because with all that stability and predictability the artists should not be there anymore. They need to rejuvenate some other area. They need another vista to conquer. That is their natural environment.

That edge, where artists are always transforming chaos into order, can be a very rough and dangerous place. Living there, an artist constantly risks falling fully into the chaos, instead of transforming it. But artists have always lived there, on the border of human understanding. Art bears the same relationship to society that the dream bears to mental life. You are very creative when you are dreaming. That is why, when you remember a dream, you think, "Where in the world did that come from?" It is very strange and incomprehensible that something can happen in your head, and you have no idea how it got there or what it means. It is a miracle: nature's voice manifesting itself in your psyche. And it happens every night. Like art, the dream mediates between order and chaos. So, it is half chaos. That is why it is not comprehensible. It is a vision, not a fully fledged articulated production. Those who actualize those half-born visions into artistic productions are those who begin to transform what we do not understand into what we can at least start to see. That is the role of the artist, occupying the vanguard. That is their biological niche. They are the initial civilizing agents.

The artists do not understand full well what they are doing. They cannot, if they are doing something genuinely new. Otherwise, they could just say what they mean and have done with it. They would not require expression in dance, music, and image. But they are guided by feel, by intuition—by their facility with the detection of patterns—and that is all embodied, rather than articulated, at least in its initial stages. When creating, the artists are struggling, contending, and wrestling with a problem—maybe even a problem they do not fully understand—and striving to bring something new into clear focus. Otherwise they are mere propagandists, reversing the artistic process, attempting to transform something they can already articulate into image and art for the purpose of rhetorical and ideological victory. That is a great sin, harnessing the higher for the purposes of the lower. It is a totalitarian tactic, the subordination of art and literature to politics (or the purposeful blurring of the distinction between them).

Artists must be contending with something they do not understand, or they are not artists. Instead, they are posers, or romantics (often romantic failures), or narcissists, or actors (and not in the creative sense). They are likely, when genuine, to be idiosyncratically and peculiarly obsessed by their intuition—possessed by it, willing to pursue it even in the face of opposition and the overwhelming likelihood of rejection, criticism, and practical and financial failure. When they are successful they make the world more understandable (sometimes replacing something more "understood," but now anachronistic, with something new and better). They move the unknown closer to the conscious, social, and articulated world. And then people gaze at those artworks, watch the dramas, and listen to the stories, and they start to become informed by them, but they do not know how or why. And people find great value in it—more value, perhaps, than in anything else. There is good reason that the most expensive artifacts in the world—those that are literally, or close to literally, priceless—are great works of art.

I once visited the Metropolitan Museum of Art in New York. It contained a collection of great and famous Renaissance paintings—each worth hundreds of millions of dollars, assuming they were ever made available for purchase. The area containing them was a shrine, a place of the divine—for believers and atheists alike. It was in the most expensive and prestigious of museums, located on real estate of the highest quality and desirability, in what might well be the most active and exciting city in the world. The collection had been put together over a great expanse of time, and with much difficulty. The gallery was packed with people, many of whom had voyaged there as part of what must be most properly regarded as a pilgrimage.

I asked myself, "What are these people up to, coming to this place, so carefully curated, traveling these great distances, looking at these paintings? And what do they believe they are up to?" One painting featured the Immaculate Conception of Mary, brilliantly composed. The Mother of God was rising to heaven, in a beatific state, encapsulated in a mandorla of clouds, embedded with the faces of putti. Many of the people gathered were gazing, enraptured, at the work. I thought, "They do not know what that painting means. They do not understand the symbolic meaning of the mandorla, or the significance of the putti, or the idea of the glorification of the Mother of God. And God, after all, is dead—or, so goes the story. Why does the painting nonetheless retain its value? Why is it in this room, in this building, with these other paintings, in this city—carefully guarded, not to be touched? Why is this painting—and all these others—beyond price and desired by those who already have everything? Why are these creations stored so carefully in a modern shrine, and visited by people from all over the world, as if it were a duty—even as if it were desirable or necessary?"

*We treat these objects as if they are sacred.* At least that is what our actions in their vicinity suggest. We gaze at them in ignorance and wonder, and remember what we have forgotten; perceiving, ever so dimly, what we can no longer see (what we are perhaps no longer willing to see). The unknown shines through the productions of great artists in partially articulated form. The awe-inspiring ineffable begins to be realized but retains a terrifying abundance of its transcendent power. That is the role of art, and that is the role of artists. It is no wonder we keep their dangerous, magical productions locked up, framed, and apart from everything else. And if a great piece is damaged anywhere, the news spreads worldwide. We feel a tremor run through the bedrock of our culture. The dream upon which our reality depends shakes and moves. We find ourselves unnerved.

## ONE ROOM

I live with my wife in a small semidetached house, with a living room that cannot be larger than 12' x 12'. But we worked to make that room extremely beautiful, while endeavoring to do the same with the rest of the house. In the living room hung some large paintings (not to everyone's taste, certainly: they were Soviet realist/impressionist pieces, some illustrating the Second World War, some representing the triumph of communism), as well as a variety of cubist miniatures and South American pieces heavily influenced by the native tradition. Prior to our recent renovations the room had held at least twenty-five paintings, including about fifteen smaller pieces (12" x 12"). There was even one—reminiscent of a medieval etching, although painted on canvas—on the ceiling, where I had attached it with magnets. It was from a Romanian church. The largest was 6' high and about 8' wide. (I know perfectly well that aggregating all these paintings together in such a small space contradicts my earlier point about devoting a room or even a building to a single work of art, but I have only a single house, so I plead necessity: If I wanted to collect paintings, they had to be put where I was able to put them.) In the rest of the house, we used thirty-six different colors, and a variety of different glosses on the walls and the trim throughout the building—all from a palette that matched a large realist painting of a railway yard in Chicago in the 1950s, created by the same artist who helped us plan and then renovate our home.

I bought the Soviet pieces on eBay from Ukrainian junk dealers specializing in Soviet-era artifacts. At one point, I had a network of about twenty people in the Ukraine sending me photographs of whatever paintings they had scrounged from the ruins of the Soviet bureaucracy. Most were awful. But some were amazing. I have a great painting, for example, of Yuri Gagarin, the first man in space, standing in front of a rocket and a radar installation, and another from the 1970s of a lonesome soldier writing his mother in front of a large radio. It is really something to see relatively modern events memorialized in oil by talented artists. (The Soviets kept their academies functioning continuously from the nineteenth century onward and, although tremendous restrictions were placed on what could be produced, those who passed through them became highly skilled painters.)

The Soviet paintings eventually took over our house. Most of them were small and insanely inexpensive, and I bought dozens of them. The Soviet era produced its own impressionism, often depicting landscapes, rougher and harsher than the classic French versions but much to my taste and reminiscent of where I grew up in western Canada. While seeking them out, I exposed myself to a larger number of paintings, I like to think, than anyone else in history. For at least four years, starting in 2001, I searched eBay, looking at roughly a thousand paintings a day,* seeking the one or two in that number that were of genuine

---

*So that's 1,000 pictures of paintings x 300 days per year x 4 = 1,200,000 paintings. That has to be some sort of record (not that it matters, but it's comical to consider), mostly because I do not think it would have been possible to see that many paintings before internet technology made massive databases possible.

quality. It was most often a Russian or Soviet landscape selling for a song—better paintings than I had ever seen in galleries or museum collections in Toronto. I would place them in a list of items I was interested in—an eBay feature—print them out, lay them on the floor, and then ask my wife, Tammy, to help me narrow my choices. She has a good eye and a fair bit of training as an artist. We would discard anything we found to be flawed and purchase what remained. Because of this, my kids grew up surrounded by art, and it certainly left an impression. Many of my paintings now hang in their respective dwellings. (They tended to avoid the more political Soviet propaganda, which I was interested in because of its historical significance and because of the ongoing war on the canvases between art—a consequence of the painter's undeniable talent—and the propaganda that art was doomed to serve. I can tell you that the art shines through the propaganda as the years pass by. That is something very interesting to observe.)

I also tried, at about that time, to make my university office beautiful. After I was transferred from an office I had already put some work into, the same artist who helped redesign the interior of our house (and from whom I also purchased many large paintings, which also hang in our house) tried to help me transform my new factory-like, fluorescent-lit catastrophe of a 1970s sealed-windows hellhole office into something that someone with some sense could sit in for thirty years without wanting to die. Faculty members were forbidden to undertake any major modifications to these spaces, due to union requirements (or administration interpretations of those requirements). So, my artist friend and I devised an alternate plan.

We decided to insert some heavy, nickel-plated hooks into the cinderblock, in pairs about four feet apart and seven feet above the ground, and then to hang from those hooks good three-quarter-inch sanded and stained wood sheets with cherry veneer on one side. Voila:

wood-paneled office, for the cost of about eight seventy-five-dollar pieces of plywood, plus some labor. We were going to install these on a weekend, when there was no one else around. Then we planned to paint the drop ceilings (carefully, as asbestos lurked above the tiles). Hell is a place of drop ceilings, rusted ventilation grates, and fluorescent lights; the dismal ugliness and dreariness and general depression of spirit that results from these cost-saving features no doubt suppresses productivity far more than the cheapest of architectural tricks and the most deadening of lights saves money. Everyone looks like a corpse under fluorescents. Penny-wise and pound-foolish indeed.

We were going to paint the ceiling with a paint called Hammerite, which looks like beaten metal once it dries. That would have transformed the unavoidable industrial aesthetic, which can be attractive if handled wisely, into something thoughtful and unique. This could also have been done for minimal cost. A good carpet, perhaps Persian (also very inexpensive on eBay), some reasonably high-quality curtains, and a decent industrial desk: one weekend of secretive work, and an office that a civilized person could inhabit without resentment and self-contempt.

But I made a fatal error. I spoke to one of the senior administrators of the psychology department about my plans. She and I had previously discussed the sheer ugliness of the floor our area inhabited and the dismal state of all the offices, and I thought we had established consensus that improvement was warranted. I assumed she was on board. We had even talked about transforming her corner office. I began to excitedly share my intentions. She looked displeased instead of happy, and said unexpectedly, "You cannot do that." I shook my head in disbelief and thought: "What? I am planning to make something exceedingly ugly better, quickly, with no trouble, for no money to speak of—and your response is, 'You cannot do that!?'" I said, "What do you mean?"

She said, "Well, if you do it, everyone else will want to do it." Four responses flashed through my mind: One: "No, they would not." Two: "Everyone *could* do it, because it would be dirt cheap." Three: "I thought we were sane adults, having a productive conversation about improving something important in a university, but we are actually children squabbling in a kindergarten playground." Four: "I thought I was speaking with someone sane and reasonable, but I was clearly wrong." She finished the conversation with a direct threat: "Do not push me on this." Stupid me. I asked for permission. (Not really: I was trying to communicate something motivating, beautiful, and exciting. But it boiled down to a power game.) I shared none of my four responses, however—although I was sorely tempted to voice all of them—and immediately recalibrated my strategy.

My artist friend and I were already more than conversant with the essential insanity and intransigence of mid-level bureaucracies, so we had already dreamed up a less expansive plan B. This involved the careful choosing of paint for the walls (rather than the much preferable wood), with some accent painting where that was possible, and matching carpets and drapery. I still had to fight the administration to get the precise colors I had chosen (which suited the industrial feel of the office), but won that battle. Plan B was not as good as plan A, but it was still much better than the status quo. Later, I added a dropped copper ceiling, using lightweight adhesive plastic tiles that mimic decorative metal quite accurately, hung a few paintings, and added a couple of suitable statues. Students, colleagues, and visitors come in and do a double take. My office is a place of creativity and beauty, and not a bloody horrible fluorescent-lit factory. Visitors are surprised, therefore—surprised, relieved, and pleased.

Not long after, I discovered that the department was now bringing potential new hires into my office to show them what kind of creative freedom was possible at the University of Toronto. I thought that was insanely comical. I thought about all of that for a long time. The resistance I encountered was somewhat incomprehensible in its strength. I wondered, "God, people seem to be afraid of what I am doing in this office. Perhaps there is a reason—an important reason—I do not understand." Then I came across a story by the biologist Robert Sapolsky. It was about wildebeest.[5] Wildebeest are herd animals and very difficult to distinguish from one another (maybe not for other wildebeest, but certainly for those who wish to study them). They blend together. At one point in the past, this presented a serious problem to biologists needing to observe individual animals for enough time to derive some conclusions about their behavior. They would watch a wildebeest, look away for a moment to make notes, and be unable to locate the same animal when they glanced back up.

Eventually, they settled on a potential solution. The biologists drove up adjacent to the herd in a Jeep, armed with a bucket of red paint and a stick with a rag on it. They dabbed a red spot on one of the wildebeest's haunches. Now they could track the activities of that particular animal, and hopefully learn something new about wildebeest behavior. But guess what happened to the wildebeest, now differentiated from the herd? The predators, always lurking around the herd, took it down. Lions—a major wildebeest threat—cannot easily bring a single wildebeest down unless they can identify it. They cannot hunt a blur of indistinguishable herd animals. They cannot track down four wildebeest at a time. They must organize their hunt around an identifiable individual. Thus, when lions go after the little ones or the ones that limp, they are not culling the weak, in some natural display of beneficial altruism. They would rather dine on a nice, healthy, delicious, juicy wildebeest than one that is tiny, old, or ill. But they must be able to identify their prey. What is the moral of the story? Make yourself colorful, stand out, and the lions will take you down. And the lions are always there.

If you stick your neck out, then the sword will come. Many, many cultures have a saying like that. The English version? "The poppy that grows higher than the rest is the first one to have its head removed by the scythe." In Japan: "The nail that sticks up above the rest is the first to get hit by the hammer." This is a nontrivial observation: hence its commonality. Artistic, creative endeavor is high risk, while the probability of return is low. But the probability of exceptionally high return does exist, and creative endeavor, while dangerous and unlikely to be successful, is also absolutely vital to the transformation that enables us to keep our footing. Everything changes. Pure traditionalism is doomed for that very reason. We need the new, merely to maintain our position. And we need to see what we have become blinded to, by our very expertise and specialization, so that we do not lose touch with the Kingdom of God and die in our boredom, ennui, arrogance, blindness to beauty, and soul-deadening cynicism. Plus, are we helpless prey animals, cowering and protecting ourselves, hiding and camouflaging, or are we human beings?

## NOT DECORATION

People are often upset by abstract art, or by art that appears to devote itself to producing negative reactions such as disgust or horror merely for the shock value. I have a tremendous respect for ideals of traditional beauty and, therefore, some sympathy for that response, and there is little doubt that many who merely disdain tradition mask the sentiment with artistic pretension. However, the passage of time differentiates truly inspired work from the fraudulent sort, even if imperfectly, and what is not crucial is generally left behind. It is easy to make the opposite error, as well: that art should be pretty and easily appreciated, without work or challenge: it should be decorative; it should match the living-room furniture. But art is not decoration. That is the attitude of a naive beginner, or of someone who will not let their terror of art allow them to progress and learn.

Art is exploration. Artists train people to see. Most people with any exposure to art now regard the work of the impressionists, for example, as both self-evidently beautiful and relatively traditional. This is in no small part because we all perceive the world now, at least in part, in the manner that only impressionists could manage in the latter half of the nineteenth century. We cannot help doing so, because the impressionist aesthetic has saturated everything: advertisements, movies, popular posters, comic books, photographs—all forms of visual art. Now we all see the beauty of light that only the impressionists could once apprehend. They taught us this. But when the impressionists first displayed their paintings—in the Salon des Refusés of 1863, as the traditional Paris Salon had rejected them—the pieces were met with laughter and contempt. The idea of perceiving that way (paying particular attention to light, essentially, rather than form) was so radical that it caused people to have emotional fits.

I am often struck by how common even the tropes of cubism, much more extreme and strange in some ways than impressionism, have become part and parcel of our visual vernacular. I have seen the multidimensional but flattened faces of the genre even in comic books. The same is true of surrealism, which has become popularly integrated almost to the point of cliché. It is worth repeating: Artists teach people to see. It is very hard to perceive the world, and we are so fortunate to have geniuses to teach us how to do it, to reconnect us with what we have lost, and to enlighten us to the world. It is for such psychological reasons that lines such as Christ's can be profitably considered:

> At that time the disciples came to Jesus and asked, "Who, then, is the greatest in the kingdom of heaven?"
>
> He called a little child to him, and placed the child among them.
>
> And he said: "Truly I tell you, unless you change and become like little children, you will never enter the kingdom of heaven. (Matthew 18:1–3)

Beauty leads you back to what you have lost. Beauty reminds you of what remains forever immune to cynicism. Beauty beckons in a manner that straightens your aim. Beauty reminds you that there is lesser and greater value. Many things make life worth living: love, play, courage, gratitude, work, friendship, truth, grace, hope, virtue, and responsibility. But beauty is among the greatest of these.

> What though the radiance which was once so bright
> Be now for ever taken from my sight,
> Though nothing can bring back the hour
> Of splendour in the grass, of glory in the flower;
> We will grieve not, rather find
> Strength in what remains behind;
> In the primal sympathy
> Which having been must ever be;
> In the soothing thoughts that spring

Out of human suffering;
In the faith that looks through death,
In years that bring the philosophic mind.

—WILLIAM WORDSWORTH, "ODE: INTIMATIONS OF IMMORTALITY
FROM RECOLLECTIONS OF EARLY CHILDHOOD"

Try to make one room in your home as beautiful as possible.

---

# IF OLD MEMORIES STILL UPSET YOU, WRITE THEM DOWN CAREFULLY AND COMPLETELY

## BUT IS YESTERDAY FINISHED WITH YOU?

Imagine you undertook some truly terrible actions in the past. You betrayed or hurt people in a genuinely damaging manner. You damaged their reputation with gossip and innuendo. You took credit for their work. You robbed them materially or spiritually. You cheated on them. Or imagine, instead, that you have been the target of some such events—and let us also assume you have become wise enough to try to avoid repeating the experience. In both circumstances (as perpetrator or victim) the actual events and the associated memories evoke fear, guilt, and shame. Why?

In the first case, you have betrayed yourself. You did not play the medium- to long-term game properly, and are suffering the consequences. You are not the sort of person other people choose to have around. You might not even be the sort of person you want to have around. In the second case, you were badly mistreated by someone else. In some real sense, however, it does not matter whether you were suffering because of self-betrayal or at the hands of others. What does matter is that you do not desire any recurrence.

Now, if you recall the memory, or if it comes back unbidden, complete with terror, shame, and guilt, this means something specific. It means that you fell into a hole—a pit, more accurately—or were pushed there. And that is not good. But what is worse is that you do not know why. Perhaps you trusted other people too easily. Perhaps you were too naive. Perhaps you were willfully blind. Perhaps you encountered genuine malevolence, on the part of another or yourself (and that is the worst situation, and the one most difficult to overcome). But at one level of analysis, whether you fell or were pushed makes little difference—not to the emotional systems that have emerged over the course of evolution and now serve to protect you. They care about one thing and one thing only: that you do not repeat a mistake.

The alarms those systems activate are fear-based (that is too weak a phrase—terror-based is more accurate, the kind of terror limited to neither time nor place), and all they care about is reminding you of the still-extant danger. A part of reality, and a perilous part, has remained unmapped, low resolution, lacking sufficient detail—and so has a part of you. You are not sharp, alert, dangerous, wary, wise, or kind enough—who knows?—so that the terror systems protecting you are confident in your ability to wend your way successfully through the same maze if it once again manifests itself in front of you.

Learn from the past. Or repeat its horrors, in imagination, endlessly.

Frequently, people do not so much repress the terrible things that happened in the past as refuse to think them through, pushing them out of their mind or occupying themselves with other activities. They have their reasons. And sometimes traumatized people appear literally unable to understand what befell them. It can be prohibitively difficult for abused children, for example, to generate a worldview philosophically sophisticated enough to span the full spectrum of human motivation. They simply cannot understand why someone might torment them physically or abuse them sexually. If they are young enough, it is likely that they do not even explicitly comprehend what is happening. Comprehending such matters is exceptionally challenging, even for adults. But in some unfortunate and arguably unjust sense, it does not matter. Refusal or inability both leave a geographic area in memory— unexplored, active, and rife with danger. It is a psychological truism that anything sufficiently threatening or harmful once encountered can never be forgotten if it has never been understood.[1]

To orient ourselves in the world, we need to know where we are and where we are going. Where we are: that concept must optimally include a full account of our experience of the world to date. If you do not know what roads you have traversed, it is difficult to calculate where you are. Where we are going: that is the projection of our ultimate ideal—by no means simply a question, say, of accomplishment, love, wealth, or power, but development of the character that makes all fortunate outcomes more likely and all unfortunate outcomes less likely. We map the world so that we can make the move from where we are—from point A—to where we are going—to point B. We use our map to guide our movement, and we encounter successes and obstacles along the way.

The successes are both confidence building and exhilarating. Not only are we moving toward our ultimate desire, we appear to be doing so properly (and are therefore not only moving ahead but validating our map). The obstacles and failures are, by contrast, anxiety provoking, depressing, and painful. They indicate our profound ignorance. They indicate that we do not understand with sufficient depth where we have been, where we are, or where we are going. They indicate that something we have built with great difficulty and wish above all to protect is flawed—to a degree both serious and not fully understood.

We must recollect our experiences and derive from them their moral. Otherwise, we remain in the past, plagued by reminiscences, tormented by conscience, cynical for the loss of what might have been, unforgiving of ourselves, and unable to accept the challenges and trag-edies facing us. We must recollect ourselves or suffer in direct propor-tion to our ignorance and avoidance. We must gather everything from the past that we avoided. We must rekindle every lost opportunity. We must repent for missing the mark, meditate on our errors, acquire now what we should have acquired then, and put ourselves back together. And I am not saying this is always possible. I have seen people so lost that there was not enough spark left to survive. The person in the present had been rendered too insignificant to confront, in his or her current condition, what was avoided even by a once-healthier self in the past. And cynicism about the future rationalizes the avoidance and deception. That is hell, and there is no limit to its depth. The humility required to clamber out of such hell exists in precise proportion to the magnitude of the unrequited errors of the past. And that is enough to send a shudder of true terror down the spine of anyone even partly awakened. We are not allowed, it seems, to avoid the responsibility of actualizing potential. And if we have made a mistake in the past, and left what could be unmanifest—regardless of the reason—then we pay the price for that in the inability to forget, and in the emotion that constitutes the pangs of conscience for past misbehavior.

Imagine that when you are very young, the map of the world you use to guide your immature self is correspondingly underdeveloped, like a child's drawing of a house: always straight and centered, por-traying only the front; always (or close enough) with a door and two

windows; always with a square for the outside wall and a triangle for
the roof; always with a chimney and smoke (which is a surprise, because smoking chimneys are not all that common now). The sun is
shining irrepressibly—a circle with rays emanating from it. There are
a few flowers—single lines with the schematic of a bloom at the top,
and two leaves halfway up the "stems." It is a very low-resolution representation of a house. It is more hieroglyph than drawing; more concept than sketch. It is something that represents the idea of house, or
perhaps home, generically, like the words "house" or "home" themselves. However, it is almost always enough: The child who drew the
picture knows it is a house, and the other children and the adults who
see the picture know it is a house. The drawing does the trick. It ful-
fills its purpose. It is a good-enough map.

But all too often appalling events occur within houses. These are
not so easy to represent. Maybe the house has adults in it—parents,
grandparents, uncles, or aunts—who say such things as "Never—and
I mean never—speak to anyone about what happens here." A few
squares, a triangle, a smattering of flowers, and a benevolent solar orb
offer only an inadequate representation of the horrors characterizing
such a dwelling place. Maybe what is happening inside the house is
beyond both tolerability and understanding. But how can what is terrifying be beyond understanding? How can trauma even exist without
comprehension? Is not understanding in some sense a prerequisite to
experience itself? These are all great mysteries. But everything is not
experienced at the same level of conception. We have all been petri-
fied by the unknown, even though that seems a contradiction in terms.
But the body knows what the mind does not yet grasp. And it remembers. And it demands that understanding be established. And there is
simply no escaping that demand. If something befalls us—or, perhaps
worse, we engage in some act—that freezes us in terror and nauseates

us to recall, we are bound by implacable fate to transform raw horror into understanding, or suffer the consequences.

## DO NOT FALL TWICE INTO THE SAME PIT

I had a client who began speaking to me almost immediately after we met of the sexual abuse she suffered in childhood at the hands of of an older cousin, with whom she lived. She became markedly tearful and upset when she recounted her experiences. I asked her how old she was when the abuse occurred. She told me she was four. She described her attacker as much larger, stronger, and older than her. I allowed my imagination to roam freely as she spoke, making the assumptions I believed (or my fantasy presumed) were justified by the nature of her description. I envisioned the nefarious, sadistic, and criminal machinations of a late adolescent or young adult. Then I asked her how much difference in age there was between her and her victimizer. She replied, "Two years. He was two years older than me." This came as a genuine surprise. It changed the picture in my mind almost completely.

I told her what I had been imagining, because I wanted her to know what assumptions I had been formulating as she related her story. Then I said, "You know, you are all grown up now, and have been for a long time. But you told me your story in the same way that you might have told it when you were four, when the molestation was still occurring—or at least with many of the same emotions. And there is no doubt that you remember your cousin as much larger and stronger and older than you. A six-year-old is, after all, half again as old as a four-year-old, and from that younger child's perspective, perhaps more akin to an adult. But your cousin was six—almost as much a child as you. So, here is another way you might consider thinking about what happened. First, recall the six-year-olds with whom you are now familiar. You know that they are still immature and cannot be held accountable as adults might be for their actions, even though they might also not be altogether innocent. I am not trying to minimize the seriousness of what happened to you, and I am not questioning the intensity of your emotions. But I am asking you to consider the situation as if you became aware of its occurrence among two children you presently know. Kids are curious. They play doctor. And if the adults around them are not paying attention properly, such games can get out of hand. Would it be possible to consider that you were not molested by an overpowering and malevolent force—the way you might be if you were raped now? Maybe, instead, you and your cousin were very poorly supervised children."

In some important way, the memories she retained of her childhood experiences had not altered as she matured. She was still experiencing the terror of a four-year-old, helpless in the hands of someone old enough to be perceived as grown-up. But her twenty-seven-year-old self needed to update that memory. She was no longer at risk for such treatment, in any obvious manner. And it came as a great relief to her to reframe what had happened. She could now consider it as a potential consequence of curiosity untrammeled by adult attention. This shifted her view of her cousin, the situation, and herself. She could now see the event from the perspective of an adult. This freed her from much of the terror and shame still associated with the memories, and it did so with remarkable rapidity. She confronted the horrors of the past voluntarily, finding a causal explanation that was much less traumatic—lacking, as it did, the vision of her cousin as a malevolent, powerful perpetrator and her as the inevitably hapless victim of such a force. All this transformation occurred in a single session. Such can be the power of the story surrounding the terrible events of our pasts.

This experience left me with a profound philosophical quandary. The memories my client brought into my office had remained unchanged for decades. The memories she walked out with were markedly altered. Which, then, were real? It could easily be argued that her original story was more accurate. It was, after all, as direct an imprint as might be left on the open book of a four-year-old's mind. It had not been altered (and therefore changed) by any previous therapeutic intervention. Was it not, then, the genuine article? But it is also the case that an event that means one thing one day might come to mean something quite different another. Is it so unusual for us to better understand what motivated the otherwise inexplicable behavior of our parents, for example, as we ourselves enter parenthood? And which memory is more accurate: the partial picture of adult motivation we have as children, or the revised recollections made possible by maturity? If it is the latter—and that does not seem unreasonable (and certainly seemed true in the case of my client)—how is it that an altered memory can become more accurate than one retaining its original configuration?

## POSSESSED BY GHOSTS

I recall another client who remembered, in a striking sense, and changed. His memories were shrouded much more profoundly in mystery, and his remembrance was of a slower, more surprising, and unlikelier sort. He was a young, gay African American man who was suffering from a set of incomprehensible mental and physical symptoms. A psychiatrist had recently diagnosed him with schizophrenia, but his aunt, who had taken him to the hospital for evaluation, believed that insufficient time had been spent on her nephew's evaluation. She contacted me for a second opinion and brought him to my office. I saw him alone.

He was shy and reserved, but neatly and carefully dressed, and appeared fully oriented when I started to gather his history. Furthermore, he wore eyeglasses—and they were well taken care of, lacking tape on the bridge or arms, and with lenses that were perfectly clean. These observations were all relevant, as far as I was concerned. Schizophrenics lose the ability to monitor themselves effectively, so unkempt clothing and damaged eyeglasses—particularly with badly smudged lenses—are telling features (not invariably: so those of you with subpar eyewear are not required to consider yourself classified). In any case, he also had a full-time job of reasonable complexity (another rarity for someone with schizophrenia), and he could carry on a conversation with no problem, apart from his tendency toward shyness. I accepted him as a client, and we began to meet regularly.

I had to see him a few times before I could determine why the psychiatrist had diagnosed him with such a serious disorder. He began by telling me that for the last four years he had been depressed and anxious. There was nothing markedly uncommon in that. His symptoms followed on the heels of a serious fight with his boyfriend and the permanent cessation of their relationship, which had lasted several years. Nothing in that was unusual, either. The two had been living together. Their partnership was important to him, emotionally and practically—and the dissolution of an intimate relationship produces unhappiness and confusion in most everyone, and can trigger more severe and lasting anxiety and depression in people who are so predisposed. The duration was out of the ordinary, however. People typically pick up the pieces and move on in under a year. That is not a hard-and-fast rule, but four years is a long time. That piqued my curiosity. He

also revealed something else very much out of the ordinary. He told
me that he experienced strange, convulsive bodily movements—every
night—while attempting to sleep. His body would contort into a fetal
position, and his arms would cross over his face. Then he would relax,
only to find himself repeating the movements. So it went, for hours.
Apart from being concerning because of its incomprehensibility, it was
interfering badly with his sleep. This had been going on for about the
same amount of time as the anxiety and depression, and the poor sleep,
if not the movements themselves, was certainly a contributing factor. I
asked him what he thought was happening. He said, with a laugh, "My
family thinks I am possessed, and I am not sure they are wrong."

My client's familial background was somewhat unusual. His parents,
immigrants to Canada from the southern United States, were unedu-
cated to a marked degree, very superstitious and religious, and apparently serious in the belief that spirits inhabited their son. I asked him,
"Did you by chance tell the psychiatrist about being possessed?" He
said, "Yes." I thought, "Well, that explains why he diagnosed you with
schizophrenia." That explanation, in tandem with the strange physical
symptoms, would have been sufficient, in my experience.* However,

*A word of advice for anyone seeking mental health help in a large city clinic, where the
psychiatrist seeing you might take fifteen minutes to assess your life and determine the
nature of your illness: do not casually mention any odd experiences or beliefs. You may
well live to regret it. It takes very little to accrue a diagnosis of schizophrenia in the
conditions that prevail in an overloaded mental health system—and once the diagnosis
has been established, it is very hard to shake. It is difficult, personally, not to take a
medical description seriously. It is harder than you might think to disbelieve a qualified
psychiatrist (who should, after all, know what he or she is talking about), particularly if
you are experiencing strange symptoms. It is difficult practically, as well, because once
such a diagnosis becomes part of your permanent medical record, it is very difficult to
have it modified. Anything out of the ordinary about you will, from then on, attract
undue attention (even from yourself), and any displays of normality will be downplayed.
Now, I say all that knowing full well that some people who have odd beliefs are in fact
schizophrenic—but a fair bit of digging is usually in order to establish that diagnosis,
and busy psychiatrists in public hospitals seldom have the time for careful excavation.

after meeting with this man for several sessions, it was clear to me that whatever was plaguing him was not schizophrenia. He was perfectly rational and lucid. But what in the world could be causing these strange, nightly, seizure-like convulsions? I had never encountered anything of the sort. My first hypothesis was that he suffered from a very severe form of sleep paralysis. This is a reasonably common condition. It generally occurs when people are sleeping on their backs (which he tended to do). A person with sleep paralysis semi-awakens, but not enough to stop dreaming, nor to escape from the inability to move that characterizes the rapid-eye-movement (REM) phase of sleeping. When you are dreaming, the same brain areas that govern active movement when you are awake are often stimulated (you experience this as the sense of moving while in your dream). You do not move around in sync with that brain activation because your voluntary musculature is switched off, physiologically, by a specialized neurochemical mechanism that has exactly that function.[2] Otherwise you would get out of bed and act out your dream and get yourself into trouble very quickly.

During a sleep paralysis episode, the sufferer wakes up enough to be semi-aware of the real world, but is still in REM paralysis and dreaming. All sorts of strange experiences can occur in such a state. Many people have, for example, claimed to have been abducted and medically examined by aliens.[3] This otherwise inexplicable nighttime phenomenon (barring the existence of curious and surgically inclined extraterrestrials) has been blamed on this condition of immobility and the often bizarre and frightening fantasies that accompany it.[4] He was quite bright, literate, and curious, so I gave him a book called *The Terror That Comes in the Night*,[5] which illuminates the strange phenomena that can accompany sleep paralysis. The author, David Hufford, describes the night terror his title refers to as a variant of the "Old Hag" experience (a term from folklore). Those who have had such an experience (up to

15 percent of the population) describe fear and paralysis, sensations of suffocation, and encounters with malign entities. My client read the book, but told me that he did not believe what Hufford described accurately characterized her experience. He felt the same way about the sleep paralysis hypothesis more generally. For one thing, the convulsions occurred before he fell asleep; second, he did not experience the inability to move.

I learned much more about him as we continued to get to know one another. I learned, for example, that he had studied history as an undergraduate, and had completed his degree. I learned that his parents had been exceptionally strict with him through his childhood and teenage years. They never allowed him to stay overnight at his friends' houses, and they monitored his behavior very closely until he escaped to university. He also related a fair bit more about the fight that occurred immediately before the breakup of his last relationship. He had returned with his boyfriend to their shared apartment after having a few drinks and arguing in public. At home, the fight escalated to physical conflict. They began pushing each other around, with increasing violence. After one particularly aggressive shove, my client fell to the living room floor. While lying there, he swept his boyfriend's feet out from underneath him. Then my client picked himself up off the floor and headed for the door. He returned several days later when he knew he would not be at home to pack up his belongings and move. That was the end of their existence as a couple.

But there was an element of his personality at play in this conflict that was not obvious. In consequence, he was struck very deeply by his boyfriend's assault. He told me while discussing this sequence of events that he did not believe people were capable of violence. I said, "What do you mean by that? You earned a history degree. You have obviously read about the horrors and atrocities of the human past. You watch the news . . ." He said that, as a matter of fact, he did not watch the news. "Fair enough," I replied, "but what about everything you learned in university? Did not that teach you that human aggression is both real and exceptionally common?" He said, "I read the books, but I just put everything I had learned into a compartment and did not think any further about it." I thought that was a striking answer, particularly in combination with something else he told me. "When I was a child," he said, "I picked up the idea that people were only good. My parents taught me that adults were angels." I asked, "What do you mean by that? That adults never did anything bad or wrong?" He said, "No, you do not understand. My parents taught me and my sister and brother that adults were literally God's angels, and that they were only good." I said, "You believed this?" He said that he had believed it deeply, partly because he had been so sheltered, partly because his parents had been so insistent, and partly, of course, because it was comforting.

I suggested that something had to be done about his naivete. It was not doing him any good. He was far too old and intelligent to maintain faith in such a childish dream. We discussed this in detail, speaking about the horrific events of the twentieth century and the mass shootings and other terrors of the more recent past. I asked him to explain such occurrences, and to pay more attention to any examples of his own anger and hostility. However, he denied the very existence of the latter and could not generate any convincing explanations for the former.

So, I assigned him a book called *Ordinary Men*.[6] That book excruciatingly details how a group of ordinary policemen from Germany were turned into cold-blooded executioners in Poland during the Nazi occupation. To call the account chilling is to say almost nothing. I told him with all due seriousness that he had to read the book as if it really happened, and more, as if he and the people he knew were capable of the same heinous acts. It was time for him to grow up. We had established a very solid rapport by this time, and when I told him that his rose-colored view of the world was presenting him with danger sufficient to destroy his life he took me seriously. The next time I saw him, a week later, he had finished the book. His face had hardened. He looked older and wiser. I had seen this happen frequently in my clinical practice when people incorporated the darker parts of themselves, instead of—let us say—compartmentalizing them. They no longer had the habitual look of deer caught in the headlights. They looked like people from whom decisions emanated, rather than people to whom things merely happened. Then I asked him to read *The Rape of Nanking*,[7] about Japanese atrocities in China in 1937. It is a horrifying book. The woman who wrote it committed suicide. My client read that, too, and we talked about it. He emerged sadder, but wiser. His nighttime symptoms, however, did not abate.

Nonetheless, his comments about adults-as-angels, claims to have compartmentalized his knowledge of evil, and the presence of the inexplicable convulsions had started some wheels turning in the far recesses of my brain. Many years earlier, I had another client (a young woman, as is more typically the case) who had hysterical epilepsy—a classic case of Freudian hysteria, where bodily symptoms were expressing psychological problems. She had been raised in the rural Midwest, in a very repressed, Victorian-like Christian fundamentalist atmosphere. She had one of her "seizures" in my office—full grand mal. The sight of it left me cold. I watched impassively as she thrashed and convulsed violently for several minutes, eyes rolled back. I did not worry. I did not feel sorry for her. I did not feel anything. I thought, "Why is this not affecting me? My client is having, by all evidence, a serious convulsive episode." I did not call an ambulance. When she came out of it and sat back down, dazed, I told her that I had responded to her seizure neither physically nor emotionally as if it were real, despite its otherwise fully credible manifestation. Previously, after pulling similar stunts (consciously? unconsciously? some mixture of the two?), she had barely skirted consignment to a psychiatric ward. She had also risked a diagnosis of psychosis and prescription for the medication accompanying that. We had some very serious talks about what she was doing. I let her know that I did not buy her epilepsy—that I had experienced it as false, even though it seemed quite real to her. (She had been tested, by the way, for epilepsy, and the results had come back equivocal.)

So, she was plausibly someone who "somatized," or physically represented their psychological symptoms. Freud noted that such somatization was often symbolic—that the manner in which the physical disability or oddity manifested had some meaningful relationship with the trauma that had precipitated it. Her hysterical epilepsy appeared to originate in her ambivalence and ignorance about sex, a substantial degree of childish immaturity, and some dangerous game-playing on her part. We made a lot of progress in our discussions. She was far from unintelligent, and the wiser part of her prevailed. Her seizures came to an end, along with the equally dangerous drama. Even better, she avoided the psych ward and continued with her university career. In any case, I learned then that Freudian hysterics existed, because I had just worked with one.

I began to hypothesize that my current client was suffering, in a similar manner, from a somatization disorder. I knew about the fight that had terminated his last relationship, just before the onset of his symptoms. Perhaps his strange movements were somehow associated with that event? I also knew from his own account that he compartmentalized—that he put things in a corner of his mind where he would not think about them again. I did not have much experience with hypnosis but knew both that people capable of compartmentalization tended to be highly hypnotizable, and that hypnosis had been used with some success (albeit many years ago) with somatization disorders. Freud used hypnosis to treat his hysterical clients, who were apparently quite numerous during the Victorian period, at least in the upper class, fixated as they were on the sexual, the theatrical, and the dramatic.[8] So, I thought I might try hypnosis to treat my client.

Now, I often used guided relaxation techniques on my clients, sitting them comfortably in their armchair in my office, asking them to focus on different parts of their body, from the soles of their feet, step by step up their legs and torso, with a brief detour down their arms, to the top of their head, focusing on their breathing and relaxing. After seven or eight minutes of the relaxation instructions, I would count back from ten to one, requesting after each count or two that they relax more deeply. It was a reasonably good, quick treatment for agitation, anxiety, and insomnia. I decided to start this way, because hypnosis employs essentially the same technique, adding questions about past trauma or other relevant issues once relaxation had been established. Its effectiveness varies substantially from person to person.[9] (That is why stage performers who use hypnosis on audience members will bring twenty people to the front of the theater, run through the initial hypnotic suggestions, and then retain only the few who are obviously responsive.) In any case, I told my client that I thought hypnotizing him and talking about the night he fought with his boyfriend might be useful. I told him why (suggesting that his nighttime movements might be associated with that event). Then I told him exactly how we were going to do it, and that he was free to refuse or agree. I would stop whenever he asked me to, if he asked; and he would remember everything when we were finished.

He agreed to try, so I began: "Sit comfortably in your chair. Place your hands on the arms of the chair or in your lap—wherever you are most comfortable. Close your eyes. Listen carefully to the noises that you hear in the world around you, and then turn your attention inward to your breathing. Breathe in deeply. . . . Hold it. . . . Breathe out. Move your attention down your body from your breathing to your thighs, and lower legs, and feet. Let your feet rest heavily on the floor. Pay attention to your toes, and the soles of your feet, and your ankles, and remember to breathe slowly, regularly, and deeply. Let all the tension flow out of your feet. Do not forget to breathe slowly, regularly, and deeply. Pay attention to your calves, and your shins . . ." and so on, up the whole body. Usually.

My client fell spontaneously into a deep hypnotic trance before I got past his feet. His head lolled heavily. I asked if he could hear me. "Yes," he said, barely audibly. I had to advance my chair and put my ear within inches of his mouth to make out what he was saying. I asked him if he knew where he was. "In your office," he said. That was good. I said, "We are returning to the time when you had a fight with your boyfriend, before you moved out. Tell me what happened." He said, "We had just returned to our apartment. We had both been drinking. We were fighting about finances and our future at the bar. We both got angry. We walked through the doorway of our house—there." He half gestured with his arm, although it was still mostly limp, like the rest of his body. I was watching his eyes dart back and forth, like those of someone in REM sleep, under three-quarter-closed lids. "I was walking backward. We were moving toward the living room. I pushed him. Then he pushed me back. I pushed him again. He pushed me backward over our coffee table and onto the floor. He picked up our floor lamp and held it over his head. I looked directly into his eyes. I had never seen an expression so hostile. I curled into a ball and crossed my hands over my face to protect myself." He said all this very slowly, gesturing awkwardly and minimally all the while, pointing as if toward the area in the apartment he was imagining. It was uncannily as if he were reliving the experience in real time. I glanced at the clock. The explanation, preparation, relaxation, and the slow recounting had taken us up to the one-hour mark—our normal session duration. I said, "I do not want to push you too far. We are running out of time. When you are ready, and comfortable, you might open your eyes and wake up fully. We could continue next week." But he did not respond. His head continued to loll forward, and his eyes kept moving. I called his name. No change.

This worried me, quite frankly. I had never heard of someone failing to emerge from a trance when requested. I was not sure what to do. Fortunately, however, he was the last client I was seeing that evening, so I had some time. I thought, "Well, he is in a deep trance and truly immersed in this account. Maybe he needs to tell the whole story. Let us continue and see what happens. When he is finished with his account, I will try to bring him around again." I went out to the hallway to speak with his waiting aunt, and informed her that we required a bit more time. I returned to my office and sat back down, near him as before. I said, "What happened then?" He replied, "The expression on his face—I had never seen someone look like that before. I was forced to realize then that my boyfriend could want to hurt me; that one person—even if adult—could truly desire to bring harm to another. It was the first time I truly learned that such events were possible." He began to weep, but continued his account: "I knocked his feet from under him, got up, and started running. He chased me out of the living room, down the hallway of our house, and through the front door. I could run faster, and got ahead of him. It was about four in the morning. It was still dark. I was terrified. I got far enough ahead of him to hide behind some nearby cars. He could not find me. I watched him looking for a long while. Then he gave up and turned around." He was sobbing openly by this point. "When I was sure he was gone, I went to my mother's place and stayed there. I could not believe what had happened. He might have killed me, and he was going to do it on purpose. I couldn't stand it. I pushed it from my mind and tried never to think about it again."

He fell silent. I called his name. He responded. I asked him, "Do you know that you are in my office and sitting in the chair you usually occupy?" He nodded. "Are you finished telling me your story?" He replied in the affirmative. I said, "You did well. It was very brave of you to go through all that. Are you ready to open your eyes?" He said that he was. I said, "Take your time. When you are ready, come back fully awake, slowly. You are going to feel relaxed and well. You will remember everything you just told me and everything that happened here." He nodded. A few moments later he opened his eyes. I asked him what had happened—what he remembered. He briefly recounted the evening's events, including our initial discussion about hypnosis. I then called in his aunt and told her that he needed to rest at home, with someone in attendance, because the session had been intense. Adults were not angels, and people could not only hurt each other— they could desire that hurt with all their heart. But my client did not know what to do with such knowledge, sheltered as he was, deluded as he was by his parents—blind as he allowed himself to remain with his "compartmentalization." This did not stop the inarticulate elements of his being from endeavoring to dramatically represent and bring toward consciousness both the fact of intended harm and everything more broadly evil such intent implied. He found himself compelled to duplicate precisely the defensive bodily movements he had made to during the fight with his boyfriend.

The next week, my client did not show up for his session. I thought "Oh, God. Maybe I did him some serious damage." However, he arrived on time the next week. He apologized for missing the last session, but said that he had become extremely upset and was in consequence too scrambled to attend or even to contact me. I asked why. He said, "The day after we last met, I was sitting in a restaurant downtown, and I saw my old boyfriend!" It was an uncanny coincidence. "It really rattled me, you know," he continued, "but nothing came of it, and I calmed down in a day or two. And guess what?" "What?" I said. "I only had convulsions one night this week! And they only lasted a few minutes!" I said, "That is great! That is really great! What a relief! What do you think changed?" He said, "What really got to me in that fight was not our disagreement about what future we wanted. It was not the physical contact—the pushing and shoving. It was the fact that he truly wished me harm. I could see it in his face. His look truly terrified me. I could not handle it. But I can understand it better now."

I asked him if I could hypnotize him again. "You are obviously better," I said, "but I want to make sure that we got everything." He agreed, and we began. He fell into a trance just as easily. But this time, he condensed the story. He got through the whole account in fifteen minutes, as opposed to the ninety required previously. He had extracted what was important: the fact that he was in danger; the fact that someone wanted to hurt him; the fact that he had defended himself successfully—the fact that the world was a place inhabited by demons, so to speak, as well as angels. When I asked him to come out of the trance, in the same way I had before, he opened his eyes almost immediately, and was calm and fully aware.

The change in his condition was remarkable. The next week, he said that his symptoms had disappeared completely. No more convulsions—and no more belief in the untarnished goodness of mankind. He had grown up and faced the reality of his own experience, as well as the nature of the world. It was something to see. Conscious acceptance of the presence of malevolence cured him of years of suffering. He now understood and admitted enough of the potential dangers that surrounded him to make his way in reasonable safety through the world. It was no longer necessary for what he had learned but refused to acknowledge to force itself upon him in its dramatic, embodied manner. He made what he now knew part of his personality—part of the map that would guide him henceforth in his actions—and freed himself from the ghosts that possessed him.

## UNCOMPREHENDED MALEVOLENCE

I had another client, a young man who was terribly bullied in his first year of vocational college. When he first came to see me, he could barely talk, and was taking a high dose of antipsychotic medication. When he sat in the chair in front of the desk in my office, he would twist his head and shoulders back and forth in a very abnormal and mechanical manner. When I asked him what he was doing, he told me that he was trying to make the shapes go away. Apparently, he could perceive geometric images of some kind in front of him, and felt compelled to manipulate them. I never did understand exactly what that signified, except that he was in a world of his own.

I spent several months working with him, and did it in a more structured manner than previously—having, in the interim, developed the tools to do so. This client could only communicate a little at the beginning of our work together, but that was enough to start the ball rolling. Some girl at the college had developed a crush on him. He informed her that her romantic interest was not reciprocated. She became exceedingly vindictive, and set out to make his life hell. She

spread rumors about his sexual habits. She encouraged some of her
male friends to physically threaten him at school. She had people on
hand to humiliate him constantly and unmercifully in transit to and
from campus. Noting his distress, his parents alerted the school, but
nothing was done to stop the ongoing torment. Unable or unwilling to
tolerate the mounting peer pressure, the friends he had only recently
made began to avoid and then entirely abandoned him. He began to
break down, and as his behavior became stranger, his outcast status
was cemented into place. And he broke.

I asked him to let me know exactly what happened—and to reach a
long way back while formulating his answer. I wanted to understand
what, if anything, made him vulnerable to the situation he found himself in, and what exactly had happened when he was being tormented
by his spurned admirer. And I structured this so that he could write,
as well as talk (more accurately, so that he could talk about what he
was writing). My colleagues and I had developed an online writing
exercise* to provide some helpful structure for those delving into and

---

*The Past Authoring Program at www.selfauthoring.com. Dr. James W. Pennebaker of
the University of Texas at Austin, and a host of colleagues working directly with him
and independently, have demonstrated that writing that reduces existential uncertainty
(there's no simpler general way of putting it) reduces anxiety, improves mental health,
and boosts immunological function. All of these effects appear associated with a general decrease in complexity-induced stress and the hormones—harmful in excess—
consequentially produced. Pennebaker demonstrated, for example, that students who
wrote for three days, consecutively, about the worst events in their lives experienced,
first, a decline in mood (no doubt elicited by calling forth such memories) but significant
improvement in their lot over the period of the following months. Other researchers
showed similar effects when students wrote about their future. Pennebaker initially assumed that it was something akin to emotional expression, or catharsis (following
Freud), that produced these positive effects—the opportunity to express anger or regret or sorrow—but found, as the result of a careful semantic analysis, that it was the
development of a cognitive and causal understanding of the reason for the events and
their significance that was curative. The effects of writing about the future seemed
similar, in that the plans thereby generated reduced uncertainty and put forward a simpler and more well-defined structure around what might otherwise have been the intol-

making sense of their past. I asked my young client to try it. Because he was too impaired in his motivation and his thoughts to complete the process at home, I had him do his writing in my office. I set him at my computer and asked him to read each question in the exercise aloud to me before writing his answer, and then to read that aloud as well. If I failed to understand something he had written or felt that more detail was required, I suggested he clarify the issues at hand with more writing and read me his revisions.

The exercise opened by asking him to break his life into key epochs—sections of his autobiographical past that lent themselves naturally to categorization as a unit or theme. That might be, say, age two through kindergarten, elementary school, junior high, high school, college, etc.—although some people are inclined, particularly as they get older, to group their experiences according to the various relationships of which they were a member. After he subdivided his past in the manner he chose, the exercise then asked him to identify key experiences during each of those epochs: events that he believed, in retrospect, shaped him as a person, for better or worse. Obviously, events of the latter type are likely to be marked in memory by negative emotions such as anxiety, anger, or the desire for revenge—and, perhaps, by a strong tendency to avoid remembering and considering altogether.

My client broke his life into the epochs that seemed relevant to him, and then identified the key events, both positive and negative, characterizing each period. Next, he analyzed them causally, coming to understand why some things had gone well, while others had deteriorated so terribly. He concentrated most intensely on what gave rise to the most disturbing events of the past—assessing particulars of his

---

erably unspecified looming weeks and months ahead. For a review, see J. W. Pennebaker and J. F. Evans, *Expressive Writing: Words That Heal* (Enumclaw, Wash.: Idyll Arbor Inc., 2014).

own behavior, motivations of other people, and characteristics of time and place. He considered what effects those produced, for better and worse (because we can learn things from difficult experiences), and thought through what might have happened or been done differently. The consequence of all this, at least in principle, was the mining of past experiences for their true perceptual and behavioral significance, and an update of his autobiographical map.

As his account progressed from day care through public schooling—he had divided his life into sections defined by school grade—he became increasingly articulate. Recollecting his life was putting him back together. As he wrote, read what he wrote, and answered the questions I put to him while listening, his account of the past became more detailed and his understanding of it deeper. We discussed the undesirable things that children do to each other, and that led us to the topic of malevolence and evil—in the adult world, as well. He was very naive about this. He expressed the belief that people were universally good (even though he had experience to the contrary). He had no theory of motivation for destruction, cruelty, and the desire for mayhem.

We walked through his life, developing a particularly detailed account of everything he had suffered at the hands of his tormentor. He became sophisticated enough to articulate some initial understanding of her motivations. She had been spurned and was, in consequence, hurt, embarrassed, and angry. He had not realized either how much impact his rejection might produce or how much impact rejection can have on people in general. He did not seem to understand, furthermore, that he had the right to defend himself. We talked about what he could have done differently, or might do differently in the future, to protect himself. He realized that he had taken far too much insult at school without reaching out for help. He could have let the appropriate administrative staff at the college know what was going on. He could have confronted his tormentor directly, publicly, earlier in the abuse, and demanded that she stop. He could have let his classmates know that the only reason he was being tormented was because he had refused a date, and that she was so fragile and brittle that she could not handle the rejection and was inventing lies for revenge. In the extreme, he could have had her charged with criminal harassment and defamatory libel. None of these strategies would have been sure to work, but they would have been worth trying, and were certainly justified and necessary under the circumstances.

As he worked through the memories of his recent month at college, his psychotic symptoms receded dramatically. At every session he attended, he was more clearheaded. He stopped manifesting his strange behaviors. He enrolled in summer school and finished his remaining coursework. It was a near-miraculous recovery.

## POTENTIAL INTO ACTUALITY

It is far from uncommon for people to worry, sometimes unbearably, about what lies ahead of them. That worry is a both a consequence of and an investigation into the multiple pathways extending from now into the future. Concerns line themselves up, often involuntarily, for consideration: troublesome issues at work, problems with friends and loved ones, practical issues of economic and material survival. Each concern requires multiple decisions: What problems should be solved? In what order should action proceed? What strategy should be employed? All of this requires something like choice—free choice, free will. And the choice to act seems voluntary; it is a simple thing (although very psychologically unsatisfying) to succumb to paralysis of will.

To decide, by contrast, voluntarily and freely, is difficult and demanding. It feels nothing like the automatic processes of reflexive or habitual pathways moving us thoughtlessly forward. We do not appear to ourselves to be driven by the past, in some fundamentally deterministic manner, like a mechanical clock in which the spring drives the gears that turn the hands and tell the time. Instead, when we decide, we actively confront the future. We seem destined to face something akin to unformed potential and to determine what will emerge as the present—and then the past.

We literally make the world what it is, from the many things we perceive it could be. Doing so is perhaps the primary fact of our being, and perhaps of Being itself. We face a multitude of prospects—of manifold realities, each almost tangible—and by choosing one pathway rather than another, reduce that multitude to the singular actuality of reality. In doing so, we bring the world from becoming into Being. This is the most profound of mysteries. What is that potential that confronts us? And what constitutes our strange ability to shape that possibility, and to make what is real and concrete from what begins, in some sense, as the merely imaginary?

There is something else of perhaps equal import allied with this, impossible as that might seem, given the very unlikeliness of the role we appear to play in the shaping of reality. Not only do our choices play a determining role in transforming the multiplicity of the future into the actuality of the present, but—more specifically—the ethics of our choices play that role. Actions based upon the desire to take responsibility; to make things better; to avoid temptation and face what we would rather avoid; to act voluntarily, courageously, and truthfully—these make what comes into Being much better, in all ways, for ourselves and for others, than what arises as a consequence of avoidance, resentment, the search for revenge, or the desire for mayhem. This means that if we act ethically, in the deepest and most universal of senses, then the tangible reality that emerges from the potential we face will be good instead of dreadful—or at least as good as we can make it.

Everyone seems to know this. We are universally tormented by our consciences for what we know we should have done yet did not do. We are tormented equally by what we did but know we should not have done. Is this not a universal experience? Can anyone escape the pangs of conscience at four o'clock in the morning after acting immorally or destructively, or failing to act when action was necessary? And what is the source for that inescapable conscience? If we were the source of our own values and masters of our own houses, then we could act or fail to act as we choose and not suffer the pangs of regret, sorrow, and shame. But I have never met anyone who could manage that. Even the most psychopathic of people seemed motivated at least to mask their malfeasance with a layer of lies (with the depth of that layer precisely proportionate to the severity of the impropriety in question). Even the most malevolent, it appears, must find justification for his or her evil.

If we fail to hold ourselves to that standard of responsibility, then other people regard us as lacking in ethics and integrity. And it does not end there. Just as we hold people (including ourselves) accountable for the wrongs they have done, or the good they have failed to do, we also believe (or at least act out the proposition) that someone who has made a good decision freely, deserves whatever benefit might come of that decision. It is for that reason that we believe each person should justly receive the fruit of their honest and voluntary labor. There seems something natural and inevitable about such judgments; something at work within them that is universal and inescapable, psychologically and socially. What all this means is that everyone—child, adult, self, others—will rebel against being treated as a cog in a wheel, incapable of choice and devoid of freedom, and (similarly) that it is practically impossible to establish a positive relationship with any other (or even our private selves) without that attribution of personal agency, free will, and responsibility.

## THE WORD AS SAVIOR

The twin ideas that we all are, as sovereign individuals, first, voluntarily participating in the act of creation itself and, second, determining the quality of that creation with the ethics of our choices finds reflection in myriad manners within our relationships, private and public. These ideas are also encapsulated and represented in the narratives, the fundamental narratives, that sit at the base of our culture. These stories—whatever their ultimate metaphysical significance—are at least in part a consequence of our watching ourselves act across eons of human history, and distilling from that watching the essential patterns of our actions. We are cartographers, makers of maps; geographers, concerned with the layout of the land. But we are also, more precisely and accurately, charters of courses, sailors and explorers. We recall the places we started from, the positions we occupied when our stories began. We remember the pitfalls and successes of the past so that we can avoid the former and repeat the latter. To do so, we need to know where we have been, where we currently are, and in what direction we are headed. We reduce that account to its causal structure: we need to know what happened and why, and we need to know it as simply and practically as possible.

It is for such reasons we are so captivated by people who can tell a story—who can share their experiences concisely and precisely, and who get to the point. That point—the moral of the story—is what they learned about who and where they were or are, and where they are going and why. Such information is irresistible to us all. It is how (and why) we derive wisdom from the risks taken by those before us, and who lived to tell the story: "This is what life was like then. This is what we wanted, and why. This is what we envisioned, and how we strategized, planned, and then acted. Sometimes, we succeeded and realized our aims. But too often (and this is what is crucial to a great story): here is how what we did not expect occurred, here is how we were knocked off the path, here are the tragedies we encountered and the mistakes we made—and here is how we put the world back together (or failed to do so)." We value such stories particularly if they have attained the pinnacle of generalizability, representing heroic battles with the unknown, as such, or the dissolution of tyrannical order into revivifying chaos and the (re)establishment of benevolent society.[10] This can be seen everywhere that people tell and listen avidly to stories: and that is literally everywhere.[11]

The most fundamental stories of the West are to be found, for better or worse, in the biblical corpus. That collection of ancient and eminently influential books opens with God Himself, in His Fatherly guise, portrayed as the ordered entity who confronts chaos and creates habitable order in consequence:

> And the earth was without form, and void; and darkness was
> upon the face of the deep. And the Spirit of God moved upon
> the face of the waters. (Genesis 1:2)

This formlessness, void, darkness, and water (a confusing conglomeration of attributes) is a consequence of the translation of a biblical Hebrew phrase, *tohu wa-bohu* (תהו ובהו), made up of two words, *tohuw* and *bohuw*. *Tohuw* is even more complicated than mere formlessness,

etc.; it also means "that which is laid waste," "vanity" (which might be
something likely to be laid to waste, psychologically speaking), and
"desert" (which is uninhabitable and void).[12] It is also associated with
another Hebrew word, *tehom* (תְּהוֹם), which is the source of the phrase
"the deep." *Tehom*, in turn, means "the abyss," and is associated with an
earlier Sumerian term, Tiamat,[13] who is the great mother goddess/
dragon (and denizen of salt water) who creates the world with her consort, Apsu, in the Mesopotamian creation myth *Enuma Elish*.

According to the Genesis account, there exists something—a potential, let us say, associated symbolically with the abyss, with the
oceanic depths—but also with desert, dragons, maternality/matriarchy,
emptiness, formlessness, and darkness.[14] This is all the attempt of poetry and metaphor to give initial, ordered, conceptual form to the form-
less. The abyss is what terrifies, what is at the end of the earth, what we
gaze upon when contemplating our mortality and fragility, and what
devours hope. Water is depth and the source of life itself. The desert
is a place of abandonment, isolation, and loneliness, as well as the in-
terregnum between tyranny and the promised land. The dragon is the
ancient image of the predator as such—the fire-breathing tree-cat-
snake-bird[15]—eternally lurking in the forest beyond the familiar confines of tribe and village. It is as well the Leviathan hidden in the salt
water, the depths—the terrible monster Jehovah refers to overcoming
in Job 41:25–34 and in many other places in the Old Testament accounts.[16]

God has an attribute, or an alternative Person, or a faculty, or a
tool that aids Him or that He relies on when confronting possibility
and the void. That is the Word, from the Christian perspective—but
certainly the capacity for speech, regardless of religious framework,
Jewish or Christian. There is a continual insistence in Genesis on the
importance of speech. The act of creation on each day begins with the

phrase "and God said" (with additional emphasis on the act of naming: "and God called"). The seven days of creation begin:

> And God said, Let there be light: and there was light.
>
> And God saw the light, that it was good: and God divided the light from the darkness.
>
> And God called the light Day, and the darkness he called Night. And the evening and the morning were the first day. (Genesis 1:3–5)

Almost immediately after God first reveals Himself, His creative actions, and the initial creation (thus, almost instantly after we are introduced to Him), He creates human beings. Three features of that creation stand forth, in addition to its immediacy: the insistence that mankind is to have dominion* over the rest of creation; the shocking and incomprehensibly modern and egalitarian insistence that God created man and woman equally in His own image (stated twice; Genesis 1:27); and the equally unlikely and miraculous insistence that the creation of humanity was, like the rest of the Creation, good. If God is, above all, as He is initially described, that implies that the men and women created in His image share with Him something of import— or, more to the point, they share an analogous destiny, necessity, or responsibility.

The Word—the tool God uses to transform the depths of potential—is truthful speech. It appears necessarily allied, however, with the courage to confront unrealized possibility in all its awful potential, so that reality itself may be brought forth. Perhaps both this

---

*Responsibility, stewardship, service; not from physical strength (Cambridge Bible for Schools and Colleges); the power of governing and controlling; but most important, the same dominion as God has over or for man.

Truth and Courage must finally be subsumed, in turn, under the broader principle of Love—love for Being itself, despite its fragility, tyranny, and betrayal; love that has as its aim what is best for the best in everything. It is that combination of Truth, Courage, and Love comprising the Ideal, whose active incarnation in each individual does in fact take the potential of the future and make the best of it. And who would deny this? No one teaches a beloved son to cringe in terror and cowardice from what confronts him. No one teaches a beloved daughter that deceit will set the world right, and that whatever works expediently is to be practiced, honored, and mimicked. And no one tells anyone he or she cares for that the proper response to Being is hatred and the desire to produce pain, suffering, mayhem, and catastrophe. Thus, it can be assumed from analysis of our own behavior that we know the difference between the pathway of good and the pathway of evil, and that we believe above all (despite our conscious resistance and prideful argument) in the existence of both. But there is yet more: the insistence of God on the goodness of creation reflected the fact that Truth, Courage, and Love were united in His creative action. Thus, there is an ethical claim deeply embedded in the Genesis account of creation: everything that emerges from the realm of possibility in the act of creation (arguably, either divine or human) is good insofar as the motive for its creation is good. I do not believe there is a more daring argument in all of philosophy or in theology than this: To believe this, to act it out, is the fundamental act of faith.

There is an argument presented much later in the biblical narrative, in the New Testament. Christ says the following words to His followers. It is a commentary on the potential for completing your life, for reclaiming what you have lost—or even discovering what you did not know was there:

And I say unto you, Ask, and it shall be given you; seek, and ye shall find; knock, and it shall be opened unto you.

For every one that asketh receiveth; and he that seeketh findeth; and to him that knocketh it shall be opened.

If a son shall ask bread of any of you that is a father, will he give him a stone? or if he ask a fish, will he for a fish give him a serpent?

Or if he shall ask an egg, will he offer him a scorpion?

If ye then, being evil, know how to give good gifts unto your children: how much more shall your heavenly Father give the Holy Spirit to them that ask him? (Luke 11:9–13)

This is not a casual statement. It is not naive. It is not a matter of asking for a present, unearned. God is no granter of casual wishes.* It is a matter, first, of truly Asking. This means being willing to let go of anything and everything that is not in keeping with the desire. Otherwise there is no Asking. There is only an immature and too-often resentful whim and wish: "Oh, that I could have what I want, without doing what is necessary." That will not suffice. So, to ask, seek, and knock is to do everything required to gather what has been left unfinished and to complete it, now. And to ask, seek, and knock is, as well, to determine what must be asked for. And that has to be something that is worthy of God. Why else would it be granted? How else could it possibly be granted?

Imagine for a moment you have been given all you need. There is possibility within you, waiting for the proper demand to release itself. There is all that is outside of you, waiting to inform and teach you.

---

*Perhaps it is for this reason that Christ insists "it is also written: 'Do not put the Lord your God to the test.'" (In this instance I prefer Matthew 4:7 of the New International Version to the same verse in the King James Version.)

But all of it is necessary—the good, bad, and unbearable. You know that when something does not go well, you should analyze the problem, resolve it, apologize, repent, and transform. An unsolved problem seldom sits there, in stasis. It grows new heads, like a hydra. One lie— one act of avoidance—breeds the necessity for more. One act of self-deception generates the requirement to buttress that self-deceptive belief with new delusions. One devastated relationship, unaddressed, damages your reputation—damages your faith in yourself, equally— and decreases the probability of a new and better relationship. Thus, your refusal or even inability to come to terms with the errors of the past expands the source of such error—expands the unknown that surrounds you, transforms that unknown into something increasingly predatory.

And, while that is happening, you get weaker. You are less than you could be because you did not change. You did not become who you could have become as a consequence of that change—and worse: you have now taught yourself, by your own example, that such turning away is acceptable, and you are therefore more likely to commit the same error in the future. And what you failed to face is now larger. This is not the kind of causal process, the kind of positive feedback loop, that you want to find yourself trapped within. So, you must confess, at least to yourself, and repent, at least within yourself, and you must change, because you were wrong. And you must humbly ask, and knock, and seek. And that is the great barrier to the enlightenment of which we are all capable in principle. This is not to claim that the courage necessary to confront the full horrors of life is easy to muster. But the alternative is worse.

It is our destiny to transform chaos into order. If the past has not been ordered, the chaos it still constitutes haunts us. There is information—vital information—resting in the memories that affect us negatively. It is as if part of the personality is still lying latent, out in the world, making itself manifest only in emotional disruption. What is traumatic but remains inexplicable indicates that the map of the world that guides our navigation is insufficient in some vital manner. It is necessary to understand the negative well enough so that it can be circumvented as we move into the future if we do not wish to remain tormented by the past. And it is not the expression of emotion associated with unpleasant events that has curative power. It is the development of a sophisticated causal theory: Why was I at risk? What was it about the world that made it dangerous? What was I doing or not doing to contribute to my vulnerability? How can I change the value hierarchy I inhabit to take the negative into account so that I can see and understand it? How much of my old map do I have to let crumble and burn—with all the pain dying tissue produces—before I can change enough to take my full range of experience into account? Do I have the faith to step beyond what should and must die and let my new and wiser personality emerge? To some great degree, we are our assumptions. They structure the world for us. When basic axioms of faith are challenged ("People are basically good"), the foundation shakes and the walls crumble. We have every reason to avoid facing the bitter truth. But making what is—and what was—clear and fully comprehended can only protect us. If you are suffering from memories that will not stop tormenting you, there is possibility—possibility that could be your very salvation—waiting there to be discovered.

If old memories still upset you, write them down carefully and completely.

# PLAN AND WORK DILIGENTLY TO MAINTAIN THE ROMANCE IN YOUR RELATIONSHIP

## THE UNBEARABLE DATE

I am not a couples' therapist. But sometimes, when I see a client, it becomes necessary to include his or her intimate partner in one or more sessions. I do that only when directly asked. I also make it clear that the couple should seek out a marital counseling specialist if that is their central goal. However, if one of the primary problems my client is addressing is dissatisfaction in the marriage, it is often counter-productive to speak with only one member of the couple. Finally, it is often the case (and no wonder, really) that the partner in question does not trust his or her better half's therapist—me—and a meeting with all three of us can go a long way toward rectifying that.

Prior to meeting with a couple, I will have discussed some basic rules for relationship improvement with my client. Let us say he or she has decided to make some time for romance: four hours a week or something like that (I am speaking here of adults, with their full share of responsibilities). Maybe that much can be managed. Maybe even more is possible. But there is not that much time in seven days, and the situation must be set up correctly and carefully. And when all this is first practiced—all this conscious negotiation and enactment—it is going to be done badly and stupidly, with all the attendant pain, resentment, and vengefulness. And then such negative emotion can be nursed and the relationship damaged—sometimes permanently.

Perhaps my client and his or her partner have become estranged from one another over several years when we first start to discuss their situation. They are not happy, and they hate me—maybe even more than they hate each other. They sit there, distant, arms crossed and eyes rolling (hopefully not the latter: that is a bad sign[1]). Neither will give an inch. I ask them when they last did something romantic together; when they last went out together for a date. They laugh ruefully, if things have not gone too far, or scoff outright. I suggest, nonetheless, that they try going out with each other; or more, that they start making dates a regular practice. The former suggestion is bad enough; the second, intolerable. They indicate: "We are not going on any damn dates. We dated before we got married, when it was appropriate. Besides, all we will do is fight."

And here is my take on that angry, bitter, and shallow response: "This is the theory you are putting forth: You are never going to accompany each other on another date in your entire married life. (So much for romance and intimacy.) Instead, you are just going to give that up. Why not, instead, risk the time? Take each other somewhere nice. Dare to put your arm around your partner, or your hand on a knee (and not your own, either). I know you are angry with each other, and probably for good reason. I have met both of you: I understand why you both feel that way :-). But just try it. You do not have to like it. You do not have to expect to be good at it, or give up your anger, or have a good time. You just have to tolerate it."

They both leave incensed at me for suggesting such an irritating idea. But they agree grudgingly, and at their next session inform me: "It happened just as we told you: we had an absolutely wretched time. We fought before we went out, while we were out, and again, when we returned home. We are certainly not going to risk a date again." They often evince a certain pride at reaching such a conclusion, as both had generally decided ahead of time that the whole idea was pointless. So, I ask: "That is the plan, is it? You are going to be married for sixty years. You put a small amount of begrudging effort into having one date. You were already not getting along, so there was a negligible probability you were going to take any pleasure in it. Besides that, irritated at me as you were for my childish suggestion, you were both motivated to make it go horribly, just as it did. So, you are done with it. And now you have decided that this is how you are going to conduct yourselves across the decades you have promised each other: with spite and bitterness instead of mutual regard?

"Let us try thinking about it this way, instead: Neither of you have any skill at dating. One attempt is therefore going to be insufficient. Maybe you need fifteen dates—or forty—because you have lost the knack, need the practice, and must develop the habit and goodwill. Perhaps neither of you are very romantic to begin with; or if you were once, those days have long gone. This is a skill you must learn, not an unearned gift from Cupid."

Assume you are married—or the equivalent. Assume, as well, that you have, or could have, a romantic interlude twice a week. It may be less; it may be more: but we will do the arithmetic for twice weekly. That is a hundred times a year. Let us imagine that you are going to be married thirty more years. Thirty times one hundred is three thousand times. Is there not some possibility that you could devote a fraction of all that time to perfecting your technique, seduction, communication, and lovemaking? What does it matter, therefore, if you have fifteen miserable dates before managing one that verges on acceptable? That is fifteen times out of a possible three thousand. That is half a percent of the romantic time you could possibly spend together. Maybe you could dare even more to determine if things could be set right between you. Why would you possibly assume that something as complex as maintaining a marriage could be managed without commitment, practice, and effort?

"So maybe the first date is wretched and horrible. You never want to repeat it but you do, because you would rather save your marriage than quit outright. And maybe the next one is five percent better. And maybe after some repeated attempts you remember for at least a brief moment why you once liked the person you married. Perhaps you manage something a little more exciting than putting your arm around him or her, and perhaps receive a bit of a response from someone who actually cares for you somewhere in their now cold and shriveled heart. And if you are in it for the long run, as indicated by the original marital vows, perhaps you will put in the time to get it right."

And maybe the couple has enough sense to do the arithmetic and contemplate all that wasted time, as well as the bitterness, resentment, and deadness of life without romance, and they agree to go on another date, or two, or three, or ten—and by the tenth session they come to see me, smiling, and tell me they had a pretty good time. And then we have an even more serious discussion about just what it takes to maintain love and respect, and invoke desire and response. How do you find the mystery in the other person over the long run? Can you muster up the will and the romantic imagination and the playfulness to manage that, each time you are together intimately, for the next three thousand occasions? That is going to require some thoughtful effort.

For each person is in truth an unfathomable enigma. With care, you might keep rediscovering, in the person you have chosen, enough residual mystery to maintain the spirit that first brought you together. With care, you can avoid stowing each other away in a conveniently sized box, punishment at hand should either of you dare to emerge, and contempt for the consequent predictability you both now face lurking not so far beneath the surface. If you are fortunate, you might rekindle that glimpse you had when you first were attracted to each other, of what your life could be like if you were better people than you are. That is what happens two people fall under the spell of love. For a while, both become better than they were, and see that, but then that magic fades away. Both receive that experience as a gift. Both have their eyes open and can see what is visible to no one else. Such love is a glimpse of what could be, if the relationship remained true. It is delivered as a gift initially, from fate, but requires tremendous effort to realize and maintain. And once that is understood, the goal is clear.

## BEDROCK

The sexual aspect of a relationship can often tell us a great deal about the whole, but not always. I have known couples who fought like proverbial cats and dogs and who had a wildly successful sex life (at least in the short term), and other couples who were well suited to each other temperamentally but one or the other could not find the spark. People and their relationships are too complex to reduce to a single aspect—but it is still reasonable to note that a good marriage is accompanied by mutual desire, mutually requited. Unfortunately, desire is not something that can be managed in isolation: "Let us fix our sex life" is a resolution too narrow in ambition to fulfill its aim.

There must be a broader, relationship-wide strategy in place to maintain romance with your partner across time. Regardless of what that strategy might be, its success is going to depend on your ability to negotiate. To negotiate, you and the person you are negotiating with must first know what you each need (and want)—and second, be willing to discuss both forthrightly. There are many serious obstacles both to knowing what you need and want, and to discussing it. If you allow yourself to know what you want, then you will also know precisely when you are failing to get it. You will benefit, of course, because you will also know when you have succeeded. But you might also fail, and you could well be frightened enough by the possibility of not getting what you need (and want) that you keep your desires vague and unspecified. And the chance that you will get what you want if you fail to aim for it is vanishingly small.

Aim is likely a problem for you. If you have a partner, the problem may be compounded. The person you have chosen is unlikely to be any smarter about you than you are, except in minor instances (and is in fact likely to be even more in the dark with regard to your innermost desires). Your failure to specify your desires means your unfortunate lover will have to guess what would please and displease you, and is likely to be punished in some manner for getting it wrong. Furthermore, given all the things you could want—and do not want—it is virtually certain that your lover will get it wrong. In consequence, you will be motivated to blame them, at least implicitly, or nonverbally, or unconsciously, for not caring enough to notice what you are unwilling even to notice yourself. "If you really loved me," you will think—or feel, without thinking—"I would not have to tell you what would make me happy." This is not a practical approach to a happy marriage.

That is all bad enough, but there is a second and equally severe problem lurking in the byways. If you have solved the problem of knowing what you want, admitted it to yourself in a verbalizable form, and let someone else know your wishes, you have then granted them a dangerous source of power. The person whom you have made your confidant is now in a position to fulfill your desires, but could equally deprive you of what you want, embarrass you for wanting it, or hurt you in some other manner, because you have now made yourself vulnerable. Naive people are possessed of the delusion that everyone is good, and that no one—particularly someone loved—would be motivated to cause pain and misery, either for revenge, as a consequence of blindness, or merely for the pleasure of doing so. But people who have matured enough to transcend their naivete have learned that they can be hurt and betrayed both by themselves and at the hands of others. So why increase the odds of being hurt by letting someone in? It is to defend against such betrayal that naivete is often replaced by cynicism, and it must be said in all truth that the latter is an improvement over the former. But such substitution is not the final word in wisdom, and thank God for that. Trust in turn trumps cynicism, and true trust is not naivete. Trust between people who are not naive is a form of courage, because betrayal is always a possibility, and because this is consciously understood. This applies with particular force within the confines of an intimate relationship. To trust is to invite the best in your partner to manifest itself, with yourself and your freely given trust as the enticement. This is a risky business, but the alternative is the impossibility of true intimacy, and the sacrifice of what could have been two minds in dialogue working in tandem to address the difficult problems of life for a single mind striving in solitude.

Romance requires trust—and the deeper the trust, the deeper the possibility for romance. But trust has its requirements, as well, apart from the courage required of the individuals wise enough to distrust but brave enough to risk putting their faith in a partner. The first of those requirements is truth. You cannot maintain trust in yourself if you lie. You cannot maintain trust in yourself, likewise, if you act in a manner that would require a lie if it was discovered. Similarly, you cannot maintain trust in your partner if he or she lies, or betrays you in action or in silence. So, the vow that makes a marriage capable of preserving its romantic component is first and foremost the decision not to lie to your partner.

There are also immense practical advantages to this, if practiced properly. There will come a time in your life when you have done something you should not have done or failed to do something that you should have done. You may need advice. You may need support. You may need exactly what your partner could provide, if only you dared to allow them to help. And at some time they are going to find themselves in exactly the same position. Life is too difficult to negotiate alone. If you tell your partner the truth, and you strive to act so that you can tell the truth about how you act, then you have someone to rely on when the seas become high and your ship threatens to founder. This can literally be a matter of life or death. In a relationship where romance remains intact, truth must be king.

## CHRIST IN THE CANDLE

I have a friend of Scandinavian descent, although he is Canadian. He married a Canadian woman, also of Scandinavian descent. They decided to get married in Sweden, as a tribute to their joint ancestry. They were both at least nominally Christian, so they were married in a ceremony reflecting that. During their exchange of vows, the bride and groom held a lit candle aloft between them. I spent a long time thinking about the significance of that ritual.

There is an ancient conceit in the book of Genesis (2:21–22) that Eve was taken out of Adam—created from his rib. Woman from man: this presents something of a mystery, reversing, as it does, the normative biological sequence, where males emerge from females at birth. It also gave rise to a line of mythological speculation, attempting to account for the strangeness of this creative act, predicated on the supposition that Adam, the original man produced by God, was hermaphroditic— half masculine and half feminine—and only later separated into the two sexes. This implies not only the partition of a divinely produced unity, but the incompleteness of man and woman until each is brought together with the other.[2] The fact that the candle is held jointly indicates the binding of the two celebrants. The fact that the candle is held aloft, lit, implies that something higher—something superordinate—is representing or performing the union. Light, light in the heavens, light in the darkness, illumination, enlightenment. Prior to the invention of modern electric lights, candles were often used for this purpose. Evergreens, the standard choice for Christmas trees, represent life unending, as they do not "die" annually in the same manner as their deciduous counterparts. Such trees therefore symbolize the Tree of Life, which serves as the very foundation of the cosmos.[3] So, we illuminate the Tree of Life, at or near December 21, the darkest time of year, at least in the Northern Hemisphere.[4] That is why Christmas is located where it is on the calendar; the reappearance of the light is associated with the birth of the Universal Savior—signifying the eternal reemergence of light in the Stygian blackness.

Christ has long been regarded as the second (perfected) Adam and, just as there was speculation about the hermaphroditic nature of the first Adam prior to God's creation of the independent sexes, there is a line of speculation about Christ's spiritual perfection being a consequence of the ideal balance of masculine and feminine elements.*[5] It is very difficult for individuals joining themselves together to become desperate enough to cease their hiding and avoidance, live in truth, and repair themselves in the light cast by their joint existence. It is for this reason that both swear the dread vow of permanence ("What God has joined together, let not man put asunder" [Matthew 19:6]). "I am bound to you," claims one party to the agreement. "And I to you," says the other, and both think, if they have any sense, that they should each transform themselves and one another, to forestall any unnecessary suffering. So, what is the superordinate principle to which both marital partners must bow? It is not illumination as mere verbal abstraction. It is not that they are only supposed to think and speak the truth. It is that they are supposed to act it out. And that is the ancient idea that the Word should be made flesh.

The individuals who make up a married couple might well engage in a lifelong struggle concerning a single inappropriately conceptualized question: "Who is subordinate to whom in a marriage?" After all, each might reason, as people commonly do, that such an arrangement is a zero-sum game, with one winner and one loser. But a relationship does not have to be and should not be a question of one or the other as winner, or even each alternating in that status, in an approximation of fairness. Instead, the couple can decide that each and both are subordinate to a principle, a higher-order principle, which constitutes

---

*The same idea emerged constantly in the centuries of alchemical literature, which tended overwhelmingly to represent the perfect person (the possessor, in a spiritual or psychological sense, of the philosopher's stone) as a consequence of the mystical marriage between the feminine and masculine elements of the psyche. We discussed this in some detail in Rule II: Imagine who you could be and aim single-mindedly at that, with regard to the figure of the Rebis.

their union in the spirit of illumination and truth. That ghostly figure, the ideal union of what is best in both personalities, should be constantly regarded as the ruler of the marriage—and, indeed, as something as close to divine as might be practically approached by fallible individuals. That is what the ceremony of the candle represents: Neither participant rules the other. Instead, both bow to the principle of illumination. In that circumstance, it is not that one must abide by what the other wants (or vice versa). Instead, it is that both should be oriented toward the most positive future possible, and agree that speaking the truth is the best pathway forward. That orientation and truthfulness will engender a transformative dialogue, verbal and non-verbal, if the partners in the arrangement commit to abiding by the consequence of that dialogue. Voluntary subordination to this higher-order principle of illumination both unifies and revitalizes.

Imagine that you have just participated in such a ceremony. What does your participation signify? Do you *believe* in the ideas that you have just acted out? Do you believe that man and woman were once together, as a single being, were then separated, and must be restored as a unity? You can believe it dramatically, poetically, and metaphorically instead of merely rationally and mechanically, and that can lead you to deep truths. Do you want to find your soul mate? It is a romantic trope, obviously, but there are deep reasons for the existence of romantic fictions. Maybe you take someone on a date to a romantic movie. You both watch the movie hero and heroine find their soul mates. If you are fortunate, while you are watching you are thinking, "Well, maybe this person I am sitting with is the one for me, too." In the best of all situations, that is also what your date is hoping for. Maybe that is too much to hope for in real life. But the romantic part of you is longing for it regardless.

There is an inevitable yearning in our natures for the completion that someone else might provide. There is a sense that you are missing something, otherwise, and that only the proper romantic union will provide it. It is true, too—you are indeed missing something. If you were not, sex would never have evolved. The entire biological course of our destiny, since reproduction progressed past the mere division of cells, appears driven by the fact that it was better for two dissimilar creatures to come together to produce a comparatively novel version of themselves than to merely clone their current embodiment. You have your idiosyncrasies, your blind spots, your biases. Some of these are implicit. They are often paired inextricably with your unique talents: you seldom gain an advantage without a corresponding disadvantage, and you are a particular person, with particular attributes. If you are on your own, you are inevitably lopsided, one-sided. That is often not for the best.

There is unrealized utility in the marital institution about which we have become cynical—a consequence of our immaturity and naivete. A marriage is a vow, and there is a reason for it. You announce jointly, publicly: "I am not going to leave you, in sickness or health, in poverty or wealth—and you are not going to leave me." It is actually a threat: "We are not getting rid of each other, no matter what." You are shackled together, like two angry cats at the bottom of a barrel with the lid on. In principle, there is no escape. If you have any sense (besides the optimism of new love) you also think, "Oh, God. That is a horrifying possibility." The part of you that claims to desire freedom (but really wants to avoid any permanent and therefore terrifying responsibility) desires a trapdoor through which escape might be made, if and when it is necessary. That seems convenient—and it is true that there are unbearable marriages—but it is an option with extreme perils. Do you really want to keep asking yourself for the rest of your life—because you would always have the option to leave—if you made the right choice? In all likelihood, you did not. There are seven billion people in the world. At least a hundred million (let us say) might have made good partners for you. You certainly did not have time to try them out, and the probability that you found the theoretically optimal person approaches zero. But you do not *find* so much as *make*, and if you do not know that you are in real trouble. Furthermore, if you have an escape route, there will not be enough heat generated in the chamber you find yourself jointly trapped in to catalyze the change necessary in both of you—the maturation, the development of wisdom—because maturation and the development of wisdom require a certain degree of suffering, and suffering is escapable as long as there is an out.

You are not going to get along with your partner—not easily, unless you agree to be tyrannized and silent (and even then you will take your revenge)—because you are different people. No one just simply gets along, precisely because of that. And not only are you different from your partner, but you are rife with inadequacies and so is he—or she. And that is not bad enough. There is also the fact that even people of good will and character locked together in matrimony will face the mundane, quotidian, dull, tragic, and terrible together, because life can be—and certainly will be at some point—difficult to the point of impossibility. It is going to be tough. Even if you strive to pull your-selves together, and succeed at that admirably, there are going to be brutal times, and they are not necessarily going to be brief. Maybe life will be better if you stay together—that is the hope, and the likeli-hood, as far as I can tell—but the brutal times will still be there. What is going to make you voluntarily deal with your differences and estab-lish a genuine agreement, a true consensus? You are going to have to negotiate in good faith, continually, to come to some sort of peaceful and productive accommodation. And if you do not? You are going to have your hands around each other's throats for sixty years.

In clinical practice, I have seen whole families in that situation. Imagine five people in a circle. Imagine further that each has their hands around the neck of the person in front of them. All are squeezing with just enough force to kill in a few decades. This is a decision, formulated over years of unspoken argument and refusal to negotiate: "I am going to kill you. It is just going to take me a lifetime." It is very possible that you have someone you might like to slowly throttle in your family, or who is currently doing it to you. Perhaps not, hopefully not (perhaps you would not admit it even if you knew it was true)— but it is common enough. If you do not negotiate peace with your partner, that is the situation you will find yourself in. There are three fundamental states of social being: tyranny (you do what I want), slavery (I do what you want), or negotiation. Tyranny is obviously not so good for the person enslaved, but it is also not good for the tyrant— because he or she becomes a tyrant, and there is nothing ennobling about that. There is nothing but cynicism, cruelty, and the hell of unregulated anger and impulsivity. Slavery is not good either, likewise for the slave and the tyrant. Slaves are miserable, wretched, angry, and resentful. They will take any and all chances whatsoever available to them to take revenge on their tyrants, who will in consequence find themselves cursed and damaged by their slaves. It is not easy to get the best out of someone by arbitrarily brandishing a stick at them, particularly when they try to do something good (and that diminution of spirit is the cruelest trick of the tyrant). But you can be certain, you want-to-be tyrants, that your slaves will take their revenge where they can, even if that means merely being much less than they could be.

My wife told me a terrible story once, about a couple she observed while volunteering in a palliative care ward. The husband was dying, and his wife was trimming his nails—a little too close. With each clip, there was blood, as she trimmed close enough to damage the quick. You see something like that, and wisdom speaks its terrible truth: "I know *exactly* what is going on there." That is the end stage of an unbelievably deceitful and brutal relationship. It is subtle. It does not announce itself loudly as murderous. No one knows, except the couple (even though they are perhaps striving with all their might, under the circumstances, not to know) and the careful observer, who sees a dying man and a wife who has determined, for whatever reasons, to make his death a little worse. That is not a desirable outcome. You do not want to end up in that situation, or anything like it. You want to negotiate. The question is, "What is going to make you desperate enough to negotiate?" And that is one of the mysteries that must be addressed if you wish to keep the romance alive in your relationship.

## NEGOTIATION, TYRANNY, OR SLAVERY

Negotiation is exceptionally difficult. We already discussed the problems associated with determining what you want and then mustering up the courage to tell someone exactly that. And there are the tricks that people use, too, to avoid negotiation. Perhaps you ask your partner what he or she wants—perhaps during a difficult situation. "I don't know" is a common answer (you get that from children, too, and even more often from adolescents). It is not acceptable, however, in a discussion that cannot in good faith be avoided. Sometimes "I don't know" truly means what it is supposed to mean—the person who utters the phrase is at a genuine loss—but often it means, instead: "I don't want to talk about it, so go away and leave me alone." Irritation or outright anger, sufficient to deter the questioner, often accompanies this response. That brings the discussion to a halt, and it can stay halted forever. Maybe that has happened once or twice or a dozen times too often, so you—the questioner, in this instance—have had enough of your partner's refusal, or you have decided that you are done being cowardly or a victim of your own misplaced compassion and you are not about to take "I don't know" for an answer. In consequence, you persist in pursuing your target. "Well, *guess*," you might say. "Throw something on the table, for God's sake. I do not care what it is. Even if it is wrong, it is at least a start." "I don't know" means not only "Go away and leave me alone." It also frequently means "Why don't you go away, do all the work necessary to figure out what is wrong, and come back and tell me—if you're so smart," or "It is intolerably rude of you to refuse to allow me to remain in my willful or dangerous ignorance, given that it obviously bothers me so much to think about my problems." It is not rude, though—or even if it is, you still need to know what your partner wants, and so does he or she, and how in the world are either or both of you going to figure it out if you cannot even get the conversation off the ground? It is not rude. It is a cruel act of love.

Persistence under such conditions is a necessity, a terrible necessity, akin to surgery. It is difficult and painful because it takes courage and even some foolhardiness to continue a discussion when you have been told in no uncertain terms by your partner to go the hell away (or worse). It is a good thing, however—an admirable act—because a person bothered by something they do not wish to talk about is very likely to be split internally over the issue at hand. The part that wants to avoid is the part that gets angry. There is a part that wants to talk, too, and to settle the issue. But doing so is going to be cognitively demanding, ethically challenging, and emotionally stressful. In addition, it is going to require trust, and people test trust, not least by manifesting anger when approached about something touchy just to determine if the person daring the approach cares sufficiently to overcome a serious barrier or two or three or ten to get to the horrible bottom of things. And avoidance followed by anger is not the only trick in the book.

The next serious hurdle is tears. Tears are easily mistaken for the distress due to sadness, and they are very effective at bringing tender-hearted people to a dead halt as a consequence of their misplaced compassion. (Why misplaced? Because if you leave the person alone because of their tears, they quit suffering right then, but continue with their unresolved problem until they solve it, which might be never.) Tears, however, are just as often anger (perhaps more often) as they are sadness or distress. If the person you are chasing down and corner-ing is red-faced, for example, in addition to their tears, then he or she is probably angry, not hurt (that is not inevitably the case, but it is a reasonably common sign). Tears are an effective defense mechanism, as it takes a heart of stone to withstand them, but they tend to be the last-ditch attempt at avoidance. If you can get past tears, you can have a real conversation, but it takes a very determined interlocutor to avoid the insult and hurt generated by anger (defense one) and the pity and compassion evoked by tears (defense two). It requires someone who has integrated their shadow (their stubbornness, harshness, and capac-ity for necessary emotionless implacability) and can use it for long-term benefit. Do not foolishly confuse "nice" with "good."

Remember the options previously discussed: negotiation, tyranny, or slavery. Of those, negotiation is the least awful, even though it is no joke to negotiate, and it is perhaps the most difficult of the three, in the short term, because you have to fight it out, now, and God only knows how deep you are going to have to go, how much diseased tis-sue you will have to remove. For all you know, you are fighting with the spirit of your wife's grandmother, who was treated terribly by her alcoholic husband, and the consequences of that unresolved abuse and

distrust between the sexes are echoing down the generations. Children are amazing mimics. They learn much of what they know implicitly long before they can use language, and they imitate the bad
along with the good. It is for this reason that it has been said that the
sins of the fathers will be visited on the children to the third and fourth
generation (Numbers 14:18).

Hope, of course, can drive us through the pain of negotiation, but
hope is not enough. You need desperation, as well, and that is part of the
utility of "till death do us part." You are stuck with each other, if you are
serious—and if you are not serious, you are still a child. That is the
point of the vow: the possibility of mutual salvation, or the closest you
can manage here on Earth. In a truly mature marriage, if your health
holds out, you are there for the aforementioned sixty years, like Moses
in the desert searching for the Promised Land, and there is plenty of
trouble that must be worked through—all of it—before peace might be
established. So, you grow up when you marry, and you aim for peace as
if your soul depends upon it (and perhaps that is more serious than your
life depending on it), and you make it work or you suffer miserably. You
will be tempted by avoidance, anger, and tears, or enticed to employ the
trapdoor of divorce so that you will not have to face what must be faced.
But your failure will haunt you while you are enraged, weeping, or in
the process of separating, as it will in the next relationship you stumble
into, with all your unsolved problems intact and your negotiating skills
not improved a whit.

You can keep the possibility of escape in the back of your mind.
You can avoid the commitment of permanence. But then you cannot
achieve the transformation, which might well demand everything you
can possibly muster. The difficulty, however, that is implicit in the
negotiation carries with it a tremendous promise, which is part of a
radically successful life: *You could have a marriage that works.* You could

make it work. That is an achievement—a tangible, challenging, exceptional, and unlikely achievement. There are not many genuine achievements of that magnitude in life; a number as small as four is a reasonable estimate. Maybe, if you strive for it, you have established a solid marriage. That is achievement *one*. Because of that, you have founded a solid and reliable, honest and playful home into which you could dare bring children. Then you can have kids, and with a solid marriage that can work out for you. That is achievement *two*. Then you have brought upon yourself more of the responsibility that will demand the best from you. Then you will have new relationships of the highest quality, if you are fortunate and careful. Then you will have grandchildren so that you are surrounded by new life when yours begins to slip away. In our culture, we live as if we are going to die at thirty. But we do not. We live a very long time, but it is also all over in a flash, and it should be that you have accomplished what human beings accomplish when they live a full life, and marriage and children and grandchildren and all the trouble and heartbreak that accompanies all of that is far more than half of life. Miss it at your great peril.

You meet people, usually young, unwise but laden with the unearned cynicism that substitutes for wisdom in youth, and they say, categorically—even pridefully—"I do not want children." Plenty of nineteen-year-olds say that, and that is acceptable, in some sense, because they are nineteen, and they have time, and what do they know at nineteen, anyway? And some twenty-seven-year-olds say that, but not so many, particularly if they are female and the least bit honest with themselves. And some forty-five-year-olds say the same thing, in the past tense, and some of them, perhaps, are telling the truth; but most are celebrating closing the barn door after the cattle have bolted. No one will speak the truth about this. To note outright that we lie to young women, in particular, about what they are most likely to want in life is taboo in our culture, with its incomprehensibly strange insistence that the primary satisfaction in the typical person's life is to be found in career (a rarity in itself, as most people have jobs, not careers). But it is an uncommon woman, in my clinical and general professional experience, regardless of brilliance or talent, training, discipline, parental desire, youthful delusion, or cultural brainwashing who would not perform whatever sacrifice necessary to bring a child into the world by the time she is twenty-nine, or thirty-five, or worse, forty.

Here is a pathway to misery I would strongly recommend avoiding, aimed primarily at the women who read this book (although wise boyfriends and husbands should take equal note). Decide that you want children when you are twenty-nine or thirty, and then be unable to have them: I would not recommend that. You will not recover. We are too fragile to play around with what life might offer us. Everyone thinks, when they are young and do not know any better, "Well, pregnancy can be taken for granted." That is only true if you absolutely do not want and should not have a child, and you have sex in the backseat of a car when you are fifteen. Then, for sure, you will find yourself in trouble. But a successful pregnancy is not a foregone conclusion, not by any stretch of the imagination. You can push trying for children to the older end of that spectrum—and many people are encouraged or encourage themselves to do exactly that—but up to 30 percent of couples experience trouble becoming pregnant.[6]

You encounter something similar—that is, the incaution about what life will and will not offer—when people whose marriages have stagnated begin to develop the delusion that a romantic affair will address their unmet needs. When I had clients considering such a move—or perhaps involved in an affair, currently—I tried to bring them back down to earth. "Let us think it through, all the way. Not just for this week, or this month. You are fifty. You have this twenty-four-year-old, and she is willing to break up your marriage. What is she thinking? Who must she be? What does she know?" "Well, I am really attracted to her." "Yes, but she has a personality disorder. Seriously, because what the hell is she doing with you, and why is she willing to break up this marriage?" "Well, she does not care if I stay married." "Oh, I see. So, she does not want to have an actual relationship with someone, with any degree of long-term permanency. Somehow that is going to work out well for you, is it? Just think about that. It is going to be a little rough on your wife. A lot of lies are going to go along with that. You have children—how are they going to respond when all this comes out, as it most certainly will? And what do you think about the ten years in court that are now beckoning, that are going to cost you a third of a million dollars and put you in a custody battle that will occupy all your time and attention?"

I have seen people who were in custody battles who would seriously have preferred cancer. It is no joke to have your arm caught in the dangerous machinery of the courts. You spend much of the time truly wishing you were dead. So that is your "affair," for God's sake. It is even more delusional than that, because, of course, if you are married to someone, you often see them at their worst, because you have to share the genuine difficulties of life with them. You save the easy parts for your adulterous partner: no responsibility, just expensive restaurants, exciting nights of rule breaking, careful preparation for romance, and the general absence of reality that accompanies the privilege of making one person pay for the real troubles of existence while the other benefits unrealistically from their absence. You do not have a life with someone when you have an affair with them. You have an endless array of desserts (at least in the beginning), and all you have to do is scoop the whipped cream off the top of each of them and devour it. That is it. You see each other under the best possible conditions, with nothing but sex in your minds and nothing else inter-fering with your lives. As soon as it transforms from that into a rela-tionship that has any permanency, a huge part of the affair immediately turns right back into whatever it was that was bothering you about your marriage. An affair is not helpful, and people end up horribly hurt. Particularly children—and it is to them you owe primary allegiance.

I am not trying to be unreasonably categorical about marriage and family. You cannot expect every social institution to work out for ev-eryone. Sometimes, you have married someone who is a psychopathic brute, a congenital and incorrigible liar, a criminal, an alcoholic, a sa-dist (and maybe all five at once). Then you must escape. But that is not a trapdoor. That is a catastrophe, like a hurricane, and you should move out of its path. You might be tempted to conclude: "Well, how about we live together, instead of getting married? We will try each other out. It is the sensible thing to do." But what exactly does it mean, when you invite someone to live with you, instead of committing yourself to each other? And let us be appropriately harsh and realistic about our appraisal, instead of pretending we are taking a used car for a test jaunt. Here is what it means: "You will do, for now, and I pre-sume you feel the same way about me. Otherwise we would just get married. But in the name of a common sense that neither of us pos-sesses we are going to reserve the right to swap each other out for a better option at any point." And if you do not think that is what living together means—as a fully articulated ethical statement—see if you can formulate something more plausible.

You might think, "Look, Doc, that is pretty cynical." So why not we consider the stats, instead of the opinion of arguably but not truly old-fashioned me? The breakup rate among people who are not married but are living together—so, married in everything but the formal sense—is substantially higher than the divorce rate among married couples.[7] And even if you do get married and make an honest person, so to speak, of the individual with whom you cohabited, you are still much more rather than less likely to get divorced than you would be had you never lived together initially.[8] So the idea of trying each other out? Sounds enticing, but does not work.

It is of course possible that people who are more likely to get divorced, for reasons of temperament, are also more likely to live together, before or without marriage, rather or in addition to the possibility that living together just does not work. It is no simple matter to disentangle the two causal factors. But it does not matter, practically. Cohabitation without the promise of permanent commitment, socially announced, ceremonially established, seriously considered, does not produce more robust marriages. And there is nothing good about that—particularly for children, who do much worse in single parent (generally male-absent) families.[9] Period. So, I just do not see it as a justifiable social alternative. And I say that as someone who lived with my wife before I married her. I am not innocent in this regard. But that does not mean I was right. And there is something else, and it is far from trivial. You just do not have that many chances in life to have an intimate relationship work out properly. Maybe it takes you two or three years to meet the potential Mr. or Ms. Right, and another two or three to determine if they are in fact who you think they are. That is five years. You get old a lot faster than you think you will, no matter how old you are now, and most of what you could do with your family—with marriage, children, and so forth—is from twentysomething to about thirty-five. How many good five-year chances do you therefore have? Three? Four, if you are fortunate?

This means that your options decrease as you wait, rather than increase. If you are a widower, or a widow, and you must hit the dating scene when you are forty or fifty, so be it. You have been struck by tragedy, and that is life. But I have watched friends do it, and it is not a fate I would casually wish on anyone I loved. Let us continue to be reasonable about this: All sixteen- to eighteen-year-olds have much in common. They are unformed. They are malleable. That is not an insult. It is just a fact. It is also why they can go off to college and make a lifelong friend (no cynicism whatsoever intended) from a roommate within a single semester. By the time you are in your midforties, however—if you have lived at all—you have become somewhat of a singular and unique person. I have known people I met at that time of my life for a decade or more whom I still seem to consider new acquaintances. That is a pure function of the complexity of increasing age. And that is mere friendship, not love—not a joint life and perhaps even the bringing together of two disparate families.

And so you have your marriage and your children, and that is working out well because you are stubborn and sufficiently terrified of the hell that awaits anyone who fails to negotiate for peace and make the sacrifices necessary to establish it. You are undoubtedly more prepared now for your career—or more likely, your job. That is the *third* of the four achievements you might manage, with good fortune and an undaunted spirit, in the brief flash of your existence. You have learned how to establish productive harmony in the close confines of your most intimate and private relationships, and some of that wisdom spills over into your workplace. You are a mentor for younger people, a helpful peer and reliable subordinate, and instead of the hash you could so easily make of the place you inhabit, you improve it. And if everyone did that the world would be a much less tragic and unhappy place. Maybe it would even be a self-evidently good place. And perhaps you learn how to make good use of your time away from family and work— your leisure—and you make that meaningful and productive. And that is the *fourth* of the four achievements—and one, like the others, that can grow. Perhaps you get better and better at such things so that you can work on solving more and more difficult problems, and become a credit, in your own way, to the spirit of humanity itself. And that is life.

Back to marriage. How do you plan and diligently maintain the romance in your relationship? Well, you have to decide: "Do you want some romance in your life or not?" If you really think about it, without resentment—without the joy of depriving your partner, now alienated, of the pleasure that might come with such an attempt—the answer is generally yes. Sexual romance: the adventure, pleasure, intimacy, and excitement people fantasize about experiencing, when they are feeling in need of a touch of the divine. You want that. The joys of life are rare and precious, and you do not want to forsake them without due cause. How are you going to accomplish that? With luck, it will happen between you and someone you like; with better luck, and sufficient commitment, it will happen between you and someone you love. Little about this is easy. If you set up a household with someone, you are going to have to do an awful lot of negotiation to keep both "like" and "love" alive.

## THE DOMESTIC ECONOMY

Here are some practical considerations. They may seem far from the topic of romance. The discussion is necessary, however, because we transcended—or lost—our traditional roles, and have not formulated replacements for them. Before that—perhaps before the invention of the birth control pill, which was a biological revolution—men did male things, whatever they were, and women did female things, whatever they were. Traditional roles are far more helpful than modern people, who vastly overestimate their tolerance for freedom and choice, tend to realize. In a less rapidly mutable society, everyone has some sense of their respective duties. That does not eliminate the tension (nothing eliminates the tension), but at least there is a template. If there is no template for what either of you should be doing when you live together with someone, then you are required to argue about it—or negotiate about it, if you are good at that, which you are probably not. Few people are.

If you are going to set up a household in peace with someone you love and hopefully like, and wish to continue loving and liking, you are going to have to determine in some manner who is going to do what. That is the replacement for roles. Who makes the bed? When should it be made? At what level of perfection does the bed have to be made to be mutually acceptable? And if this is not handled well, the conversation becomes counterproductive rapidly: "I made the bed." "Well, you did not do a very good job." "Nothing's ever good enough for you. If you do not think I did a good enough job making the bed, maybe I will just stop, and you can make it yourself!" "Well, maybe you should raise your standards a bit, and maybe not just about the bed!" It is going to take days to sort that out—if it ever does get sorted out—and that is just the bed. That is just the first ten minutes of the morning. So maybe it remains unmade or made badly and bitterly for the next sixty years (there is that time span again), and there are many more domestic issues to address than just the bed. But if that is not sorted out, then it is a problem every morning of every day and every day of every week and month and year and everyone is angry at least under the surface as soon as they awaken or every time they enter the bedroom and other things begin to fall out of order. There is nothing good about that.

Whose career is going to take priority? When and why? How will the children be educated and disciplined, and by whom? Who does the cleaning? Who sets the table? Takes out the garbage? Cleans up the bathroom? How are the bank accounts set up and managed? Who shops for groceries? Clothes? Furniture? Who pays for what? Who adopts responsibility for the taxes? Et cetera, et cetera, et cetera. Two hundred things, perhaps, to run a household properly—as complex a problem as running a business, with the additional difficulty of trying to manage it with a family member, much of it repeated daily. Your life is, after all, mostly composed of what is repeated routinely. You either negotiate responsibility for every single one of these duties or you play push and pull forever, while you battle it out nonverbally, with stubbornness, silence, and half-hearted attempts at "cooperation." That is not going to do your romantic situation any good. It is of vital necessity, in consequence, to place the domestic part of the household economy on firm ground.

It is an incredibly difficult set of problems to solve, because it means you must consciously sort the hierarchy of responsibilities between the partners in the household. You are required to negotiate every damned and apparently trivial detail (but the apparent triviality is a delusion): Who prepares the meals? When do they prepare the meals? What is that worth in terms of trade-off for other tasks? How do you thank someone for conducting themselves properly in the kitchen? Who loads the dishwasher? Who does the dishes? How fast do the dishes have to be cleared off the table after you eat? Which dishes are going to be used? What are we going to eat? What role are the kids going to play? Do we sit down together? Do we have regular mealtimes? Each of these questions can become a bloody war. One person thinks one thing, and the other person thinks another thing, and who knows who's right? So, you have to have a struggle with it, and you have to come to a consensus. Doing so is difficult. Maybe it means hundreds of fights. It certainly means dozens. But they are fights with a purpose, and that purpose is to fight it out until a solution arises, so that fights about that issue are no longer necessary. That makes peace the goal, and it cannot be established except through negotiation, and that requires a commitment strong enough to withstand serious and deep conflict.

The next thing you have to do—I know this from both my clinical and marital experience (thirty years of each)—is actually talk to your partner for about ninety minutes a week, purely about practical and personal matters. "What is happening to you at work?" "What is going on, as far as you are concerned, with the kids?" "What needs to be done around the house?" "Is there anything bothering you that we can address?" "What do we have to do that is necessary to keep the wolf from the door next week?" Just pure, practical communication: partly because you have a story, your partner has a story, and you have a joint story. To know your story, you must tell it, and, for your partner to know it, he or she must hear it. It is necessary for that communication to happen on an ongoing basis. It does not have to be ninety minutes all at once. Maybe it can be fifteen minutes a day. But you keep those lines of pragmatic communication open, so you know where the other person is, and vice versa. If you dip below ninety minutes a week, you generate a backlog, and your mutual story begins to unwind. At some point, that backlog is so large that you do not know who you are yourself, and you certainly do not know who your partner is, and you become mutually alienated. Your relationship loses its coherence. That is a bad situation.

When I am helping someone straighten out their marriage, let us say, we do very mundane things. I am not interested in vacations, special occasions, or anything that happens that is out of the ordinary. It is not that those things are unimportant, but they are not vital in the same sense that daily routines are vital. It is the latter that must be set right. I want to know what interrelationships constitute the bulk of your typical day. You wake up together, perhaps; you eat together. You do such things every day. Maybe waking up, preparing for the day, and eating make up five hours a day. That is a third of your waking time and, therefore, a third of your life. It is thirty-five hours every seven days—a whole workweek; an entire career. Get it right. Ask yourself and each other: How do we want these times to be structured? How can we make the morning awakening pleasant? Can we attend to each other politely and with interest and perhaps without electronic distractions while we eat? Could we make our meals delicious and the atmosphere welcoming? Consider coming home in the evening. Let us say that routine takes ten minutes. So that is another hour plus per week; fifty hours a year—one and a half workweeks. You spend one and a half workweeks a year being greeted as you come in the door. It is a sizable fraction of your existence. Does somebody meet you at the door and indicate a certain degree of happiness to see you, or are you ignored because everyone is using their smartphones, or met with a litany of complaints? How would you like to organize that, so you do not dread the moment you arrive at home? There are things you do together that are mundane things; those things you do every day. But they are your whole life. You get those things right and you have established yourself much more effectively than you might realize. If you can successfully fight the war that establishes harmony in the domestic economy, you have both won a major victory. And then you can concentrate on what might happen during a romantic vacation to a boutique hotel, or your parents' cottage, or an all-inclusive resort, or an adventure holiday—or just during that twice-weekly date we discussed earlier that you are both so reluctant to attempt.

Start by getting these things straight, and see what happens. Then you will have peaceful mealtimes, for example, and you will not die of frustration or high blood pressure. You will have to fight for such an accomplishment. What matters, however, is not whether you fight (because you have to fight), but whether you make peace as a consequence. To make peace is to manage a negotiated solution. And you want and need to come to a negotiated solution about every responsibility and opportunity you share as a couple—and about every obstacle you encounter. At least then you will have someone to talk things through with when your life gets complex, as it inevitably will. And you have the advantage of two heads, even though they will not see eye to eye. What all this means is that the problems of knowing what you want and discussing it with your partner must be solved before the romance in your relationship can be maintained.

Other people keep you sane. That is partly why it is a good idea to get married. Why? Well, you are half insane, and so is your spouse (well, maybe not half—but plenty). Hopefully, however, it is not generally the same half. Now and then you meet couples who have the same weakness, and they compound that failing in each other. Maybe they are both too fond of wine, for example, and they drift together toward alcoholism. What you might want, to avoid such a fate, is that one person in the couple is fond of alcohol, but not both. This will cause a certain amount of short-term conflict, in situations where drinking is occurring or likely to occur, but the long-term consequences (avoiding either of you becoming an alcoholic) are likely to be beneficial. The one who does not drink will have a drink or two on a social occasion, just to avoid being too rigid and horrible, and the one who likes to drink will get what is hopefully a salutary reprimand if he or she does not exercise proper control.

It is a fortunate happenstance, generally speaking, that your idiosyncrasies are likely to be somewhat randomly distributed, and that if you unite with someone else you are likely to find some strength where you are weak and vice versa. When you unite the two of you to recreate that original being—that is the symbolic idea—then you have a chance of producing one reasonable, sane being. That is good for you both, even better for your children (who now have a fighting chance of adapting to what constitutes generally sane behavior), and it is good for friendship and the broader world, too.

A lot of that movement toward functional unity is a consequence of dialogue and communication. If you are old enough, you know that people are badly broken. When you are young and not very experienced, you are likely to make two assumptions, in a rather unquestioning and implicit manner, that are simply not true. The first is that there is someone out there who is perfect. You are likely even to encounter this hypothetically perfect person, whom you view through your delusion, and to fall desperately and foolishly in love with them (foolishly because you are in love with your projection of perfection, rather than the person—which is very confusing to the target of your affection). The second assumption is that there is someone out there who is perfect *for you*. From these assumptions, you are making at least three errors, which is quite an accomplishment, given you have made only two assumptions.

To begin with, there is not anyone out there who is perfect. There are just people out there who are damaged—quite severely, although not always irreparably, and with a fair bit of individual idiosyncrasy. Apart from that, if there was someone out there who was perfect, they would take one look at you and run away screaming. Unless you are deceiving someone, why would you end up with anyone better than you? You should be truly terrified if you have been accepted as a date. A sensible person would think of their new potential romantic partner: "Oh, my God! You are either blind, desperate, or as damaged as me!" That is a horrifying idea—signing up with someone who is as at least as much trouble as you. It is by no means as bad as being alone with yourself, but it is still out of the frying pan and into the fire—and at least the fire might transform you. Thus, you get married, if you have any courage—if you have any long-term vision and ability to vow and adopt responsibility; if you have any maturity—and you start to transform the two of you into one reasonable person. And it is even the case that participating in such a dubious process makes the two of you into one reasonable person with the possibility of some growth. So, you talk. About everything. No matter how painful. And you make peace. And you thank providence if you manage it, because strife is the default condition.

## FINALLY: ROMANCE

There was not much point in this chapter in talking about romance immediately—at least not about its maintenance. Romance is play, and play does not take place easily when problems of any sort arise. Play requires peace, and peace requires negotiation. And you are lucky even then if you get to play.

The issue of marital romance—intimacy and sex—is a complex one, with a dragon lurking under every question. For example: What do you owe each other sexually if you are entangled in a marriage? The answer is not "no sex." That is not the answer, because part of the contractual arrangement is to organize your romantic life in a mutually satisfactory manner. It is an implicit precondition for the stability of the marriage. It is probably not sex fifteen times a day, and it is probably not sex begrudgingly once a year. It is somewhere between extremes, and that is where you must begin to negotiate.

My observation has been that the typical adult couple—when they have a job, children, and the domestic economy we just discussed, and all that worry and responsibility and concern—might manage once or twice a week, or even three times a week (not likely), for a reasonable romantic interlude. That frequency, if handled well, seems to work out acceptably for both partners. I have observed that twice is better than once, but once is much better than zero. Zero is bad. If you go to zero, then one of you is tyrannizing the other, and the other is submitting. If you go to zero, then one of you is going to have an affair—physical, emotional, fantastical, or some combination of the three. I do not say that lightly. Something has to give, and there has to be a *no* there, somewhere, when the romance disappears and the frequency of sexual intimacy hits rock bottom; there has to be a strong indication that "that is not good enough." I am not recommending the affair, but that is what you are setting yourself up for if your sex life vanishes. Maybe you want to take that pathway and facilitate the affair because you want to play the martyr: "My wife left me to have an affair, and poor me." And why did she do such a thing? "Well, perhaps our sex life was not all it could have been" (and this is an answer that may require a fair bit of digging). "What exactly do you mean by 'was not all it could have been'?" "Well, we had not made love for two years, and she went and had an affair."

That is not a shock. You should begin by assuming that your partner is a relatively normal human being, and that there is a certain amount of sexual satisfaction that is a reasonable requirement—let us say twice a week, or once a week, under conditions of intense busyness. In the early days of marriage it might be no problem to express romantic interest in your partner, but there is so much that must be done to live. Dating is a pain, even if you are single. I am perfectly aware that there is adventure there, too, but a lot of that occurs in movies, and not on internet dating sites, in text exchanges, coffee shops, restaurants, and bars, where the first awkward encounters occur.

You really have to work at it, and you will, if you are single, because you are lonesome, starved for attention, and desperate for physical intimacy. (Single people have far less sex, on average, than married people, although I suppose that a small percentage are making out like bandits. But I cannot see that even those successful in that manner are doing themselves any favors.)

So, as a single person, you will work at dating, because you are lonesome and deprived, but it is no simple matter. You must make space in your life for it. You have to plan. You must use your imagination, spend money, find an acceptable dating partner, and, as they say, kiss a lot of frogs to find a prince (or to find a princess, as well). People are often relieved when they get married, because they do not have to make all that so often counterproductive effort anymore. But that does not at all mean that you are now off the hook; that you can just lay back in your worn white underwear and socks and assume that all the hypothetical pleasures of Hugh Hefner are going to automatically manifest themselves in your household. There is still plenty of effort required, unless you want the romance to vanish. You have to talk about it. You have to have the difficult and embarrassing conversation: "What is it going be, dear? Tuesday and Thursday? Wednesday and Friday? Monday and Saturday?" You think, "Oh, God. That is so cut and dried. That is so mundane and planned. That is so scheduled, predictable, bourgeois, antiromantic, and robotic. It is demeaning and constricting, and it just turns sex into a duty. Where is the fun? Where is the spontaneity, the light jazz, cocktails, and excitement of sudden unexpected attraction? Where is the tuxedo and the little black dress?" That is what you expect? Even unconsciously, in your foolish fantasies? How often did you manage that when you were dating? Ever? And (remember, we are adults talking here) you want two jobs (two careers, two incomes), two kids, a reasonable standard of living—and spontaneity? And you are not about to "settle" for anything less?

Good luck with that. It is not going to happen—not in my clinical (and personal) experience—not without a lot of effort. What will happen is that the absolute necessities of life will inexorably start to take priority over the desirable necessities. Maybe there is a list of ten things you will do in a day, and sex is number eleven. It is not that you do not think sex is important, but you do not ever get past number five on the list of ten. You must make space and time, and, as far as I can tell, you have to do it consciously. You might think, "What would it be like to spend some time with this person I was once romantically attracted to?" You have to think that through. Maybe you only have time to watch half an hour of a TV show before you hop into bed. Maybe you have an hour and a half, or an hour, because life is too hectic. It would not be too bad an idea to have a shower. A little lipstick—that could be good. Some perfume. Some clothing that is attractive and erotic. Buy some lingerie for your wife, if you are a man, and wear it, with some courage, if you are a woman. Maybe you, if you are a man, can find something to wear that is reasonably sexy in a men's shop or a place that sells erotic clothing that is not too extreme and does not scream of poor taste and produce intense and counterproductive self-consciousness. And a compliment or two when all that courage is manifested is not such a bad idea. Maybe each time it happens for a year. You are trying to build some confidence. Try some nice soft lighting—maybe some candles (and someone has to buy the candles, and should be encouraged to do so; and the cynicism should be kept to an absolute minimum, if you do not want to banish what is fragile out of existence altogether). Here is a rule: do not ever punish your partner for doing something you want them to continue doing. Particularly if it took some real courage—some real going above and beyond the call of duty—to manage.

How about trying to set up the whole situation in the romantic manner that you might imagine, if you were imagining having an affair, because that is the sort of thing that people imagine when they imagine an affair (if they have any imagination). Try having an affair with your wife or husband. Maybe the latter can set up the bedroom while the former is preparing in the bathroom. We already mentioned candles. How about some music? How about making sure that the room is clean and—God willing—aesthetically attractive? That might be a start. And maybe, the two you of will not get old and fat, unhealthy and hypochondriacal as fast as possible just to spite each other, which many couples certainly do. And then, maybe, you could both have what you need, and maybe even what you want. But you would have to admit your desires, and you would have to negotiate with your partner. What do you like? What does she like? And are you going to let each other know? Are you going to risk practicing badly? Are you going to learn some new tricks, even if you feel like a fool when you first try?

None of this is easy. People will do things with or to each other that they will not talk about with each other, which is not helpful if they are married. It could be, maybe, if you were in a trading mood and approaching this with goodwill, that you could decide what you need and want, and arrange exactly the right trade. You might ask yourself, "Look, how do I have to set this up so I am likely to continue being romantically interested in my wife or my husband for the next twenty years, so that I do not wander off and do something stupid, like so many people do? What is my minimal precondition for erotic satisfaction?" You might try to convince yourself that it is not necessary; that you can put up with what you have, even if it is nothing. But you cannot. Not if you have any self-respect or sense. There is something that you are going to want and need. It is possible that, if you communicate openly what that something is, and at the same time leave yourself open to the same communication coming from your partner, that you both could get not only what you want from each other, but even more than you expect.

Arrange some dates, and then practice making those dates and going on them until you are expert at it. Negotiate, and practice that, too. Allow yourself to become aware of what you want and need, and have the decency to let your partner in on the secret. After all, who else are you going to tell? Devote yourself to the higher ideal upon which an honest and courageous relationship is necessarily dependent, and do that with the seriousness that will keep your soul intact. Maintain your marital vows, so that you are desperate enough to negotiate honestly. Do not let your partner brush you off with protestations of ignorance or refusal to communicate. Do not be naive, and do not expect the beauty of love to maintain itself without all-out effort on your part. Distribute the requirements of your household in a manner you both find acceptable, and do not tyrannize or subject yourself to slavery. Decide what you need to keep yourself satisfied both in bed and out of it. And maybe—just maybe—you will maintain the love of your life and you will have a friend and confidant, and this cold rock we live on at the far end of the cosmos will be a little warmer and more comforting than it would otherwise be. And you are going to need that, because rough times are always on their way, and you better have something to set against them or despair will visit and will not depart.

Plan and work diligently to maintain the romance in your relationship.

---

# DO NOT ALLOW YOURSELF TO BECOME RESENTFUL, DECEITFUL, OR ARROGANT

## THE STORY IS THE THING

You have your reasons for being resentful, deceitful, and arrogant. You face, or will face, terrible, chaotic forces, and you will sometimes be outmatched. Anxiety, doubt, shame, pain, and illness, the agony of conscience, the soul-shattering pit of grief, dashed dreams and disappointment, the reality of betrayal, subjection to the tyranny of social being, and the ignominy of aging unto death—how could you not degenerate, and rage, and sin, and come to hate even hope itself? I want you to know how you might resist that decline, that degeneration into evil. To do so—to understand your own personality and its temptation by darkness—you need to know what you are up against. You need to understand your motivations for evil—and the triad of resentment, deceit, and arrogance is as good a decomposition of what constitutes evil as I have been able to formulate.

Is it possible to understand the world in a manner that provides

protection against the temptation to traverse that lowest of roads? It
is an axiom of human wisdom that clearer formulation and deeper
comprehension of a problem is salutary. We will begin just that attempt with a conceptual shift—one that is difficult and perplexing for
the committed materialists we moderns are. First, a question: *What is
the world made of?* To answer this, we will need to consider reality—the
world—as it is fully experienced by someone alive and awake, with all
the richness of subjective being left intact—dreams, sensory experiences, feelings, drives, and fantasies. This is the world that manifests
itself to—or, better, that you meet head-on with—your unique individual consciousness.

Consider the act of awakening in the morning. If you were asked
what you perceive, at that moment, you might well mention the same
concrete objects that anyone else might see, if they woke up in bed
beside you. You might describe all that you have gathered around you
in your bedroom—the desk, the chairs, the clothes (messy or neatly
arrayed, depending on your temperament and preference and, perhaps, your condition last night). You are likely to answer in this very
objective, realistic manner, claiming, essentially, to see the furniture
of the stage. There is, of course, some truth to your answer, although
you may pay less attention to the familiar things around you than you
think. Why waste time and energy perceiving what you can simply
remember?

However, the furniture and other contents of your bedroom are *not*
truly what you perceive when you first wake up. You are already familiar with the place where you sleep, and what it contains. There is
no reason to continue to effortfully and consciously apprehend what
you already understand. Instead, you are liable to perceive your surroundings *psychologically*. You begin to consider how you are going to
conduct yourself on the stage you will inevitably occupy, and what is

going to happen in consequence. What you see upon waking is an array of possibilities, many of them concerning the day at hand, and others associated with the weeks, months, and years to come. What you are truly concerned with upon waking is the answer to a question: "What shall I make of the possibilities that I see in play in front of me, complex, worrisome, exciting, dull, restricted, unlimited, fortunate, or catastrophic as they may be?"

Out there in the potential is everything you could have. It is the realm of unrealized possibility, and no one knows its full extent. There appears to be no limit, in principle, to what can be made from what has not yet manifested itself. Everything that might yet be makes its home there. You could well consider what remains to be encountered as an eternal treasure house—a horn of plenty (which are in fact two of its representations). But that is only half the story (and there is the rub). If the potential you confront manifests improperly (because of a mistake on your part; because of the sheer arbitrariness of the world), then you can find yourself in terrible trouble. Out there, in the unknown—in the future, which is what you truly contend with, when your consciousness reawakens—awaits everything good, but also everything terrible, painful, hellish, and deadly. Whatever *potential* might be, therefore, it does not follow the simple rules of material logic. Objects that play by the rules of the game we consider real (when we assume that what is real is also logical) can only be one thing at a time, and certainly not themselves and their opposite, simultaneously. Potential, however, is not like that. It is not categorizable in that manner. It is tragedy, comedy, good and evil, and everything in between at the same time. It is also not tangible, in the sense that the things we consider must be tangible. It does not even exist—except as *what could be* exists. Perhaps it is best considered as the structure of reality, before reality manifests itself concretely in the present, where reality appears to most self-evidently exist. But creatures such as us do not contend with the present. It may therefore be that it is not the present that is most real—at least as far as our consciousness is concerned. We have to fight to "be here now," the advice of the sages. Left to our own devices, we turn our minds instead to investigating the future: *What could be?* Attempting to answer that question—that is life. That is the true encounter with reality. *What is?* That is the dead past, already accomplished. *What could be?* That is the emergence of new being, new adventure, brought about by the conjunction of living consciousness with the great expanse of paradoxical possibility.

And if it is possibility that is most real, rather than actuality (as evidenced by the fact that it is possibility we are destined to contend with), then it is the investigation into possibility that is the most important of all investigations. But how do we investigate something that is not here, or there, or anywhere? How do we examine what has not yet manifested itself; explore what only could be but is not yet? And how can we possibly communicate with each other intelligibly about that attempt, trade information about the most effective conceptualizations, approaches, and strategies? The answer to that, as far as I can tell, is by communicating through stories about what is and, equally, what could be. And what that implies is that if possibility is the ultimate element of reality with which we contend, then it is stories that hold the wisdom that we most need to know.

We naturally think of our lives as stories, and communicate about our experience in that same manner. We tell people automatically where we are (to set the stage) and where we are going, so that we can create the present out of the possibility that springs forth as we journey toward our destination. No one finds such an account out of the ordinary. But we are doing more than portraying our lives, and those of others, as a sequence of events. It is something deeper than that.

When you depict a person's actions in the world, you describe how they perceive, evaluate, think, and act—and, when you do so, a story unfolds (and the better you are at such descriptions, the more storylike your accounts are). Furthermore, we experience the world as populated by figures that represent exactly what we must contend with. The unknown, unexpected, and novel—the world of possibility—is represented in dramatic form, as is the world that we expect and strive to bring into being, and ourselves, as actors faced with the unknown and the predictable alike. We use the story to represent all of this.

Could it be that we communicate in stories (and everyone else understands them) because what everyone is doing in the world *is* fundamentally a story? Could that mean that the world of experience is, in truth, indistinguishable from a story—that it cannot be represented in a manner more accurate than that of the story? We are, in principle, adapted to the world—adapted to its realities. Thus, if we naturally construe the world as a story, then perhaps the world is most accurately, or at least most practically, construed as a story (and *accurate* and *practical* are not so easy to distinguish). You might argue, contrarily, that the scientific view of the world is more accurate, in some sense, and that the scientific view is not fundamentally a story. But, as far as I can tell, it is still *nested inside* a story: one that goes something like "careful and unbiased pursuit of the truth will make the world a better place for all people, reducing suffering, extending life, and producing wealth." Why practice science otherwise? Why would anyone take on the difficulties and rigors of scientific training without that motivation? There are more effective ways of making money, for example, if you have the intelligence and discipline to become a genuine researcher. And in terms of intrinsic motivation, the love of science is not precisely disinterested learning. The great experimenters and scientific writers I have known are passionate about their pursuit. Something emotional drives them.

They hope that their learning (disinterested though it may be, as at present it has no specific aim except that of learning) will have some genuinely positive outcome: making the world a better place. That provides the entire pursuit with a narrative element, the motive that accompanies any good plot, and the transformation of character that makes up the best of stories.

We conceptualize what we experience as a story. That story is, roughly speaking, the description of the place we are at right now, as well as the place that we are going to, the strategies and adventures that we implement and experience along the way, and our downfalls and reconstitutions during that journey. You perceive and act inside a structure like that all the time, because you are always somewhere, going somewhere else, and you are always evaluating where you are and what is going on in relation to your goal. Part of this thinking in stories is our tendency to see the world as a selection of characters, each of which represents either where we are or are going, the unexpected occurrences we may encounter, or ourselves as actors. We see animated intent everywhere[1]—and we certainly present the world that way to our children. That is why Thomas the Tank Engine has a face and a smile, and the sun has a face and a smile. That is why—even among adults—there is a man in the moon, and deities scattered across the stars. Everything is animated. That is a reflection of our proclivity to treat things as if they are personalities with intent, regardless of what they are, regardless of whether they are animate or inanimate. That is why it is okay with you that your car has a face (on the front, where faces belong), which it most certainly does.

We act (perceive, think, react) that way because each member of the human species does almost everything he or she does in the presence, for better or worse, of other people. And that has been the case forever. Virtually everything we encountered in the long biological rise to our current form was social. If we were not interacting with people, then it was with animals. Maybe we were hunting them, or herding them, or playing with them, once they had been domesticated—or maybe they were hunting us, and we had to understand them to escape them or defend ourselves. All that tribal, intertribal, and cross-species interaction molded our brains, shaped our fundamental categories, rendering them social, not objective—not like the categories of science. It is not as if we are born with an instinct for the periodic table of the elements. No. We only managed to get that straight a few hundred years ago, and it took a lot of conscious time and effort to formulate. Furthermore, even though it was other people who did the terribly hard work necessary to establish that remarkable chemical category system, it is difficult to learn. It is not that interesting, intrinsically (at least for most people), because there is no story associated with it. It is an accurate and useful representation of the objective reality of what is, beyond the shadow of a doubt, but it is a struggle to master perception of that abstracted sort.

Conversely, if someone is telling you a story, it attracts your attention immediately. It can be a complicated and cognitively difficult story—something requiring hours of concentration. It might even be the story of how the periodic table of the elements was discovered, and the triumphs and difficulties that accompanied the process. It does not matter. If it is well told, it is gripping, and likely to be remembered. If you want to teach a child something and get them to attend, tell them a story. They will repeatedly ask you to do that. They do not grab your pant leg and beg, "Dad, one more line from the periodic table of the elements before bed!" But they are highly motivated to hear a story—sometimes even the same one every night. That is an indication of the depth and importance of stories. You might think the story is simple, but your child, listening intently, is processing the multiple levels of meaning represented in any decent tale—meanings of which you are very unlikely to be aware, if the story you are telling is traditional and deep.

We are all human. That means there is something about our experience that is the same. Otherwise, we would not all be human. We would not even be able to communicate. To communicate, paradoxically, there must be things about you and others that can go without saying. Imagine telling someone, "I got really angry this morning." If there is any indication you want the conversation to continue and they are agreeable, they might ask you why; but they are not likely to ask you, "What do you mean, 'angry'?" They do not ask the latter question because they already know, from their own experience, what "angry" means. It can be assumed, rather than explained. In fact, the only reason you can talk about anything at all is because there are some things you do not ever have to talk about. You can just take them for granted. We know, worldwide, for example, that there are basic sets of emotions shared by all humans—and by many animals.[2] Everyone understands a growling mother bear standing in front of her cubs, teeth bared for all to see. It is those things that you do not have to talk about that most precisely make us human, that constitute the essence, mutable though it remains through the actions of society and environment.

So, on to the story—to the story of the story, in fact. We will begin by meeting the characters whose existence universally structures our understanding of the potential of the world. And, with luck, as you meet them, you will begin to understand their relationship to resentment, arrogance, and deceit well enough so that understanding will offer you some protection.

# THE ETERNAL CHARACTERS
# OF THE HUMAN DRAMA

## THE DRAGON OF CHAOS

When my son, Julian, was about four years old, he watched the movie *Pinocchio* obsessively—particularly the sequence that portrays the whale, Monstro, transforming into a fire-breathing dragon. He must have seen it fifty times. And it was not obvious that he enjoyed it. He was clearly afraid of the climactic scene. I could see it on his face. He had good reason for his fear. The characters he had come to identify with had laid it all on the line. There was a strong motif of danger and sacrifice. Nonetheless, it was the scene that fascinated him the most.

What in the world was he doing, watching the film repeatedly? Particularly if the emotion it produced was fear? Why would a child voluntarily subject himself to that? Julian was using all the faculties of his newly forming mind, rational and unconscious alike, to process the relationships in such a tale. *Pinocchio* and tales like it are dense, layered, and complex in ways that seize the imagination of children and will not let go. That is not accidental. Kids are small and young and, in some ways, they do not know anything, because they have very little personal experience. But they are also very ancient creatures, in another manner, and by no means stupid or inattentive. The fact that they are gripped by fairy tales and stories like *Pinocchio* is an indication of just how much depth children perceive in those stories, even if you, as an adult observer, do not notice it anymore.

That whale is the Dragon of Chaos. This is the symbolic representation of potential, of possibility, for better and for worse. Representations of this figure appear everywhere, and children see them, even if they have no idea what those figures mean. In the Disney classic *Sleeping*

*Beauty*, for example, the Evil Queen, Maleficent, entraps Prince Phillip. She chains him in her castle dungeon and tells him a charming fairy tale of sorts. She delights in describing to him the ruined and ancient man he will be, six or seven decades in the future, when she deigns to release him from his cell. She portrays him as nothing but the parody of a hero, and has a fine time doing so, locking the door to his prison cell on her departure, climbing the stairs back to her palace, laughing evilly all the while. She is the classic devouring Oedipal mother, preventing her son from manifesting his destiny by refusing to allow him to leave home.

The prince escapes from the dungeon, with the help of the positive feminine: three helpful fairies, who are clearly the mythical counterparts to Maleficent. The Evil Queen sees him mount his horse and make his dangerous way through her army, across her crumbling, quickly closing drawbridges, and down the road leading outside the would-be death trap of her castle. With ever-increasing dismay, she leaps from turret to turret, until she makes her way to the uppermost place. There she stands, enraged, calling up the fires of hell themselves, and transforms herself into a gigantic, fire-breathing dragon. Everyone viewing the movie accepts that as a given: "Of course the Evil Queen turns into a dragon. There is no problem with that." Why, exactly, is that universally acceptable? On the face of it, the transformation makes no sense at all. One moment, she is standing, a perfectly understandable although exceedingly irritated Evil Queen. Next, she spins around a few times and—poof!—she is a gigantic fire-breathing reptile. Perhaps you are all thinking as you read this, "Why are you making an issue of this? Even my four-year-old understands that!" I do not have a problem with an Evil Queen turning into a dragon. It is so self-evident that it can happen even in the middle of a popular movie and be accepted at face value—so self-evident that it is very difficult to draw people's attention to the idea that something very strange has happened.

However, if Queen Elizabeth II suddenly turned into a giant fire-breathing lizard in the midst of one of her endless galas, a certain amount of consternation would be both appropriate and expected. People—even monarchs of a great kingdom—do not just transform into dangerous reptiles and attack their guests (well, not at most parties). But if it happens within the context of a story, then we accept it. That does not explain the mystery, however. Not just any old transformation can happen within a story. It would not have made any sense if Maleficent had donned a sparkly pink outfit and begun to cast roses on the pathway Prince Phillip galloped down to escape his confinement. That was not in Maleficent's nature, nor in the set of narrative expectations that every audience implicitly brings to every movie (and is unlikely to appreciate having disrupted, unless done with exceptional finesse and higher-order purpose). But it is no problem for her to become a dragon. Why? It is partly because nature can and constantly does revert from her dangerous but still understandable guise into total chaos. This happens, for example, when the campfire we just built to cook our hot dogs and sit around singing campfire songs catches a sudden gust of hot, dry air and the long-parched forest hypothetically sheltering our tents ignites into a raging inferno. Dangers we can handle can suddenly turn themselves into dangers we cannot handle. That is why it is no surprise to anyone when the Evil Queen becomes the Dragon of Chaos.

Imagine, for a moment, that you are a prehistoric protohuman being. You are camped for the night, and that site is defined territory—safety and predictability, for the time. Your friends are there, your tribal kin. You have your spears. You have your fire. It is safe—or at least what passes for safe under such conditions. But if you carelessly wander a

mere two hundred feet away from the campfire, then something horrible with teeth and scales eats you. That is what is out there in the
terrible unknown. That idea is deeply embedded inside of us. We
know that human beings are innately afraid of reptilian predators, for
example—and that there is good reason for that. It is not merely that
we are prepared to learn fear of them (which we certainly are): the fear
itself is innate.[3] For all intents and purposes, there is an image that exists inside of us of the terrible hunter that lurks in the night. That is
why children become afraid of the dark once they are old enough to
move around by themselves.[4] "There is a monster in the dark, Dad!"
they insist, at nighttime. And Dad assures his son or daughter that
there is no such thing as a monster. Well, the adult is wrong, and the
child is exactly right. There might not be a monster in that particular
section of the dark, right now, but that is of small comfort when you
are three feet high and tasty, and there could be—will be—a monster
there in the future. That is why it might be of more use to let your
child know directly and through your own actions that there is always
something sinister and dangerous in the dark, and that it is the job of
the well-prepared individual to confront it and take the treasure it
archetypally guards. It is something that an adult and child can act out
with great results.

About a year and a half before his encounter with Pinocchio, I took
Julian to the Boston Science Museum. There was a Tyrannosaurus rex
skeleton there. It was impressively large, as far as I was concerned. But
it was even larger, from his perspective. He would not get closer than
100 feet. At 150 feet, his curiosity drove him forward. But things came
to a stop when we got closer. That was a neurological phenomenon,
too. His curiosity drove him forward, toward the monster, so he could
collect some useful information—until the fear froze him. I could see
exactly where that boundary lay. Maybe it defined how far away he

would need to be to remain safe if that thing suddenly whipped its head around to grab him.

There is an idea embedded deep within the human psyche that potential can be a place of maximal horror, home to an infinite predator—or an infinite variety of predators. Practically speaking, it is true, as human beings have been prey animals since the beginning of time, although we made it very difficult for the predators once we effectively armed and banded together. (Personally, I am happy about that. I have camped where the grizzly bears were plentiful. It is nice that they are on the planet and all that, but I prefer my grizzlies shy, not too hungry, and far enough away to be picturesque.) But there are spiritual and psychological forces operating in a predatory manner that can destroy you, as well—and they can present an even greater danger. The malevolence in the heart of people that makes them criminal falls into that category, as does the evil that drives the totalitarian war of revenge, rapine, greed, or sheer love of blood and destruction. And that malevolence also exists in your heart, and that is the greatest dragon of all—just as mastering that malevolence constitutes the greatest and unlikeliest of individual achievements.

You are built, neurologically, to interpret the world in this dramatic manner, at a very deep level. An ancient part of your brain known as the hypothalamus[5]—a small region, sitting atop the spinal cord— regulates many of the fundamental responses that find their expression in the conceptualization of danger and potential. One of its two modules is responsible for self-preservation (hunger, thirst, and, most important for our purposes, defensive aggression in the face of threat) as well as reproduction (sexual arousal and basic sexual behavior). The second is responsible for exploration.* Half of the hypothalamus

---

*It is possible, in fact, to remove the entire brain of a female cat—to take a common

drives our use of what has been explored previously to quell and sat-
isfy the basic demands of life, including our capability to protect ourselves in the case of attack. The other half is always asking, What is out
there? What could it be used for? How might it be dangerous? What
are its habits? So, what is the story? Eat, drink, and be merry, until the
provisions run out—but watch out, always, for the monsters. Then
venture out into the dangerous but promising unknown world and discover what is there. Why? Well, you already know a lot of things you
need to know, although you do not know nearly enough. You understand that, because life is not as good as it could be, and because you
are going to die. Obviously, under such conditions, you should learn
more. So, you are driven to explore. The fundamental representation
of reality, as an eternal treasure house guarded by an eternal predator,
is therefore a perfect representation of the way you are wired to react
to the world at the most fundamental depths of your Being.

## NATURE: CREATION AND DESTRUCTION

We all have an image of nature. It might be an image akin to a beautiful landscape—nature as benevolent and renewing. It is an image of
that kind that grounds the sentimental environmentalist view of the
world. Being from Northern Alberta, I do not share exactly the same
view of nature, since up in my hometown of Fairview nature was constantly conspiring either to freeze its inhabitants to death for six
months of the year, and to devour them with insects for at least two

---

example from the scientific literature—excepting the hypothalamus and the spinal
cord, and the cat can still maintain itself in relative normality, as long as its environment
is reasonably constrained. Furthermore, it becomes hyperexploratory. That's truly staggering, in my estimation. Think about it: if you surgically remove 95 percent of a cat's
brain, it cannot stop exploring. You would think an essentially brainless cat would just
sit there, but that's not what happens. The curious part of its brain is still there.

more. So that is the less romantic part of nature, which is red in tooth and claw. That is the part of nature that is associated with injury, disease, death, insanity, and everything else that can and will befall you, as a biological creature, on the negative end of the continuum.

There is the potential of the future that has not yet been transformed into reality (represented, as we have seen, by the Dragon of Chaos). But then there is the nature you encounter directly in your life, and which cannot be considered absolutely unknown. There is the benevolence of nature: the fact that you are here, alive—and sometimes happy; the fact that there is delicious food to eat, and attractive, interesting people to interact with, and no shortage of fascinating things to see and do. There are amazing vistas of landscape. There is the beauty and immortality and immensity of the ocean. There is all the bountiful, wondrous element of natural Being. But there is also the absolute horror that goes along with that: destruction, disease, suffering, and death. Those two elements of experience exist side by side. It is even the case that the former could not exist without the latter: even within your own body, healthy as it may be, a very delicate balance between the death of every cell that has outlasted its utility and the new life that springs forward to replace it is a prerequisite for your continued existence.

Both these elements of existence manifest themselves in our imagination in personified form. One is the Evil Queen, the Goddess of Destruction and Death; the other is her positive counterpart, the Fairy Godmother, the benevolent monarch, the young and loving mother watching with infinite care over her helpless charge. To live properly, you need to be acquainted with both these figures. If you are a child, abused by your mother, familiar only with the Evil Queen, then you are damaged by the absence of love, stunted by lack of attention, and arbitrarily subject to fear and pain and aggression. That is no way to live, and it is very difficult to grow up functional and capable and void of distrust, hate, and the desire, say, for revenge. You need to find someone to act the part of the Benevolent Queen: a friend, a family member, a fictional character—or a part of your own psyche, motivated by knowing that your mistreatment is wrong, swearing to take any opportunity that comes your way to escape your misfortunate circumstances, leave them behind, and balance your life appropriately. Maybe the first step in this direction is to posit, despite your mistreatment, that you are in fact worthy of care; and the second step is to give it, where you can, despite receiving tragically little yourself.

If you understand the polarity of nature, its terror and benevolence, you recognize two fundamental elements of experience, permanent, eternal, and unavoidable, and you can begin to understand, for example, the profound pull toward sacrifice. It is a religious trope that sacrifices keep the gods happy, and coming to understand just who the unhappy gods are, so to speak, and just how terrible they are when they are unhappy is a genuine step toward wisdom—a genuine and humbling step. Modern people have a hard time understanding what sacrifice means, because they think, for example, of a burnt offering on an altar, which is an archaic way of acting out the idea. But we have no problem at all when we conceptualize sacrifice psychologically, because we all know you must forgo gratification in the present to keep the wolf from the door in the future. So, you offer something to the negative goddess, so that the positive one shows up. You train long, difficult hours to be a nurse or a physician or a social worker. That sacrificial attitude is in fact the great discovery of the future, conjoined with the ability to negotiate and bargain and cope with that future—abandon impulsive gratification; let go of something you need and want; obtain something valuable in the long run in consequence (and keep the horror at bay). You forgo the partying and the easy hours.

You immerse yourself, instead, in the difficulties of life. You do that so that fewer of those difficulties will manifest themselves—for yourself, employed gainfully as you will become, and for all the others you will help as the strength you developed through proper sacrifice makes itself manifest. We are always bargaining in that manner. We act out the belief that we can strike a bargain with the structure of reality. Strangely enough, we often can. If you are sensible, you do that all the time. You prepare for the worst. You prepare for the arrival of the Evil Queen. You do what you have to do, knowing about her existence, and you keep her at bay—in proportion to your wisdom and in accordance with your luck. And if you succeed, Benevolent Nature smiles upon you—until she does not. But at least you have some control over the situation. You are not a sitting duck, or a babe in the woods, or a rube at the amusement park—or at least no more so than you have to be.

Nature is chaos, too, because it is always wreaking havoc with culture, its existential opposite—and the next subject of our investigation. After all, as Robert Burns has it, "The best laid schemes o' Mice an' Men / Gang aft a-gley." And it is often nature in positive and negative guise that does precisely that. It is no easy matter to balance the fragility of life and the necessity for procreation (and all the uncertainty of pregnancy and birth and child-rearing) with the desire for certainty, predictability, and order. And this is to say nothing of death (and even cancer is, after all, just another form of life). But all that is not to say, ever, that chaos is of less value than order. There is nothing but sterility without unpredictability, even though a bit less unpredictability often seems eminently desirable.

This nature/chaos combination is often seen in pop culture representations. As we mentioned, in the Disney movie *Sleeping Beauty*, for example, there is an Evil Queen—just as there is in *The Little Mermaid* (Ursula), *Snow White* (Grimhilde), *One Hundred and One Dalmatians*

(Cruella de Vil), *Cinderella* (Lady Tremaine), *Tangled* (Mother Gothel), and *Alice in Wonderland* (the Queen of Hearts). She represents the harsh element of the natural world. The example of *Sleeping Beauty* is, once again, particularly germane. Remember what happens at the movie's opening. The king and queen have waited long, and are now desperate to have a baby. The blessing arrives; the baby is born and they call her Aurora, the dawn. They are all thrilled, and so is the whole kingdom—properly so, because new life has arrived. They plan a great christening party. It is a fine idea, but they fail to invite Maleficent, the Evil Queen, to the celebrations. And it is not ignorance that prevents them. They know of her existence, and they are well acquainted with her power. It is willful blindness, and it is a bad move. They desire to shield their new and precious daughter from the negative element of the world, instead of determining how to provide her with the strength and wisdom to prevail, despite the reality of the negative. All this does is keep Aurora naive and vulnerable. Maleficent shows up anyway, as she most certainly will, and there is a message in that: invite the Evil Queen to your child's life. If you fail to do so, your children will grow up weak and in need of protection, and the Evil Queen is going to make herself known no matter what steps you take to stop her. At the christening, in fact, not only does she arrive, well behaved but uninvited, but she offers a present (in the form of a curse): the death of Aurora at the age of sixteen, brought about by the prick of the spindle of a spinning wheel. And all that because she was not invited to celebrate the young princess's christening. Only because a compassionate and powerful guest intercedes—one of the three aforementioned fairies, representative of the positive feminine—is the curse transmuted from death into profound unconsciousness, a state barely less fatal.

That is what happens to those beauties, so to speak, who remain far too unawakened when they hit sixteen: They do not want to be conscious, because they have not developed the courage and ability to face the negative element of the natural world. Instead of being encouraged, they have been sheltered. And if you shelter young people, you destroy them. You did not invite the Evil Queen, even for short visits. What are your children going to do when she shows up in full force, if they are entirely unprepared? They are not going to want to live. They are going to long for unconsciousness. And it gets worse. If you overprotect your kids, you become the very thing from which you are trying to shelter them. Depriving them of their young lives' necessary adventures, you weaken their characters. You become the Destroying Agent itself—the very witch that devours their autonomous consciousness.

I had a client many years ago who was a real-life version of Sleeping Beauty. She was tall, blonde haired, razor thin (as the saying goes), and profoundly unhappy. She was enrolled in a local junior college, attempting to upgrade so that she could attend university. She came to see me because she did not want to live. She also did not want to die, really—at least not actively. Instead, she attempted to keep herself unconscious with the use of Valium and its variants, including sleeping pills, which she procured in sufficient quantities from her (several) physicians, who were no doubt overworked enough not to keep track of exactly what she was doing. She managed to keep herself asleep fifteen or sixteen hours a day. She was smart and literate, and showed me a philosophy essay she had written on the pointlessness not only of her life but life in general. She was unable to tolerate the responsibility, by all appearances, but also could not deal with the cruelty she saw everywhere around her. She was a vegan, for example, and that was directly associated with her acute physical terror of life. She was unable even to enter the aisles of a supermarket where meat was displayed. Where others saw the cuts they were going to prepare for their family, she saw rows of dead body parts. That vision only served to confirm her belief that life was, in essence, unbearable.

Her biological mother had died in childbirth, and she was raised by her father and her stepmother. The latter was a holy terror. I met her only once, in my office, during what would have ordinarily been a clinical session with her stepdaughter. She spent the entire hour actively tearing strips off me: first for being of little use as a clinician, and second for "no doubt" blaming everything that was wrong with my client on her (step)mothering. I do not think I got more than a dozen words in edgewise. It was a remarkable performance, brought on, I believe, by my insistence that the phone calls she made two or three times a day to my client while the latter was away at school—some of which I heard in recordings—had to be reduced by a factor of ten, and certainly needed to be more pleasant. I am not saying and did not believe then that all this was the stepmother's fault. I am sure she had her reasons to be frustrated. Her stepdaughter was not fully engaged in life, by any means, and was an expensive four underperforming years into what should have been a two-year certificate. But it was clear that thrice-daily phone calls consisting mostly of anger and insults were not adding to my client's desire to be alive. I suggested that weekly phone calls should become the norm, and encouraged her to hang up if the conversation took a wicked turn. She started to put that into practice, and I presumed all that contributed to her stepmother's demand to meet and confront me.

Sleeping Beauty described her childhood as idyllic. She said that she lived the life of a fairy-tale princess; an only child, the darling of both parents. But that all changed when she hit adolescence. Her stepmother's attitude changed from trust to deep distrust, and they began the fights that continually characterized their relationship from then on (she was in her early thirties when I met her). The problem of sex had reared its ugly head. The stepmother responded by acting as if her innocent child had been replaced by a corrupt impostor; the step-daughter responded by dating a series of ne'er-do-wells whom at one level she probably thought she deserved (having lost the perfect innocence of the child princess) and at another constituted the perfect punishment for her mother.

Together, we designed an exposure-training program to help her overcome her fear of life. We first undertook to visit a nearby butcher shop. The shop owner and I had become friendly acquaintances over the years. After I explained my client's situation to him (with her permission), I asked if I could bring her into his store, show her the meat counter, and then—when she was ready—bring her to the back to watch as his team cut up the carcasses that were delivered through the alleyway loading dock. He quickly agreed. Our initial goal was merely to get to the store together. I assured her that we could pause at any time, or stop altogether, and that under no conditions would I trick, entice, or even cajole her into pushing her beyond what she could tolerate. During the first session, she managed to enter the store and place her hand on the display case. She did it shaking and in visible tears (also no easy thing to manage in public), but she did it. By the fourth session, she was able to watch the butchers use their knives and saws on the large and still animal-like carcasses they were slicing into the standard cuts they sold. There was no doubt that this was good for her. She was less inclined, for example, to medicate herself into unconsciousness and more likely to attend classes. She became tougher, harder, harsher—adjectives that are not always meant as compliments but are sometimes the precise antidote to too much sentimentality, which is dangerously infantilizing. We also made arrangements for her to spend a weekend at a local farm where a few common barnyard animals were kept (pigs, horses, chickens, goats). I asked the farmer, who had also been a client of mine, to allow her to accompany him while he attended to his livestock.

A city girl to the core, my client knew nothing whatsoever about animals, and tended, in consequence, to romanticize them, in exactly the fairy-tale manner appropriate to the conditions of her childhood. Her two-day sojourn in the country and her decision to observe the animals carefully helped her develop a much less romanticized perception of the true nature of the animals we raise and dine upon. They are sentient beings, in part, and we have a responsibility not to inflict any more suffering upon them than necessary, but they are not human beings, and they are certainly not children. This needs to be understood at an embodied level. Excess sentimentality is an illness, a developmental failure, and a curse to children and others who need our care (but not too much of it).

Sleeping Beauty was a remarkable dreamer. I have had clients who would commonly remember two or three dreams a night, though not always in great detail. She not only remembered many dreams, but remembered them fully, and she also often became lucid—conscious of dreaming—while she slept. She was the only person I ever met who could ask her dream characters what they meant—symbolically speaking—or what message they had for her, and they would tell her outright. One day she came to me with one of her many dreams: She had journeyed alone deep into the depths of an old-growth forest and met a dwarf dressed like a harlequin in the darkness and gloom. The dwarf offered to answer a question, if my client had one to ask. She asked the strange figure what she would have to do to finish her college certificate, a task that had taken her the four aforementioned years and plenty of negotiation with the requisite university authorities for permission to continue. The answer she received? "You will have to learn to work in a slaughterhouse."

Now, as far as I am concerned, dreams are statements from nature. It is not so much that we create them. They manifest themselves to us. I have never seen a dream present something I believed to be untrue. I also do not believe—contra Freud—that dreams attempt to disguise what they mean. They are, instead, an earlier part of the process by which fully developed thoughts come to be born, as they certainly do not just appear magically out of nowhere. We must confront the unknown, as such—the great Dragon of Chaos or the Terrible Queen— and we do not know how to do it, to begin with. The dream serves as the first cognitive step—in the wake of basic emotional, motivational, and bodily reactions such as fear or curiosity or freezing—in transforming that unknown into actionable and even articulable knowledge. The dream is the birthplace of the thought, and often of the thought that does not come easily to the conscious mind. It is not hiding anything; it is just not very good at being clear (although that certainly does not mean that it cannot be profound).

In any case, this dream was not difficult to interpret, particularly because its main character, the dwarf, simply spoke his mind. So, I listened carefully to my client's account (remember, this was after the butcher shop and the farm) and asked her what we might do about that. I had no idea how I might arrange a visit to an actual slaughterhouse. I did not even know if they existed in the city we inhabited, and if they did, I could not imagine they would appreciate visitors, regardless of motivation. She was convinced, however, that she had been told the truth, and that something of the sort had to be done. So we discussed the consequences of her toughening up, and the fact that she had successfully put her hypercritical stepmother on the back burner, and left it at that for the remainder of the session, although she was tasked (as was I) with determining something that might serve as a reasonable substitute for a slaughterhouse.

A week later, she returned for her scheduled session. She announced the last thing, perhaps, that I could have possibly imagined from her—or anyone else, for that matter: "I think I need to see an embalming." I did not know what to say. I did not want to see an embalming, personally—not at all. I had seen body sections in science museums, and there was something about them that refused to leave my memory. I had also gone to see one of the displays of plasticized, sculptured bodies that were so popular about a decade ago, and I was horrified by it. I became a psychologist, not a surgeon—or, for that matter, a coroner—for a reason. However, this was not about me. It was about my client, Sleeping Beauty, and her desire to awaken, and there was no way I was going to let my wishes or lack thereof interfere with whatever wisdom the dwarf who inhabited the deep forest of her unconscious mind was about to impart. I told her I would see what I could do. It all turned out to be much simpler to arrange than I expected. I simply picked up the phone and called a local mortician's office. To my great surprise, he immediately agreed. I suppose he had seen his fair share of people grieving and frightened, and was accustomed to dealing with them calmly and wisely. So that was that. I was stuck with the visit, and my client wanted to go through with it.

Two weeks later, we went to the funeral home. My client had asked me if a friend could attend with her, and I said yes. The mortician offered the three of us a tour first. He showed us the chapel and the display room for the caskets. We asked him how he managed his job, given its endless concentration on death and suffering and grief. He said that it was his heartfelt responsibility to make his clients' most terrible of times the least painful they could be, and that he took heart from that. That made sense to both of us, and helped us understand how he could continue with his work, day in and out. After the tour, we went to the embalming room. It was a small space, perhaps a hundred feet square. The naked body of an aged man was lying motionless, gray, and mottled on a stainless-steel table. Because there was not space in the small room, and to provide us both with some distance, my client, her friend, and I took our places in the hallway immediately outside the door and observed the proceedings, which were entirely unimpeded by our trivial separation from the mortician's operations. He drained the blood and other liquids from the body. They ran undramatically but in some sense all the more horribly for that, because of their mundane mode of disposal, I suppose. It seemed like something that precious and vital deserved better. He made his surgical alterations, and sewed together the eyelids, and made up the face, and injected the embalming fluid. I watched. And I watched my client. To begin with, she looked down the hallway, avoiding the scene unfolding in front of her. But as the minutes ticked by, she started to glance at the proceedings, and by the time a quarter of an hour had passed, she was spending far more time observing than looking away. I could see, however, that she had taken her friend's hand, and was gripping it tightly.

She was seeing firsthand that something she had believed would terrify her (and reasonably so) was not in fact doing so. She could manage the experience. She did not panic, become ill, run away, or even cry. She asked the mortician if she could put a hand on the body. He offered her a rubber glove, which she pulled on. She walked directly into the operating station, in a quiet and meditative state, and placed her gloved hand on the ribs of the body, and she kept it there, as if it was a comfort both to her and the poor departed soul. The procedure terminated soon after that, and we left quietly together, after offering the mortician our genuine and heartfelt thanks.

The three of us expressed our shared astonishment that we had managed such a visit. My client had learned something vitally important about her tolerance for the terrors of life. Equally importantly, she had a reference point for her fears: from that point onward (and I am by no means claiming complete success in her treatment) she had something truly awe inspiring—something truly serious and horrifying and graphic and real—to compare with the other, almost inevitably lesser, horrors of life. Were the mundane miseries of existence as challenging as the experience she had put herself through voluntarily? Was the butcher shop more frightening than human death, in all its reality, at such close proximity? Had she not demonstrated to herself that she could encounter the worst that Terrible Nature could throw at her and face it courageously? And that was to her a paradoxical and ineradicable source of comfort.

As with the Sleeping Beauty of fairy tales, my client's family had failed to invite the Evil Queen, the terrible aspect of nature, into their child's life. This left her completely unprepared for life's essential harshness—the complications of sexuality and the requirement for everything that lives to devour other lives (and to be eventually subjected to the same fate). The Evil Queen made her reappearance at puberty— in the form of my client's stepmother, whose character apparently turned 180 degrees—as well as in her own personal inability to deal with the responsibilities of maturity and stark obligations of biological survival. Like Sleeping Beauty, as well—as that tale is multistoried and deep in the way of ancient fairy tales, which can be thousands of years old— she needed to be awakened by the forces of exploration, courage, and fortitude (often represented by the redeeming prince, but which she found within herself).

## CULTURE: SECURITY AND TYRANNY

If the Dragon of Chaos and the paired Benevolent and Evil Queen are representatives of potential and of the unknown, the Wise King and the Authoritarian Tyrant are representatives of the structures, social and psychological, that enable us to overlay structure on that poten-

tial. We interpret the present through the lens of culture. We plan for
the future by attempting to bring into being what we have been taught
and what we have determined, personally, to value. All of that seems
good, but a too-rigid approach to understanding what is currently in
front of us and what we should pursue can blind us to the value of
novelty, creativity, and change. When the structures that guide us are
merely secure, rather than inflexible, we leaven our desire for routine
and predictability with the curiosity that makes us attracted to and
appreciative of what remains outside our conceptual schemes. When
those same structures degenerate into stasis, we run from and deny
the existence of what we do not yet understand and what we have not
yet encountered, and this means that we make ourselves unable to
change when change is required. Understanding that both possibilities
exist is of crucial importance to establish the balance that is required
in life.

We could use a poetic metaphor to represent the elements of experience that we have so far discussed (this is in fact how the world I
am describing is usually considered). Imagine the realm of the Dragon
of Chaos as the night sky, stretching infinitely above you on a clear
night, representing what will remain forever outside your domain of
understanding. Maybe you are standing on a beach, looking up, lost
in contemplation and imagination. Then you turn your attention to
the ocean—as grand in its way as the starry cosmos, but tangible and
manifest and knowable, comparatively speaking. That is nature. It is
not mere potential. It is there, in its unknowability, instead of removed
from comprehension entirely. It is not yet tamed, however; not brought
into the domain of order. And it is beautiful in its mystery. The moon
reflects on its surface; the waves crash eternally and lull you to sleep;
you can swim in its welcoming waters. But that beauty has a price. You
better keep an eye out for sharks. And poisonous jellyfish. And the

riptide that can pull you or your children under. And the storms that could destroy your warm and welcoming beach house.

Imagine, further, that the beach on which you stand is the shore of an island. The island is culture. People live there—perhaps in harmony and peace, under a benevolent ruler; perhaps in a war-torn hell of oppression, hunger, and privation. And that is culture: Wise King or Authoritarian Tyrant. It is of vital necessity to become acquainted with both characters, just as in the case of Evil Queen and Benevolent Goddess, to ensure the appropriate balance in attitude required to adapt properly to the vicissitudes of life. Too much emphasis on the Wise King blinds those who hold that attitude to the injustice and unnecessary suffering that is a consequence of the inevitable flaws in our all-too-human social structures. Too much insistence on the Authoritarian Tyrant means lack of appreciation for the often fragile structures that bind us together and protect us from the chaos that would otherwise certainly reign.

The ideological systems we are prone to adopting—the systems that so polarize us, politically and personally, can be profitably understood in light of the present conceptualization. They are cultural narratives usefully considered as parasites upon a more fundamental religious, mythological, or dramatic substructure—ancient, evolved, and deeply biological in its nature. Ideologies take on the structure of a story that is essentially religious, but they do so incompletely, including certain elements of experience or eternal characters while ignoring others. The power remains in the representation, nonetheless, because what is included retains its fundamentally mythological/biological nature— its instinctual meaning—but the missing elements mean that what remains, however powerful in its expression, is biased in a way that restricts its utility. That bias is desirable subjectively, as it simplifies what would otherwise be too complex to understand, but dangerous because of its one-sidedness. If the map you are using is missing part of the world, you are going to be utterly unprepared when that absent element makes itself manifest. How is it possible for us to retain the advantages of simplification, without falling prey to the accompanying blindness? The answer is to be found in the constant dialogue between genuinely different types of people.

Much of what people believe politically—ideologically, let us say— is based on their inborn temperament. If their emotions or motivations tend to tilt one way (and much of that is a consequence of biology), then they tend to adopt, say, a conservative or liberal tendency. It is not a matter of opinion. Imagine, instead, that animals have a niche—a place or space that suits them. Their biology is matched to that place. Lions are not found in the open ocean, and killer whales do not roam the African veldt. The animal and its environment are of a piece.

Human beings are similar, at least in the realm of abstraction. We are nonetheless capable of making ourselves at home almost every-where, geographically, because we change the geography, as neces-sary, as well as modify our own behavior. But we have perceptual or cognitive niches. Liberals, for example, are positively enthralled by new ideas. The advantages to being attracted by new ideas are obvious. Sometimes problems require new solutions, and it is people who take pleasure in novel conceptions who find them. Such people also tend not to be particularly orderly.[6] Perhaps this is because if you are gripped and driven by new ideas, and are also inclined to test or implement them, you need to be able to tolerate the intermediary chaos produced between the time the old idea disintegrates and the new idea takes control. If you are a conservative, you have the opposite advantage and problem. You are wary of new ideas, and not particularly attracted to them, and that is in part because you are less sensitive to their possi-bilities and more concerned about their unpredicted consequences.

Just because a new idea fixes one problem, after all, does not mean that it will fail to generate another, or several others. If you are conservative, you like things to be where they are supposed to be, when they are supposed to be there. You are in the place you want to be when people act conventionally, responsibly, and predictably.

Conservatives are necessary for maintaining things the way they are when everything is working and change might be dangerous. Liberals, by contrast, are necessary for changing things when they are no longer working. It is no easy task, however, to determine when something needs to be preserved or when it needs to be transformed. That is why we have politics, if we are fortunate, and the dialogue that accompanies it, instead of war, tyranny, or submission. It is necessary for us to argue vociferously and passionately about the relative value of stability versus change, so that we can determine when each is appropriate and in what doses.

It is of great interest to note that difference in fundamental political belief appears to determine which of the twinned Great Fathers are considered of fundamental reality. The liberal tends strongly to see the world as the Authoritarian Tyrant suppressing the Benevolent Goddess—as the arbitrary strictures of dead culture corrupting and oppressing citizen and foreigner alike, or as the military-industrial structure of modern society threatening Gaia, the living planet, with pollution, mass extinction, or climate change. Such a viewpoint is obviously useful when culture has become truly tyrannical—and that is by no means uncommon. The conservative tends, conversely, to see the world as Wise King—security of place, order, and predictability—bringing to heel, taming and disciplining the Evil Queen—nature as disorder and chaos. That is obviously necessary as well. No matter how beautiful the natural world, we should remember that it is always conspiring to starve, sicken, and kill us, and that if we lacked the protective shield constituted by Culture as Security we would be devoured by wild animals, frozen by blizzards, prostrated by the heat of the desert, and starved by the fact that food does not simply manifest itself for our delectation. So there are two different ideologies—both of which are "correct," but each of which tell only half the story.*

To develop a properly balanced view of the world of experience, it is necessary to accept the reality of both elements of culture. Those with a conservative bent, drawn temperamentally to regard the status quo as protective, must to come to understand that mere order is insufficient. Because the future and the present differ from the past, what worked before will not necessarily work now, and it is necessary to understand that the line between the stability bequeathed to us by our ancestors and the tyranny that can so easily become shifts and moves with the transformations of existence. Equally, however, the more liberal types, prone to see the Authoritarian Tyrant everywhere, must work to develop gratitude for the social and psychological structures of interpretation that continually shield us from the terrors of nature and the absolute unknown. It is difficult for any of us to see what we are blinded to by the nature of our personalities. It is for this reason that we must continually listen to people who differ from us, and who, because of that difference, have the ability to see and to react appropriately to what we cannot detect.

---

*I am aware, of course, that conservatives also have a proclivity to object to big government, which seems to contradict the fundamental point I am making. But, in Western democracies, that's primarily because the faith that conservatives manifest in culture is predicated more on the eternal verities of the Constitution and the more permanent elements of government (so Culture with a capital "C") than on the too variable and too unpredictable whims of whomever might be elected presently, conservative or liberal. Likewise, in the same democracies, the liberals tend to look to government for the solution to the problems that concern them, but that's because they believe more in the dynamism of the current crop of politicians (particularly, but not only, if they are liberal themselves) and less in the eternal verities of the underlying structure.

## THE INDIVIDUAL: HERO AND ADVERSARY

If the night sky is chaos, the ocean nature, and the island culture, then the individual—hero and adversary—is one brother locked in combat with his twin in the middle of the isle. Chaos, treasure and dragon, have their negative and positive element, as do Nature—Evil Queen and Benevolent Mother—and Culture—Authoritarian Tyrant and Wise King. No less the individual. The positive element is the heroic aspect: the person who can sacrifice properly to nature and strike a bargain with fate such that benevolence reigns; the person who is awake, alert, attentive, communicative, and bears responsibility, so that the tyrannical part of the state remains at bay; and the person who is aware of his or her own faults and proclivity for malevolence and deceit, so that proper orientation is maintained. The negative element is everything despicable and contemptible—particularly evident in yourself, if you have any sense, but also manifested to some degree by other people and (more clearly) in stories. Those are the hostile brothers, a very old mythological idea: the hero and the adversary. The archetypal representations of those two forces, those two personified figures, are Cain and Abel. That is one level of representation. Christ and Satan are a pair representing an even more fundamental duality. Cain and Abel, after all, are human (the first humans, born in the human manner, as Adam and Eve were created directly by God). Christ and Satan are elements of personified (deified?) eternity itself.

So, there exists a hero and an adversary; a wise king and a tyrant; a positive and negative maternal figure; and chaos itself. That is the structure of the world in six characters (with the strange seventh of chaos in some sense the ultimate birthplace of all the others). It is necessary to understand that all seven exist, and that they are all existential permanents—elements of experience with which every soul, rich, poor, blessed, cursed, talented, dull, male, and female must inevitably contend. That is life—*they* are life. Partial knowledge of the cast, conscious or unconscious, leaves you undefended; leaves you naive, unprepared, and likely to become possessed by deceit, resentment, and arrogance. If you do not know that the treasure is guarded by a dragon, or that nature, beautiful nature, can turn its teeth on you in an instant, or that the peaceful society you take for granted is threatened constantly by authoritarianism and tyranny, or that you contain within yourself the adversary who might wish that all those negative transformations occur, then you are, first, a needy acolyte for an ideology that will provide you with a partial and insufficient representation of reality; and, second, someone blind in a manner dangerous to themselves and others alike. If you are wise, your political philosophy encompasses a representation of all seven, even if you could not articulate it in those terms. We should always have enough sense to keep in mind, for example, that a great predator lurks beneath the thin ice of our constructed realities. I remember a vision I once had about my then very young daughter, portraying exactly that reality. In the winter, in Northern Alberta—where, as I said, I grew up—there were years where the snow stayed at bay for weeks after the lakes themselves had frozen, smooth, perfectly clear, rock hard, barren, and not without beauty and mystery. (A stone skipped across their expanse would chime and echo melodically as it skidded across the slippery surface.) I imagined my daughter Mikhaila—a toddler dressed only in a diaper—sitting at some distance from me, directly on the ice. Underneath her, I could see a huge fish, a whale shark (although carnivorous, in this incarnation)— hanging motionless below her, waiting, upright in the water underneath the ice, mouth gaping. That is life, and death, and the pure chaos that destroys our hard-won certainties, but it is also the prophet-swallowing whale who grants wisdom and rebirth, if it does not kill.

And what is the proper attitude of the hero, let us say, with respect to the remaining six characters (assuming we have dealt sufficiently with chaos with that last anecdote)? Obviously, we must endeavor to preserve Nature, upon whose benevolence we are finally dependent for everything that life requires. But it is also perfectly worthwhile for us to note and take seriously the fact that the same Nature is doing her best to kill us, and that we have every reason to erect the structures we do, despite their often unfortunate environmental costs.* Something similar applies to culture. We all have reason to be grateful, in the main, for the wisdom and the structure that our forebears bequeathed to us, to their great cost. That does not mean that those benefits are distributed equally, because they are not and never will be, no more than the benefits of Nature are distributed equally. That gratitude also does not justify any willfully blind optimism with regard to the nature of society. As individuals—struggling, let us say, against the adversarial tendency and the Authoritarian Tyrant simultaneously—we need to be awake to the fact that our functional hierarchical structures can become unproductive, tyrannical, and blind in the blink of an eye. We have a responsibility to ensure that they do not become radically unfair and corrupt and begin to distribute their rewards on the basis of power or unmeritocratic privilege instead of competence. We must attend to them constantly and adjust them carefully so they remain suf-

---

*There is little doubt that we create a fair bit of "unnatural" mess while we are doing so (another ideological idea, based as it is on the one-sided view of Nature as the victim of our rapine and greed), but it's not as if we are doing it for trivial reasons. That's why I have some sympathy for humanity, as well as for the individuals who compose the mass of humanity, and why I cannot find it in my heart to forgive those who say foolish things such as "the planet would be better off if there were no people on it." That's the genocidal element of the radical environmentalist ethos, and it's a consequence of an ideology that sees only the Adversary, the Authoritarian Tyrant, and the Benevolent Mother as the prime actors of being. It's something horrible to behold, if you think it through with any degree of depth.

ficiently stable and appropriately dynamic. That is a fundamental part of our roles and responsibilities as persons aiming courageously at the good. We manage that partly in democratic systems by throwing out the people in charge on a regular basis, and replacing them with their ideological opposites. That capability and opportunity constitutes one of the fundamental achievements of a democratic society. In the absence of the ability to regularly choose only the wise and good as leaders (and good luck finding them), it is worthwhile to elect a pack blind to half of reality in one cycle and another blind to the other half the next. Then at least most of society's concerns are attended to in some reasonable measure over the course of something approximating a decade.

I think that somewhat pessimistic but also eminently realistic strategy is in keeping with the vision of the people who founded the American system (and the actions and attitudes of the English and other early democrats and parliamentarians whose gradually evolving systems laid the groundwork for the explicit claims those founders made). They were not utopian in their essential viewpoint. They believed that the people who were inevitably to be their successors were going to be just as flawed as they were, and just as flawed as people before them. What do you do about that, when you are not blinded by ideology, and you see the world and all its dramatic characters clearly? Well, you do not hope for the infinite perfectibility of humanity and aim your system at some unattainable utopia. You try to design a system that sinners such as you cannot damage too badly—too permanently—even when they are half blind and resentful. To the degree that I am conservative in orientation, I believe in the wisdom of that vision. I believe that is a more appropriate way of looking at things. Let us not get too grandiose. We can design systems that allow us a modicum of peace, security, and freedom and, perhaps, the possibility of incremental improvement.

That is a miracle in and of itself. We should have the wisdom to doubt that we will produce some positive transformation of individual, society, and nature simultaneously, particularly if those improvements are to be brought about in consequence of our own intrinsic, personal goodwill, which is often in too short supply (despite our protestations to the contrary).

## RESENTMENT

Why do you and others fall prey to resentment—that terrible hybrid emotional state, an admixture of anger and self-pity, tinged, to various degrees, with narcissism and the desire for revenge? Once you understand the world as a dramatic forum, and you have identified the major players, the reasons become clear. You are resentful because of the absolute unknown and its terrors, because nature conspires against you, because you are a victim of the tyrannical element of culture, and because of the malevolence of yourself and other individuals. That is reason enough. It does not make your resentment appropriate, but it certainly makes the emotion understandable. None of these existential problems are trivial. In fact, they are serious enough to make the real question not "Why are you resentful?" but "Why is not everyone resentful about everything all the time?" We are the focus of unbelievably powerful and often malevolent transpersonal forces. There is a terrible reptilian predator, metaphorically speaking, pursuing you all the time, just like the crocodile with the ticktock of time emanating from the clock he swallowed chasing the tyrannical coward Captain Hook. And there is nature herself. She is hell-bent on doing you in, in a million horrible ways. Then there is the tyrannical element of the social structure, which has molded you—taught you, so to speak—and made you into the quasi-civilized, semi-useful creature that you are, but crushed a tremendous amount of life force out of you at the same time, pounding you like the proverbial square peg into the round hole. There were many things you could have been. Maybe some of them were more than you have become. But you were lessened and reduced by the demand for social existence.

And you are stuck with yourself, too, and that is no picnic. You procrastinate, you are lazy, you lie, and you do vicious things to your-self and others. It is no wonder you feel like a victim, given what is arrayed against you: chaos, the brute force of nature, the tyranny of culture, and the malevolence of your own nature. It is no wonder you might feel resentful. And it is certainly the case that these forces are arrayed against some of you in a manner that seems far more serious, unjust, arbitrary, continuous, and unpredictable than it seems for oth-ers. How could you fail to feel victimized and resentful under those conditions? Life contains no shortage of fundamental brutality.

There is a problem with this logic, however, inexorable though it may seem. The first is that not everyone does in fact construe him or herself as a victim and fall prey, in consequence, to resentment—and that includes a large proportion of people who have had a very hard time in their lives. In fact, I think it is reasonable to posit that it is often the people who have had too easy a time—who have been pampered and elevated falsely in their self-esteem—who adopt the role of victim and the mien of resentment. You can encounter people, contrarily, who have been hurt virtually beyond all hope of repair who are not resent-ful and who would never deign to present themselves as victims. They are not that common, but they are not so very rare either. Thus, re-sentment does not appear to be an inevitable consequence of suffering itself. Other factors are at play, in addition to the undeniable tragedy of life.

Maybe you—or just as tragically, someone close to you—contracts a serious illness. It is typical in such circumstances to ask the question (of whom? God?) "Why did this have to happen to me?" Well, what do you mean? Would you wish it instead upon a friend, neighbor, or even a random stranger? You certainly might be tempted to spread your misery, but such a response does not seem either reasonable or a choice that a good person, thinking clearly, would ever make, and it certainly would not make the situation more just. To be fair, the question "Why me?" constitutes, in part, a psychologically appropriate response. It is often the case that if something bad happens to you, you should ask yourself if there is something that you have done in the past that has increased the probability of the terrible event—as we have discussed at length—because it is possible that you have something to learn that would decrease the chances of its recurrence. But often that is not at all what we are doing. The question "Why did this have to happen to me?" frequently contains a reproachful element, based on a sense of injustice: "There are all these bad people in the world, and they seem to be getting away unpunished for this misbehavior," or "There are all these people in the world who are enjoying good health, and it seems singularly unfair for them to be in that fortunate position when I am not." That means that "Why me?" is in this manner generally contaminated with a sense of victimization, signifying injustice. This false misapprehension that the terrible experience that has befallen you somehow singularly characterizes you—is aimed, particularly, at you—is part of what turns exposure to tragedy into the very resentment we are discussing.

The fact that unfortunate things are happening or are going to happen to you is built into the structure of reality itself. There is no doubt that awful things happen, but there is an element of true randomness about them. You might think, "That is trivial compensation, and of little help." But some appreciation for the random element can be helpful, by distancing the personal element, and that can help you erect some barriers to developing that intense egotistical resentment. Furthermore, it can be of great utility to realize that each of the negatives that characterize human existence are balanced, in principle, by their positive counterpart.

Here is something I have learned in my years as a clinical psychologist. I constantly saw people who were hurt by life. They had their reasons for feeling resentful, and those reasons were often far from trivial. I would propose: "Let us take your problems apart, even though many of them are real. We will try to figure out which ones are your fault, because some of them are going to be. Some of them, alternatively, are just the catastrophe of life. We will delineate that very carefully. Then we will start having you practice overcoming whatever it is that you are bringing to the situation that is making it worse. We will start to make some strategic plans about how you might confront the parts of your life that are truly just tragic, and we will get you to do that in a truthful, open, and courageous manner. Then we will watch what happens."

People got better. Not always. Some of my clients even died. We would be halfway through their clinical issues, and they would be carried off by a sudden cancer or killed in a traffic accident. There is no certain path, even with the noblest of actions. The arbitrariness of the world is always at the ready, preparing to manifest itself. There is no reason or excuse to be stupidly naive or optimistic. But most people did get better. Encouragement prepared them to confront their problems head-on, and that voluntary confrontation dispelled some of their fear. This was not because things around them became less dangerous, but because the people facing the danger became braver. It is unbelievable how strong and courageous people can become. It is miraculous what sort of load people can bear when they take it on voluntarily. I know we cannot have an infinite capacity for that, but I also believe that it is in some sense unlimited. I think the more voluntary confrontation is practiced, the more can be borne. I do not know what the upper limit is for that.*

People not only become encouraged, so they can stave off the horror and resentment from a psychological perspective, but they also become more able. Not only are they contending with the existential burden of life more effectively from a spiritual perspective, say, but they start to be better people in the world. They start to constrain the malevolence and resentment in their own hearts that makes the horror of the world even more dismal than it must be. They become more honest. They make better friends. They make more productive and meaningful career choices. They start aiming higher. Thus, they can cope better, psychologically, but they also reduce the volume of what they and the others around them must cope with. Then they suffer less unnecessarily, and so do their families. Then, maybe, the same thing starts to happen with their communities. And then there is the other half of the story: the treasure that the dragon hoards, the benevolent element of nature, the security and shelter provided by society and culture, and the strength of the individual. Those are your weapons in times of trouble. And they are just as real, and perhaps of sufficient power, that their full use will provide you with the means to cope when your life falls apart. The issue is: can you organize the structure of reality so that you find the treasure, the positive aspect of nature smiles upon you, you are ruled by the wise king, and you play

---

*If I didn't say it before, I can certainly say it now: I was and remain in constant awe as a consequence of the absolute courage and grace that my wife, for example, manifested in the face of her trials in the first six months of 2019, after she was diagnosed with terminal cancer (and perhaps cured). Shame, too . . . because I am not at all convinced that I could have done the same.

the role of hero? The hope is that you can conduct yourself in such a manner that it tilts things in that direction. That it is all we have—and it is much better than nothing. If you confront the suffering and malevolence, and if you do that truthfully and courageously, you are stronger, your family is stronger, and the world is a better place. The alternative is resentment, and that makes everything worse.

## DECEIT AND ARROGANCE

There appear to be two broad forms of deceit: sins of commission, the things you do knowing full well they are wrong; and sins of omission, which are things you merely let slide—you know you should look at, do, or say something, but you do not. Maybe your business partner is a little bit crooked with the books, and you decide that you are just not going to audit them; or you turn a blind eye to your own misbehavior; or you fail to investigate the misdeeds of a child, adolescent, or your partner in your household. Instead, you just let it go.

What motivates these kinds of deceit? We lie, outright—the sin of commission—knowing full well that we are doing so, to make things easier for us, in theory, regardless of the effect upon other people. We try to tip the world in our own personal favor. We try to gain an edge. We endeavor to avoid a just punishment that is coming our way—often by passing it to others. We commit the sin of omission, alternatively (and perhaps more subtly), in the belief that what we are avoiding will just go away, which it seldom does. We sacrifice the future to the present, frequently suffering the slings and arrows of outraged conscience for doing so, but continuing, rigidly and stubbornly, in any case.

So, what do people use to justify bending and twisting the structure of reality, at the cost of others or even their future selves, to benefit themselves now? It is a motivation clearly embedded in resentment.

Lies are justified by the belief lurking at the bottom of the resentful soul that the terrors of the world have been aimed specifically at the sufferer attempting to justify his lying. But we need to bring arrogance into the conversation, along with resentment, to truly understand why we practice to deceive. It is not obvious that these states of mind can exist in the absence of each other, anyway. They are coconspirators, so to speak.

The first conspiracy between deceit and arrogance might be regarded as a denial or rejection of the relationship between divinity, truth, and goodness. In the early chapters of Genesis, God creates habitable chaos out of order with the Word, with the Logos: courage, love, and truth. Courage, we might say, is the willingness of God to confront the nothingness that preceded Being, which is perhaps of the same form we manage when we rise up from poverty and nothingness to thrive, or rebuild our lives when they have been reduced to chaos by disaster and catastrophe. Love is the ultimate aim—the desire to create the very best that can be created. It provides the same kind of superstructure for Being, perhaps, as the desire for a peaceful and harmonious home provides when such desire allows the truth to be spoken. The Word God uses to confront the nothingness we spoke of is the Truth, and that truth creates. But it does not just create: it appears to create the Good—the very best that love would demand. It is not for nothing that God is so insistent that what has been created is Good. Arrogance and deceit unite to oppose the idea that courageous truth aimed at love creates the Good, and replace it with the idea that any whim, large or small, has the right and opportunity to reveal itself for purposes that are instead narrow and self-serving.

The second form of arrogance that enables deceit has something to do with the assumption of the power of divinity itself. Someone who lies, through action, inaction, words, or silence, has made a choice about what element of becoming (what element of still-unformed but potential chaos) is or is not going to manifest itself. This means that the deceitful individual has taken it upon him or herself to alter the very structure of reality. And for what? For a wish based on the idea that whatever egotistical falsehood conjured up by the act of deceit will be better than the reality that would have transpired had the truth been enacted or spoken. The liar acts out the belief that the false world he brings into being, however temporarily, will serve at least his own interests better than the alternative. That is the arrogance of someone who believes that he can alter the structure of reality through pretense, and that he can get away with it. It is not clear how either of these beliefs could be sustained, if they are thought through carefully (which implies, of course, that they are generally not). First, the transgressor himself is going to know that he is not to be trusted in word or action, and then, to the degree that genuine self-regard relies on such truth, the deceitful words and acts are inevitably going to undermine the personality of the liar. At minimum, he will not be living in the real world, or in the same world as other people, and so he will be weaker than he would have been had he learned what was true instead of having substituted for it what is false. Second, for the liar to genuinely believe that he is "going to get away with it," carries with it the belief that he is smarter than everyone else—that is, the everyone who will not notice (and perhaps that belief comes to encompass God, the Creator, whether explicitly or implicitly). Perhaps he will get away with one, two, or ten lies, of increasing severity, as he is emboldened by success. Each time he succeeds, however, his arrogance will increase, as success is rewarding and will inspire efforts to duplicate and even increase that reward. This cannot help but motivate larger and riskier lies, each associated with a longer fall from the heights of pride. The strategy seems unworkable—a positive feedback loop designed to drag those who entrap themselves within it lower and lower, faster and faster.

The third form of arrogance that underlies deceit has to do with the belief that the deceitful act (which, as we already discussed, has bent or warped the structure of reality) will stand on its own powerfully, without being revealed and destroyed as reality itself straightens and reforms, as it inevitably will. That is the arrogance behind the liar's belief that the lie has somehow permanently altered the form of the world, so that now life in the world can be conducted as if that lie is somehow real. But reality is very complicated and almost everything, it seems, touches on everything else. It is very difficult, for example, to make the consequences of an adulterous affair stop spreading. People are seen. Tongues start to wag. More lies are generated and must be validated to account for the time spent on the affair. Scents linger. Affection within the relationship starts to be replaced by hatred or contempt (particularly if the betrayed person is a genuinely good person, providing no excuse for the sinful actions taken against him or her).

The fourth form of arrogance that justifies deceit has to do with a warped sense of justice, often brought about by resentment. People employ deception in this fourth set of circumstances because they are resentful and angry about their victimized positions in the hell and tragedy of the world. This response is entirely understandable, although no less dangerous because of that. The logic is simple and even compelling, particularly in the case of people who have been truly hurt: "I can do what I want because I have been unfairly treated." This reasoning can be seen as simple justice, although it is seldom the case that the people who are now being lied to or deceived are the same individuals who produced the unfair treatment used to justify the falsehood. The arrogance is in believing that the unfair treatment was specifically personal, existentially speaking, rather than being an expected part of existence itself, given its unknown natural, social, and individual dangers. If you have been the victim of what appears to be some malevolent cosmic joke, then why should not you do whatever is in your power to set things a little bit right for yourself? All that line of reasoning does, however, is make life worse. If your justification for misbehaving was that life was bad, then the rationale for continuing to misbehave cannot reasonably be that you should embark on a pattern of action that does nothing but make it more so.

## OMISSIONS

There are a variety of reasons why you stand idly by when something you know to be terrible and wrong is occurring, and do nothing (including what you know you should have done) to interfere. The first of these is nihilism. It might not be immediately obvious what nihilism and pride have to do with each other (and even less what both have to do with sins of omission). But the nihilistic attitude is one of certainty: everything is meaningless, or even negative. It is a judgment, a conclusion—and it is a sin of pride, in my estimation. I think we are properly bounded in humility by a reasonable sense of our own ignorance not to take the terrible risk of damning the structure of existence itself.

Another motive for a sin of omission? The claim that it is justifiable to take the easy path. This means living life so that true responsibility for anything important never falls on your shoulders. And you might think that is perfectly acceptable: "Why should I expend extra effort and risk when someone else is lining up for it; pushing actively for it;

or just not sophisticated enough to slip away from it when it seeks them out?" But everyone should take their turn—both at receiving the benefits of social interaction and of bearing the responsibility for ensuring that such interaction remains possible. Children who do not learn that at three do not make any friends, and there are good reasons for that. They do not know how to play a game that can sustain itself across time, which is exactly what a friendship is (as well as the attitude that makes for good superiors, peers, and subordinates in a business organization).

Critically consider, as well, the assumption that it is somehow acceptable or even wise to slip by without paying your bills in full. This is another variant of the judgment of existence. "It does not matter if I take the easy path" begins with "It does not matter," and that is Being, judged and damned, with a twist. The second part of the statement, "if I take the easy path," is a self-imposed curse. If you take your turn at the difficult tasks, people learn to trust you, you learn to trust yourself, and you get better at doing difficult things. All of that is good. If you leave all that undone, you will find yourself in the same position as the child whose parents insisted upon doing everything for him or her: bereft of the capacity to thrive in the face of the difficulties/ challenges of life. "It does not matter if I take the easy path," is true only if there is no personality element of the speaker that could be called out by a true adventure. And those who avoid their destiny by standing back when asked to step forward also deprive everyone else of the advantages that may have come their way had the person who took the easy way instead determined to be all they could be.

The final form of sins of omission is associated with lack of faith in yourself—perhaps in humanity in general—because of the fundamental nature of human vulnerability. There is a scene in the book of Genesis in which the scales fall from the eyes of Adam and Eve, and they realize they are vulnerable and naked—both part and parcel of self-consciousness. At the same time, they develop the knowledge of good and evil. These two developments coincide because it is not possible to hurt other people with true effectiveness until you know how you can be hurt yourself. And you do not know that you can be hurt until you are, more or less, fully self-conscious; until you know that you can suffer excruciating pain; until you know that you can be killed; until you realize the limits of your being. And as soon as you know all that, you have knowledge of your own nakedness, and you can apply knowledge of that vulnerability with malevolent intent to other people. And then you understand and are capable of Good and Evil.

When called upon later to account for his behavior—for eating of the forbidden fruit—Adam blames the woman for the development of his painful self-knowledge, and God for making her, saying as he does, "The woman whom thou gavest to be with me, she gave me of the tree, and I did eat" (Genesis 3:12). The first man's refusal to take responsibility for his actions is associated with resentment (for his acquisition of painful knowledge), deceit (as he knows he made a free choice, regardless of his wife's behavior), and arrogance (he dares to blame God and the woman the divinity created). Adam takes the easy way out—just as you might, when you say to yourself, "I do not need to have this fight with my wife. I do not have to stand up to my tyrannical boss. I do not have to live by what I believe to be true. I can get away with avoiding my responsibilities." Some of that is inertia and cowardice, but some of it is also motivated by a deep sense of disbelief in your own personal ability. Like Adam, you know you are naked. You are intimately aware of your flaws and vulnerabilities, and the faith in yourself dissolves. This is understandable, but neither helpful nor, in the final analysis, excusable.

## THE EXISTENTIAL DANGER OF
## ARROGANCE AND DECEIT

As Proverbs 9:10 has it: "The fear of the Lord is the beginning of wisdom." The connection between deception and the deepest of orienting instincts can be profitably comprehended in light of that. If you understand that deception corrupts and distorts the function of the most fundamental instinct that guides you through the difficulties of life, that prospect should scare you enough so that you remain careful in what you say and do. A truthful person can rely on his or her innate sense of meaning and truth as a reliable guide to the choices that must be made through life's days, weeks, and years. But there is a rule that applies—the same rule that computer programmers well know: "garbage in, garbage out." If you deceive (particularly yourself), if you lie, then you begin to warp the mechanisms guiding the instinct that orients you. That instinct is an unconscious guide, so it works underneath your cognitive apparatus, especially once it has become habitual. If you rewire the unconscious mechanisms that maintain you with assumptions derived from something you know to be unreal, then your meaningful instinct will take you places you should not go, in proportion to its corruption. There is little more terrifying than the possibility that you could come to a crisis point in your life when you need every faculty you possess, at that moment, to make the decision properly, only to find you have pathologized yourself with deceit and can no longer rely on your own judgment. Good luck to you, because nothing but luck will then serve to save you.

There is a sin somewhat mysteriously defined by Christ as unforgivable: "Whosoever speaketh against the Holy Ghost, it shall not be forgiven him, neither in this world, neither in the world to come" (Matthew 12:32). St. Paul, one of Christianity's founders, shed some light on this statement, when he associated that Third Person of the Trinity with conscience: "I say the truth in Christ, I lie not, my conscience also bearing me witness in the Holy Ghost" (Romans 9:1). Conscience is no less than the sharing of moral knowledge with the self. Deceit necessitates voluntary refusal to abide by the dictate of conscience, and risks pathologizing that very vital function. There is no walking away from that corruption unscathed. This is true even in a neurological sense. Drugs of addiction are generally characterized by their effects upon the neurotransmitter dopamine, increasing its effects in some manner. Dopamine essentially produces the pleasure associated with hope or possibility. Furthermore, your brain is wired so that if you do something that feels good (and therefore produces a dopamine kick) then the parts of you that played a role in the action under question become stronger, more dominant, more able to inhibit the function of other parts of your being. Continued use of an addictive drug therefore feeds the growth of what can be accurately conceptualized as a living monster in the user's psyche—and the attention and intention of that monster is single-mindedly devoted to the drug's effect. It wants one thing, and it comes armed with an entire philosophy about why that one thing must be considered of primary import.

Imagine you are recovering, fragilely, from addiction. Something goes wrong in your life. Resentment emerges. You think, "Oh, to hell with it!" as the initial event leading to reuse of the drug, and the experience of the subsequent dopamine hit. In consequence, the little circuits that formulate the thought "to hell with it" grow more powerful than the parts of the addict's psyche that might be motivating refusal to use the drug. "To hell with it" is a multifaceted philosophy. It means "This is worth sacrificing anything for." It means "Who cares about my life. It is not worth anything, anyway." It means "I do not care if I have to lie to those who love me—my parents, my wife and children—because what difference does it make, anyway? What I want is the drug." There is no easy coming back from that.

When you habitually engage in deceit, you build a structure much like the one that perpetuates addiction, especially if you get away with it, however briefly. The success of the lie is rewarding—and if the risks were high, and you are not caught out, that successful reward might well be intense. This reinforces the development of the neural mechanism in your brain comprising the structure of the entire system of deception. With continued success, at least in the short term, this mechanism begins to work with increasing automaticity—and comes to act, in its arrogant manner, knowing that it can get away with it. That is more obvious for sins of commission; but it is equally and more dangerously and subtly true for what you could know but refuse to—sins of omission. That is the arrogance of believing that what you know is sufficient (regardless of the evidence that accumulates around you, in the form of suffering, which is all too easily and archetypally, let us say, blamed on the structure of reality and the apparent insufficiency of God).

## THE PLACE YOU SHOULD BE

It is in our individual capacity to confront the potential of the future and to transform it into the actuality of the present. The way we determine what it is that the world transforms into is a consequence of our ethical, conscious choices. We wake up in the morning and confront the day, with all its possibilities and terrors. We chart a course, making decisions for better or worse. We understand full well that we can do evil and bring terrible things into Being. But we also know that we can do good, if not great, things. We have the best chance of doing the latter if we act properly, as a consequence of being truthful, responsible, grateful, and humble.

The right attitude to the horror of existence—the alternative to resentment, deceit, and arrogance—is the assumption that there is enough of you, society, and the world to justify existence. That is faith in yourself, your fellow man, and the structure of existence itself: the belief that there is enough to you to contend with existence and transform your life into the best it could be. Perhaps you could live in a manner whose nobility, grandeur, and intrinsic meaning would be of sufficient import that you could tolerate the negative elements of existence without becoming so bitter as to transform everything around you into something resembling hell.

Of course, we are oppressed by the fundamental uncertainty of Being. Of course, nature does us in, in unjust and painful ways. Of course, our societies tend toward tyranny, and our individual psyches toward evil. But that does not mean we cannot be good, that our societies cannot be just, and that the natural world cannot array itself in our favor. What if we could constrain our malevolence a bit more, serve and transform our institutions more responsibly, and be less resentful? God only knows what the ultimate limit to that might be. How much better could things become if we all avoided the temptation to actively or passively warp the structure of existence; if we replaced anger with the vicissitudes of Being with gratitude and truth? And if we all did that, with diligent and continual purpose, would we not have the best chance of keeping at bay those elements of self, state, and nature that manifest themselves so destructively and cruelly, and that motivate our turning against the world?

Do not allow yourself to become resentful, deceitful, or arrogant.

# BE GRATEFUL IN SPITE OF
# YOUR SUFFERING

## DOWN CAN DEFINE UP

I have been searching for decades for certainty. It has not been solely a matter of thinking, in the creative sense, but of thinking and then attempting to undermine and destroy those thoughts, followed by careful consideration and conservation of those that survive. It is identification of a path forward through a swampy passage, searching for stones to stand on safely below the murky surface. However, even though I regard the inevitability of suffering and its exaggeration by malevolence as unshakable existential truths, I believe even more deeply that people have the ability to transcend their suffering, psychologically and practically, and to constrain their own malevolence, as well as the evils that characterize the social and the natural worlds.

Human beings have the capacity to courageously confront their suffering—to transcend it psychologically, as well as to ameliorate it practically. This is the most fundamental twin axiom of psychotherapy, regardless of school of thought, as well as key to the mystery of human success and progress across history itself. If you confront the limitations of life courageously, that provides you with a certain psychological purpose that serves as an antidote to the suffering. The fact of your voluntary focus on the abyss, so to speak, indicates to yourself at the deepest of levels that you are capable of taking on without avoidance the difficulties of existence and the responsibility attendant upon that. That mere act of courage is deeply reassuring at the most fundamental levels of psychological being. It indicates your capability and competence to those deep, ancient, and somewhat independent biological and psychological alarm systems that register the danger of the world.

But the utility of such confrontation is by no means merely psychological, as important as that is. It is the appropriate pragmatic approach as well: If you act nobly—a word that is very rarely used now, unfortunately—in the face of suffering, you can work practically and effectively to ameliorate and rectify your own and other people's misery, as such. You can make the material world—the real world—better (or at least stop it from getting worse). The same goes for malevolence: you can constrain that within yourself. When you are about to say something, your conscience might (often does) inform you, noting, "That is not true." It might present itself as an actual voice (internal, of course) or a feeling of shame, guilt, weakness, or other inner disunity—the physiological consequence of the duality of psyche you are manifesting. You then have the opportunity to cease uttering those words. If you cannot tell the truth, you can at least not consciously lie.[1] That is part of the constraint of malevolence. That is something within our grasp. Beginning to cease knowingly lying is a major step in the right direction.

We can constrain our suffering, and we can face it psychologically. That makes us courageous. Then we can ameliorate it practically, because that is what we do when we care for ourselves and other people. There seems to be almost no limit to that. You can genuinely and competently come to care for yourself and your family. You can then extend that out into the broader community. Some people become unbelievably good at that. People who work in palliative care constitute a prime example. They work continually, caring for people who are suffering and dying, and they lose some of those people every day. But they manage to get out of bed every morning, go to work, and face all that pain, tragedy, and death. They make a difference under virtually impossible circumstances. It is for such reasons and because of such examples—watching people confront the existential catastrophe of life forthrightly and effectively—that I am more optimistic than pessimistic, and that I believe that optimism is, fundamentally, more reliable than pessimism. To come to such a conclusion, and then to find it unshakable, is a good example of how and why it may be necessary to encounter the darkness before you can see the light. It is easy to be optimistic and naive. It is easy for optimism to be undermined and demolished, however, if it is naive, and for cynicism to arise in its place. But the act of peering into the darkness as deeply as possible reveals a light that appears unquenchable, and that is a profound surprise, as well as a great relief.

The same holds true for the issue of gratitude. I do not believe you can be appropriately grateful or thankful for what good you have and for what evil has not befallen you until you have some profound and even terrifying sense of the weight of existence. You cannot properly appreciate what you have unless you have some sense not only of how terrible things could be, but of how terrible it is likely for things to be, given how easy it is for things to be so. This is something that is very much worth knowing. Otherwise you might find yourself tempted to ask, "Why would I ever look into the darkness?" But we seem positively

drawn to look. We are fascinated by evil. We watch dramatic representations of serial killers, psychopaths, and the kings of organized
crime, gang members, rapists, contract killers, and spies. We voluntarily frighten and disgust ourselves with thrillers and horror films—
and it is more than prurient curiosity. It is the development of some
understanding of the essentially moral structure of human existence,
of our suspension between the poles of good and evil. The development of that understanding is necessary; it places a *down* below us and
an *up* above us, and orients us in perception, motivation, and action. It
protects us, as well. If you fail to understand evil, then you have laid
yourself bare to it. You are susceptible to its effects, or to its will. If you
ever encounter someone who is malevolent, they have control over you
in precise proportion to the extent that you are unwilling or unable to
understand them. Thus, you look in dark places to protect yourself, in
case the darkness ever appears, as well as to find the light. There is
real utility in that.

## THE MEPHISTOPHELIAN SPIRIT

The great German writer Goethe, who is to Germanic culture what
Shakespeare is to English, wrote a famous play, *Faust*, the story of a
man who sells his soul to the devil for knowledge.[2] Mephistopheles is
the devil in Goethe's play—the adversary. The adversary is a mythical
figure; the spirit who eternally works against our positive intent (or,
perhaps, against positive intent generally). You can understand that
psychologically, as well as metaphysically or religiously. We all see
within ourselves the emergence of good intentions and the repeated
instructions to ourselves to act accordingly, yet we note distressingly
often that we leave undone what we know we should do, and do instead what we know we should not. There is something in all of us that

works in counterposition to our voluntarily expressed desires. There are in fact many such somethings—a chorus of demons, so to speak—working at cross-purposes even to each other; many dark and unarticulated motivations and systems of belief, all manifesting themselves as partial personalities (but with all the essential features of personality, despite their partial nature).

To realize this is uncanny. That realization is the great contribution of the psychoanalysts, who insisted above all, perhaps, that we were inhabited by spirits that were beyond not only our control but even our conscious knowledge. And that realization brings up great and paralyzing questions: If you are not in control of yourself, who or what is? If you are not, a challenge has been posed to the very idea of the centrality, unity, and even reality of the "you" whose existence seems so immediately certain. And what is that *who* or *what* that is not you up to? And toward what end is it acting? We all hope we are the sorts of creatures who can tell ourselves what to do, and who will then do exactly that, in accordance with our will. You are you, after all, and you should—virtually by definition—be in control of yourself. But things often do not work that way, and the reason or reasons they do not are deeply mysterious.

Sometimes, of course, it is simply much easier just not to do the things we should. Good actions can be and often are difficult to undertake, and there is danger—exhaustion not the least of it—in difficulty. Inertia is also a powerful reason for stasis and can provide a certain immediate safety. But there is more to the problem. It is not just that you are lazy: it is also that you are bad—and declared so by your own judgment. That is a very unpleasant realization, but there is no hope of becoming good without it. You will upbraid yourself (or your conscience will do so) for your shortcomings. You will treat yourself as if you were or are at least in part an immoral agent. That is all deeply unpleasant too, and you might well be motivated to avoid your own judgment. But no simple rationalizations will allow for your escape.

You will see, if you are willing to look, the adversarial force at work within you, working to undermine your best intentions. The exact nature of that force is grounds for endless speculation—philosophical, literary, psychological, and above all, religious or theological. The Christian conception of the great figure of evil—Mephistopheles, Satan, Lucifer, the devil himself—is, for example, a profound imaginative personification of that spirit. But the adversary is not merely something that exists in the imagination—certainly not only in the individual imagination. It is also something that manifests itself through something that is still aptly described as "possession" in the motivation for malevolent actions, as well as in the acts themselves. Everyone who has thought or said something akin to "I do not understand what came over me" after acting in a particularly unseemly manner notes the existence of such possession, even if they cannot or do not articulate that noting. In consequence, we may ask ourselves, in utter dismay, "Why would such a spirit exist? Why would it be part of each of us?"

The answer appears to be partly associated with the powerful sense that each of us shares of our own intrinsic mortal limitations, our subjugation to the suffering inflicted upon us by ourselves, society, and nature. That embitters and produces a certain self-contempt or disgust, inspired by our own weaknesses and inadequacies (and I am not speaking here yet of immorality, merely of our intrinsic and terrible fragility), and also by the apparent unfairness, unpredictability, and arbitrariness of our failings. Given all these disappointing realizations, there is no reason to assume that you are going to be satisfied or happy with yourself, or with Being itself. Such dissatisfaction—such unhappiness—can easily come to reinforce and magnify itself in a vicious circle. With each step you take against yourself or others as a consequence of your unhappiness and resentment, there is more to be ashamed of, and more reason for self-directed antagonism. It is not for nothing that approximately one person in five engages in some form of serious physical self-harm in their lifetime.[3] And this does not include the most serious act—suicide itself (or the more common tendency toward suicidal ideation). If you are unhappy with yourself, why would you work in your best interest? Maybe something vengeful would emerge from you, instead; maybe something capable of justifying itself while it metes out hypothetically deserved suffering, designed to interfere with your movement forward. If you conceptually aggregate and unite into a single personality all that opposes you in you, all that opposes your friendships, and all that opposes your wife or husband, the adversary emerges. That is precisely Mephistopheles in Goethe's play—the devil himself. That is the spirit who works *against*—and that is exactly how he describes himself: "I am the spirit that denies."[4] Why? Because everything in the world is so limited and imperfect—and causes itself so much trouble and terror because of that—that its annihilation is not only justified but ethically demanded. So goes, at least, the rationalization.

This is no mere lifeless abstraction. People struggle in a deadly fashion with such ideas. Women wrestle with them when they consider having a baby, inquiring of themselves: "Should I really bring an infant into a world like this? Is that an ethical decision?" The followers of the philosophical school of antinatalism, of whom the South African philosopher David Benatar is perhaps the leading advocate,[5] would decisively answer no to both of those questions. I debated his views with him a few years back.[6] It was not as if I failed to understand his position. There is no doubt that the world is steeped in suffering. A few years later, I debated another philosopher, Slavoj Žižek—known much more widely for his Marxist predilections than his religious

convictions. He said something during our discussion that might be
theologically debatable, but that I found of great interest. In the Christian tradition, even God Himself, in the form of Christ, despairs of the
meaning of life and the goodness of His Father in the agony of His
Crucifixion. At the peak of his suffering, just before death, He utters
the words "*Eli Eli lama sabachthani*"[7]—"My God, my God, why has thou
forsaken me?" (Matthew 27:46). This appears to strongly imply, in its
narrative way, that the burden of life can become so great that even
God Himself can lose faith when confronted with the unbearable reality of injustice, betrayal, suffering, and death.

It is hard to imagine a story more sympathetic to mere mortals. If
God Himself experiences doubts in the midst of His self-imposed
agony, how could we mere humans not fall prey to the same failing?
And it is possible that it was compassion that was driving the antinatalist Benatar's position. I saw no evidence that Benatar was malevolent in any obvious manner. He appeared to truly believe—in a manner
I found reminiscent of Goethe's Mephistopheles—that the combination of consciousness, vulnerability, and mortality is so dire that there
is simply no moral excuse for its continuance. Now, it is entirely possible that Mephistopheles's opinion is not to be trusted. Since he is
Satan himself, there is no reason to assume that the argument he puts
forward to justify his adversarial stance toward Being is valid, or even
that he himself truly believes it. And perhaps the same was true of
Benatar, who was and is no doubt prey to the frailties that characterize
each of us (and that certainly includes me, despite the stance I took in
opposition to him). But I believed then and still firmly believe now
that the consequences of his self-negating position are simply too dire.
It leads directly to an antilife or even an anti-Being nihilism so profound that its manifestation could not help but exaggerate and amplify
the destructive consequences of existence that are already the focus of

the hypothetically compassionate antinatalists themselves (and I am not being sarcastic or cynical about the existence of that compassion, misplaced though I believe it to be).

Benatar's hypothesis was that life is so rife with suffering that it is, actually, a sin—for all intents and purposes—to bring any new conscious beings into existence, and that the most appropriate ethical action for human beings to take would be to simply stop doing so: to render ourselves voluntarily extinct. Such a viewpoint is more widespread, in my opinion, than you might think, although perhaps rarely held for long. Whenever you are cut off at the knees by one of life's many catastrophes, whenever a dream collapses, or someone close to you is hurt in some fundamental way—especially a child or another loved one—then you can easily find yourself thinking, "Perhaps it would be better if the whole mess was just brought to a halt."

That is certainly what people think when they contemplate suicide. Such thoughts are generated in their most extreme variant by the serial killers, by high school shooters, by all generally homicidal and genocidal actors. They are acting out the adversarial attitude as fully as they might. They are truly possessed, in a manner that exceeds the merely metaphorical. They have decided not only that life is unbearable and the malevolence of existence is inexcusable, but that everything should be punished for the mere sin of its Being. If we want to have any hope of dealing with the existence of evil, and working toward its minimization, we must understand these sorts of impulses. It is in no small part the consciousness of suffering and malevolence that embitters people. And it is toward this embitterment that I believe the antinatalist position would, if widely adopted, inevitably drift. First, it might be the mere refusal to reproduce. But I cannot believe that it would be long until that impulse to cease production of new life was transformed into a similar impulse to destroy life that currently exists, in consequence of the "compassionate" judgment that some lives are so terrible that it is merciful to bring them to an end. That philosophy emerged relatively early in the Nazi era, for example, when individuals judged unbearably damaged by life were euthanized for purposes deemed "morally merciful." The question this line of thinking leads to is where does such "mercy" stop? How sick, old, intellectually impaired, crippled, unhappy, unproductive, or politically inappropriate do you have to be before dispensing with you is a moral imperative? And why would you believe, once the eradication or even merely the limitation of life became your guiding star, that you would not continue down that road to its hellish end?

I found the Columbine High School killers' writings particularly instructive in that regard. They are scrawled out, and are careless, incoherent, and narcissistic, but there is definitely a philosophy at the base of them: that things deserve to suffer for the crime of their existence. The consequence of that belief is the creative elaboration and extension of that suffering. One of the killers wrote that he considered himself the judge of all that exists—a judge that found Being, particularly of the human form, wanting—and that it would be better if the entire human race was eradicated. That defined the scope of his horrific vision. He and his partner shot their classmates in their local high school, but that was only a tiny fraction of what they were planning. They had incendiary devices laid out across the community, and had fantasized together about trying to take out the entire city. Such plans are just a step on the way to the ultimate genocidal vision.

You do not have those sorts of visions unless you are deeply possessed by something very much resembling the adversarial spirit. That is Mephistopheles, whose essential viewpoint might be paraphrased as follows: "Life is so terrible, because of its limitations and malevolence, that it would be better if it did not exist at all." That is the central doctrine of the spirit that works at counterpurposes to you. It is an arguable case and not surprising that it should emerge, and it seems terribly credible at moments of crisis, even though I believe it is deeply wrong. I think the reason that it is wrong, in part, is because, when it is realized, all it does is exacerbate an already admittedly bad situation. If you set about making things worse, they are likely, in fact, to get worse. I cannot see how this constitutes an improvement, if your original objection was motivated by the essential terror of our existential situation itself. It does not seem to be a pathway that a conscious creature, with a bit of gratitude, might walk down. There is an incoherency to it that is logically untenable, and that therefore seems to make the argument fundamentally specious, and cannot help but make the listener think, "There are things going on here behind the scenes that are both unspoken and unspeakable, despite the surface logic."

The failings in the adversary's logic do not mean that constructing an unshakable viewpoint to counter it is a simple matter. In the most straightforward sense, identifying that vision of objection and vengefulness is useful, in the way that negative space in a painting is useful: it defines the positive, by contrast. Good can be conceptualized— however vaguely in its initial formulation—as the opposite of whatever constitutes evil, which is usually more readily identifiable in the world than goodness. I have been trying to find touchstones on that pathway of opposition to evil, so that people can identify what that good might be. Some of these are very practical, if difficult. I have been suggesting to my viewers and listeners,[8] for example—particularly those currently burdened by the mortal illness of a parent—that it is useful to consciously take on the task of being the most reliable person in the aftermath of the death, during the grief-stricken preparations for the funeral and the funeral itself, and for the care of family members during and after the catastrophe. There is a call to your potential in doing that. There is a call to the strength of Being itself—the Being that could manifest itself in you. The human race has been dealing with loss and death forever. We are the descendants of those who could manage it. That capability is within us, grim as the task might seem.

If you truly love someone, it can seem a deep form of betrayal to stay integrated and healthy, in essence, in their absence or sadly waning presence. What does that ability indicate, after all, about the true depths of your love? If you can witness their demise and survive the loss, does that not imply that the bond was shallow and temporary, and even replaceable? If you were truly bonded, should not it destroy you (as it sometimes does)? But we cannot wish that every inevitable loss leads to the destruction of everyone affected, because we would then all be doomed, far more immediately than we currently are. And it certainly is not the case that the last wish of the dying is or should be the interminable suffering of those they love. My impression has been, instead, that people tend to feel guilty on their deathbeds (because of their immediate uselessness and the burden that causes, but even more because of their apprehension about the grief and trouble they will cause those left behind). Thus, their most fervent wish, I believe, is that those whom they love will be able to move forward and live happily, after a reasonable time of mourning.

To collapse in the aftermath of a tragic loss is therefore more accurately a betrayal of the person who has died, instead of a tribute, as it multiplies the effect of that mortal catastrophe. It takes a dying person of narcissistic selfishness to wish endless grief on their loved ones. Strength in the face of death is better for the person who is dying and for those who remain living alike. There are family members who are suffering because of their loss who need taking care of, and who may be too old and infirm and otherwise troubled to cope with the situation properly. And so someone strong has to step in and exercise the terrible authority that makes even of death something to face and over-come. To understand clearly that you are morally obliged under such circumstances to manifest strength in the face of adversity is to indicate to yourself—and, perhaps, to other people—that there is something in you of sufficient grandeur and power to face the worst forthrightly and to yet prevail. That is certainly what people need to encounter at a funeral. There is little to say, explicitly, in the face of death. Everyone is rendered speechless when they encounter the infinite expanse of emptiness surrounding our too-brief existence. But uprightness and courage in such a situation is truly heartening and sustaining.

I have suggested that strength at the funeral of someone dear and close is a worthy goal more than once during a lecture (where people might encounter it live, or on YouTube or a podcast). In consequence, a not insignificant number of people have indicated to me that they took heart in desperate times as a consequence. They set reliability and strength in a crisis as a conscious goal and were able to manage exactly that, so that the devastated people around them had someone to lean on and see as an example in the face of genuine trouble. That, at the very least, made a bad situation much less dreadful than it might have been. And that is something. If you can observe someone rising above the catastrophe, loss, bitterness, and despair, then you see evidence that such a response to catastrophe is possible. In consequence, you might mimic that, even under dire circumstances. Courage and nobility in the face of tragedy is the reverse of the destructive, nihilistic cynicism apparently justified under just such circumstances.

Again, I understand the negative attitude. I have had thousands hours of clinical experience. I have been deeply involved in some very difficult situations, along with those I was listening to and strategizing with, as well as within the confines of my private life. People have arduous lives. You think your life is hard (and it probably is, at least at times), then you meet someone and your life is so much better than theirs that, no matter what your hardships are, you cannot even conceive of how they might continue to exist in their current misery. And you find out, not infrequently, that those same unfortunate people know someone else whose life is so hard that they feel the same way about them. And even they are often left feeling guilty that they believe what they have is a hard lot, because they know just how much worse it could be.

It is not as if the suffering and betrayal, the catastrophes, are of insufficient gravity to make bitterness a real option. But there is just no good whatsoever in that option, and plenty of evident harm. So, what constitutes the alternative? I began to seriously contemplate the topic of this rule just before Thanksgiving, in 2018, when I was touring the United States. That holiday has become, arguably, the biggest shared celebration in America (and is also a major event in Canada, approximately a month earlier). The only competitor, particularly since Easter has largely faded away, is Christmas, which is also in some sense a holiday of thanksgiving, concentrating as it does on the arrival of the eternal Redeemer in the midst of the darkness and cold of winter, and so reflects the endless birth and rebirth of hope itself. The giving of thanks is an alternative to bitterness—perhaps *the* alternative. My observation of American holidays—I lived in the States for seven years, and I have spent time there on countless other occasions—is that the prominence of Thanksgiving among holidays seems to be a good thing, practically and symbolically. The fact that the primary feast of celebration characterizing a country would be one of explicitly "giving thanks" appears, in principle, as a positive commentary on the fundamental ethic of the state. It means that the individual is striving to have his or her heart in the right place, and that the group is supporting and encouraging that endeavor. Why is that, given the trouble that constitutes life? It is because you can be courageous. You can be alert, awake, attentive. You can see how demanding life is and can be, and you can see it clearly. Despite this, you can remain grateful, because that is the intrepid attitude toward life and its difficulties. You are grateful not because you are naive, but because you have decided to put a hand forward to encourage the best in yourself, and the state, and the world. You are grateful, in the same manner, not because suffering is absent, but because it is valiant to remember what you have and what you may still be offered—and because the proper thankful attitude toward that existence and possibility positions you better than any other attitude toward the vicissitudes of existence.

To be grateful for your family is to remember to treat them better. They could cease to exist at any moment. To be grateful for your friends is to awaken yourself to the necessity of treating them properly, given the comparative unlikelihood of friendship itself. To be grateful to your society is to remind yourself that you are the beneficiary of tremendous effort on the part of those who predeceased us, and left this amazing framework of social structure, ritual, culture, art, technology, power, water, and sanitation so that our lives could be better than theirs.

The temptation to become embittered is great and real. It requires a genuine moral effort not to take that path, assuming that you are not—or are no longer—naive. The gratitude associated with that state of Being is predicated on ignorance and inexperience. That is not virtue. Thus, if you are attentive and awake, and you can see the structure of the world, bitterness and resentment beckon as a viable response. Then you might well ask yourself, "Well, why not walk down that dark path?" It seems to me that the answer to that, to state it again, is courage: the courage to decide "No, that is not for me, despite the reasons I may have for being tempted in that direction," and to decide, instead, "Despite the burden of my awake mortality, I am going to work for the good of the world."

## COURAGE—BUT SUPERORDINATE, LOVE

That decision seems to me to be courage subsumed to love. If it is resentment and bitterness and the consequent hatred that emerges from that tempting us toward the torment and destruction of everything that lives and suffers, then perhaps it is active love that aims at its betterment. And that seems to me to be the fundamental decision of life, and that it is correct to identify it, at least in a vital part, as an act of voluntary will. The reasons for acrimony, anger, resentment, and malevolence are strong and plentiful. Thus, it must be a leap of faith—a decision about a mode of being not so clearly justified by the evidence, particularly in hard times—that Being should be strengthened and supported by your aims and your acts. That is something done in some deep sense despite "*Eli Eli lama sabachthani*"—something that says "despite it all, no matter what *it* is, onward and upward"—and that is precisely the impossible moral undertaking that is demanded from each of us for the world to function properly (even for it to avoid degeneration into hell).

It is within the frame of that impossible undertaking—that decision to love—that courage manifests itself, enabling each person who adopts the courageous pathway to do the difficult things that are necessary to act for the good in even the worst of times. If you determine to manifest the two virtues of love and courage—simultaneously, consciously— you decide that you are going to work to make things better and not worse, even for yourself, even though you know that because of all your errors and omissions you are already three-quarters lost.

You are going to work to make things better for yourself, as if you are someone you are responsible for helping. You are going to do the same thing for your family and the broader community. You are going to strive toward the harmony that could manifest itself at all those levels, despite the fact that you can see the flawed and damaged substructure of things, and have had your vision damaged in consequence. That is the proper and courageous pathway forward. Maybe that is the definition of gratitude, of thankfulness, and I cannot see how that is separate from courage and love.

You might well ask, "Do people actually perceive and act in this manner?"—even—"Can they?" One of the most compelling pieces of evidence I have come across is the fact of grief over the loss of someone close. Even if you are ambivalent about life itself—and maybe even if you are ambivalent, to some degree, about the person that you lost, because that can certainly be the case—your likely response to a death is grief. That response is not exactly conscious. Grief is a strange experience. It seizes you unexpectedly. You feel shock and confusion. You are not at all sure how to respond. What is it that you are supposed to do? But if it is conscious grieving—the voluntary acting out of the supposedly appropriate response—it is not real; not in the manner that genuine grief grips you of its own accord. And if you do not feel yourself seized, unwittingly, in the latter sense, you might think, "I am not feeling the way I am supposed to feel. I am not crying. I am not overwhelmed by sorrow. I am going far too normally about my day-to-day business" (something particularly likely to occur if you receive the news of a death from a distant locale). But then, as you engage in something trivial, as if things are normal, the grief will strike you like a rogue wave. That happens repeatedly, God only knows for how long. It is something that arises from the depths, and it takes you irresistibly in its grasp.

Grief must be a reflection of love. It is perhaps the ultimate proof of love. Grief is an uncontrollable manifestation of your belief that the lost person's existence, limited and flawed as it might have been, was worthwhile, despite the limitations and flaws even of life itself. Otherwise, why would you feel the loss? Otherwise, why would you feel, involuntarily, sorrowful and bereft (and that from a source self-deception cannot reach)? You grieve because something that you valued is no longer in existence. Thus, in the core of your Being, you have decided that the person's life was valuable, despite whatever trouble they caused you—and themselves. In my experience, that happens even when people die who were quite monstrous. It is a rare person whose life has gone so catastrophically wrong that their death brings no sorrow.

There is a deep part of us that makes the decision, when we grieve for someone we have lost, that their existence was worthwhile, despite it all. Maybe that is a reflection of an even more fundamental decision: Being itself is worth having, despite it all. Gratitude is therefore the process of consciously and courageously attempting thankfulness in the face of the catastrophe of life. Maybe that is what we are trying to do when we meet with our families during a holiday, wedding, or funeral. Those are often contentious and difficult affairs. We face a paradoxical, demanding tension. We bring people that we know and love close to us; we are pleased at their existence and their proximity, but also wish they could be more. We are inevitably disappointed in each other, and in ourselves, as well.

In any familial gathering, there is tension between the warmth you feel and the bonding of memory and shared experience, and the sorrow inevitably accompanying that. You see some relatives who are in a counterproductive stasis, or wandering down a path that is not good for them. You see others aging, losing their vitality and health (and that sight interferes with and disrupts your memories of their more powerful and youthful selves: a dual loss, then, of present and past). That is all painful to perceive. But the fundamental conclusion, despite all of that, is that "It is good that we are all together and able to share a meal, and to see and talk to each other, and to note that we are all here and facing this celebration or difficulty together." And everyone hopes that "perhaps if we pull together, we can manage this properly." And so you make the same fundamental decision, when you join communally with your people, that you make when you grieve: "Despite everything, it is good that we are together, and that we have one another." That is something truly positive.

The same is true of your relationship with your children. My grief at life in recent decades was exaggerated in the case of my daughter, because she was very ill for many years as a child, adolescent, and young adult. A child is a being of tremendous potential, capable of developing an admirable, productive, and ever-increasing autonomy and ability. But there is also something truly fragile about their three- or four- or five- (or even fifteen- or twenty-five-) year-old forms (because that fragility never truly disappears from a parent's perception, once it has been experienced deeply, as it certainly will be with the experience of caring for young children). All that is part of the joy of having them, but also part of the pain. The pain is the absolute certainty that the fragility will be exploited. And yet I thought that whatever steps I might take to eradicate that fragility in my children would also destroy that for which I was thankful. I remember thinking this quite distinctly with my son when he was three, because he was supercute and fun. But he was three, so he was little. He would collapse, bang his head on tables, fall down the stairs, and get into little scraps with other kids. Maybe he would be playing in the supermarket parking lot and, distracted, run off briefly. This is not a wise move in a place ruled by cars. There is an undeniable vulnerability around children that wakes you up and makes you very conscious of the desire to protect them, but also of the desire to foster their autonomy and push them out in the world, because that is how you strengthen them. It is also a vulnerability that can make you angry at life because of its fragility, and lead you to curse the fate that joins the two together.

When I think about my parents, the same thing comes to mind. They are getting old. As people get older, in some sense, you see them crystallize into the people that they are. My father and my mother both have a decided character. They were who they were in their fifties, and now they are perhaps even more so. They have their limitations and their advantages (and it is even the case that the latter are often integrally necessary to the former). They are in their eighties now and are very particularized. Sometimes it is frustrating to deal with people and their particularities. You think, "Would not it be better if they could be some other way?" I am not saying I think that about my parents more than people generally think that about each other. It is by no means a criticism of them. In addition, there is no doubt that they (and others—many others) feel the same way about me. But it is necessary to understand that, just as in the case of children, all those particularities, fragilities, and limitations are part and parcel of what it is that you come to love.

So, you might love people despite their limitations, but you also love them *because* of their limitations. That is something very much worth understanding. Doing so may help you see how gratitude remains possible. Despite the fact that the world is a very dark place, and that each of us has our black elements of soul, we see in each other a unique blend of actuality and possibility that is a kind of miracle: one that can manifest itself, truly, in the world, in the relationships we have that are grounded in trust and love. That is something for which you can be courageously thankful. That is something in which you can discover part of the antidote to the abyss and the darkness.

Be grateful in spite of your suffering.

# Coda

As I indicated in the overture, much of this book was written during long months spent in hospitals—first, visiting or staying with my daughter, Mikhaila, then doing the same over a longer period with my wife, Tammy, and finally—when it became necessary—during my repeated admissions. I do not think it appropriate to write about those personal trials in any more detail than I already have in the Overture—partly because the common circumstances of the COVID-19 pandemic have rendered everyone's life tragic in an unimaginable manner, so that it seems superfluous, in some sense, to provide a detailed account of familial or individual suffering on top of that, and partly because the current book is not about my daughter's troubles, or my wife's, or mine, directed as it is to topics of general psychological import. What I truly find necessary to relate, however, is our appreciation to all those many people who supported us during this trying time. So, some additional discussion of our various maladies appears unavoidable at this point.

On the public front, we received an outpouring of good wishes from thousands of people who had become familiar with my work. Some of this was delivered in person, when people met Tammy or me in public; some was sent by email and social media; and some of it came in YouTube comments on my videos. This was exceptionally heartening. My sister, Bonnie, gathered and printed out particularly thoughtful messages to Tammy from around the world, and posted them in bright colors on the walls of the hospital room where they could be easily seen. The messages later addressed to me helped bolster my oft-wavering conviction that I could and should prevail in the face of the difficulties I was experiencing, and that the book you are reading or listening to would maintain its relevance, even in the face of the terrible pandemic that currently envelops the world. We were also the beneficiaries of medical care, much of it extreme, but most often provided with optimism, care, and competence. Tammy's dual cancer surgeries were courageously performed by Dr. Nathan Perlis of the Princess Margaret Cancer Centre, and when the complications arising thereof became too extreme, was treated by Dr. Maxim Itkin, director of Philadelphia's Penn Center for Lymphatic Disorders.

More privately, Tammy and I were individually and jointly the grateful beneficiaries of constant support from family and friends, who interrupted their lives to spend days, weeks, or months of time with us while we were undergoing our trials. I can only hope, in the face of serious doubts about the matter, that I would have chosen to be as generous with my time and attention as they were if the tables were turned. It is particularly necessary to thank my family members—my daughter, Mikhaila Peterson, and her husband, Andrey Korikov; my son, Julian Peterson, and daughter-in-law, Jillian Vardy; my brother-in law and sister Jim and Bonnie Keller; my brother and sister-in-law Joel and Kathleen Peterson; my parents, Beverley and Walter Peterson; my brother- and sister-in-law Dale and Maureen Roberts, and their daughter, Tasha; my sister-in-law Della Roberts and her husband, Daniel Grant; as well as our friends Wayne

Meretsky, Myriam Mongrain, Queenie Yu, Morgan and Ava Abbott, Wodek Szemberg and Estera Bekier, Wil Cunningham and Shona Tritt, Jim Balsillie and Neve Peric, Dr. Norman and Karen Doidge, Gregg and Dr. Delinah Hurwitz (the former of whom also profoundly helped me edit and improve *12 Rules for Life: An Antidote to Chaos*), Dr. Cory and Nadine Torgerson, Sonia and Marshall Tully, Dr. Robert O. and Sandra Pihl, Dr. Daniel Higgins and Dr. Alice Lee, Dr. Mehmet and Lisa Oz, and Dr. Stephen and Dr. Nicole Blackwood, all of whom went above and beyond the call of duty in the attention they paid to Tammy and me over the last two years. There are, finally, three men of God who were of service, particularly to Tammy: Fathers Eric Nicolai, Fred Dolan, and Walter Hannam.

My family made arrangements to have me treated in Moscow for the consequence of a paradoxical reaction and then a dependence on the hypothetically safe but truly dangerous benzodiazepine antianxiety medication. This was arranged with exceptional efficiency, despite the time of year (the Christmas and New Year holidays in 2019–20), by Kirill Sergeevich Mikhailov, the consul general of the Russian Federation in Toronto, and the consular staff who provided an urgent visa in a matter of days. Many people, including Kelly and Joe Craft, Anish Dwivedi, Jamil Javani, Zach Lahn, Chris Halverson, Metropolitan Jonah, and the V. Rev. Victor Potapov and Dimitir Ivanov, helped expedite what was a very complex, multidimensional process. While in Russia, my safety was ensured by Alexander Usov, and my sense of isolation diminished by daily visits by Mikhaila and her husband, Andrey, who truly cannot be thanked enough. The Russian medical teams included IMC Addiction by Roman Yuzapolski, who agreed to supervise my case despite being advised by assorted experts that it was too dangerous to do so, and his staff members, Herman Stepnov, administrative directors, and Alexandr, therapist, who translated for me constantly for a two-week period, without even a change of clothes. The team of the Russian Academy of Medical Sciences took me in with undiagnosed double pneumonia and in a state of catatonia and delirium, and restored my ability to ambulate. Dr. Marina Petrova, the deputy director, and Dr. Michael, the head doctor of what was known as the Reanimatology Ward, were of particular and notable aid. Uliana Efros, nanny to my granddaughter, Elizabeth Scarlett, always had our backs and traveled with Mikhaila, Andrey, and me for eight months from Russia to Florida and Serbia, caring for Scarlett, including spending a month in quarantine. Thanks as well to Uli's daughter Liza Romanova, who helped take care of Scarlett in Russia, so that my daughter and son-in-law could visit me in the hospital. Finally, on the Russian end, I would like to thank Mikhail Avdeev, who helped us extensively with provision of medication and translation of medical information—both on very short notice.

Later, in June 2020, I sought admission at the IM Clinic for Internal Medicine in Belgrade, an institution dedicated to benzodiazepine withdrawal, and fell directly under the competent and caring treatment provided by Dr. Igor Bolbukh and his staff. Dr. Bolbukh had flown to Russia previously to consult there while I was in a state of delirium, provided months of pro bono medical guidance, moved me to a more stable condition when I arrived in Serbia, and managed my care thereafter. The IM Clinic was founded by Dr. Nikolai Vorobiev, and his staff were very patient, without resentment—a difficult feat to manage in these days of COVID and the inevitable accompanying and sudden quarantines.

There are also those who profoundly deserve credit, recognition, and gratitude on the professional front. Thank you to my agents, Mollie Glick of Creative Artists Agency, as well as Sally Harding of CookeMcDermid (Canada) and her colleagues Suzanne Brandreth and Hana El Niwairi of Cooke Agency International Canada. Thank you to the editors and publishers of *12 Rules for Life: An Antidote to Chaos*: Penguin Random House

Canada senior editor Craig Pyette, who played a diligent and instrumental role in quality control and enhancement; former CEO Brad Martin; current CEO Kristin Cochrane; publisher of the Knopf Random House Canada Publishing Group Anne Collins; vice president, associate publisher, and director of marketing strategy Scott Sellers; Penguin Random House UK editor Laura Stickney and her colleague Penelope Vogler, and CEO Tom Weldon; and Penguin Random House International CEO Markus Dohle. Thanks to the editors and publishers of the current book, a group that includes the immediately aforementioned individuals, as well as additional Penguin Random House US personnel, including publisher of the Portfolio and Sentinel imprints Adrian Zackheim and editor Helen Healey. Finally, thank you to Professor Bruce Pardy and lawyer Jared Brown for their active support of my ideas during a time when doing so could be truly hazardous to one's professional reputation and security.

The worldwide tour of 160 cities that Tammy and I undertook during the incubation period of this book as well as its preliminary formulation was organized with exceptional efficiency and good nature by Creative Artists Agency representatives Justin Edbrooke (assisted by Daniel Smith) and Ari Levin (assisted by Colette Silver), as well as Live Nation's Andrew Levitt. The Australian and New Zealand tour benefited from the attention of Australian producer TEG Dainty's Brad Drummond, tour manager Simon Christian, and security man Scott Nicholson. Gunnlaugur Jónsson and his crew were exceptionally hospitable to Tammy and me (as well as to my mother and aunt, who accompanied us for the days we were in Iceland). John O'Connell served as primary tour manager, and was extremely professional, great at problem solving, and consistently upbeat and supportive over the months of travel and organization.

Dave Rubin of *The Rubin Report* traveled with us, introduced my lectures, and emceed the question-and-answer periods that followed, adding a necessary bit of levity to what might otherwise have been a too-serious endeavor. Rob Greenwald of Rogers & Cowan helped ensure appropriate media coverage. Joe Rogan, Ben Shapiro, Douglas Murray, Gad Saad, and Steven Crowder extended their friendship and shared their extensive media presence. Zachary Lahn was there many times as needed, and Jeff Sandefer opened up his extensive connection network. Bill Vardy, Dennis Thigpen, Duncan Maisels, and Melanie Paquette served as drivers for the tour leg in North America when we used motor homes. Tammy and I would also like to thank designer Shelley Kirsch and the crew at SJOC Construction for completing the renovation of our house during these trying times with minimal supervision on our part. So much has happened in the last three years I am sure that I have missed key people, and for that I sincerely apologize.

Thanks is due, finally, to all of you who have read or listened to my books—*Maps of Meaning: The Architecture of Belief*, as well as the two 12 Rules volumes—and/or tuned in to my YouTube videos and podcasts. I have been profoundly struck, as have the people close to me, by the exceptional loyalty and care you have demonstrated over the last half decade. May all of you reading or listening to this book wend your way successfully through these difficult times. I hope you are surrounded by people you love and who love you in turn. I hope that you can rise to the challenge presented by our current circumstances, and that we all might have the good fortune to eventually turn our attention to rebuilding the world after the deluge.

# Notes

**OVERTURE**

1. This is the philosopher David Hume's famous "scandal of induction." For further reading, see D. Humes and P. Millican, *An Enquiry Concerning Human Understanding* (New York: Oxford University Press, 1748/2008).
2. J. B. Peterson, *12 Rules for Life: An Antidote to Chaos* (Toronto: Random House Canada, 2018).


**RULE I: DO NOT CARELESSLY DENIGRATE SOCIAL INSTITUTIONS OR CREATIVE ACHIEVEMENT**

1. S. Hughes and T. Celikel, "Prominent Inhibitory Projections Guide Sensorimotor Communication: An Invertebrate Perspective," *BioEssays* 41 (2019): 190088.
2. L. W. Swanson "Cerebral Hemisphere Regulation of Motivated Behavior." *Brain Research* 886 (2000): 113–64.
3. F. B. M. de Waal and M. Suchak, "Prosocial Primates: Selfish and Unselfish Motivations," *Philosophical Transactions of the Royal Society of London: Biological Science* 365 (2010): 2711–22.
4. J. B. Peterson and J. Flanders, "Play and the Regulation of Aggression," in *Developmental Origins of Aggression*, eds. R. E. Tremblay, W. H. Hartup, and J. Archer (New York: Guilford Press, 2005), 133–57.
5. J. Piaget, *Play, Dreams and Imitation in Childhood* (New York: W. W. Norton & Company, 1962).

6.  F. de Waal, *Good Natured: The Origins of Right and Wrong in Humans and Other Animals* (Cambridge, Mass.: Harvard University Press, 1997).

7.  K. S. Sakyi et al., "Childhood Friendships and Psychological Difficulties in Young Adulthood: An 18-Year Follow-Up Study," *European Child & Adolescent Psychiatry* 24 (2012): 815–26.

8.  Y. M. Almquist, "Childhood Friendships and Adult Health: Findings from the Aberdeen Children of the 1950s Cohort Study," *European Journal of Public Health* 22 (2012): 378–83.

9.  All of the adult data here is derived from M. Reblin and B. N. Uchino, "Social and Emotional Support and Its Implications for Health," *Current Opinions in Psychiatry* 21 (2009): 201–2.

10. R. Burns, "To a Louse: On Seeing One on a Lady's Bonnet at Church," *The Collected Poems of Robert Burns* (Hertfordshire, UK: Wordsworth Poetry Library, 1786 /1988), 138.

11. J. B. Hirsh et al., "Compassionate Liberals and Polite Conservatives: Associations of Agreeableness with Political Ideology and Moral Values," *Personality and Social Psychology Bulletin* 36 (2010): 655–64.

12. J. F. Fenlon, "Bible Encyclopedias, The Catholic Encyclopedia, Codex Bezae," Study Light.org, www.studylight.org/encyclopedias/tce/c/codex-bezae.html. See also *The Catholic Encyclopedia*, "Codex Bezae" (New York: Robert Appleton Company, 1913).

## RULE II: IMAGINE WHO YOU COULD BE, AND THEN AIM SINGLE-MINDEDLY AT THAT

1.  We have recently discovered, for example, that new experiences turn on new genes, which code for new proteins, which build new structures of mind and body. Novel demands therefore appear to activate biological switches, allowing thoughts and actions once latent to make themselves manifest. For a review, see D. J. Sweatt, "The Emerging Field of Neuroepigenetics," *Neuron* 80 (2013): 624–32.

2.  From the traditional spiritual "Go Down Moses," ca. 1850.

3.  C. G. Jung, *Psychology and Alchemy*, vol. 12 of *Collected Works of C. G. Jung* (Princeton, N.J.: Princeton University Press, 1968), 323.

4.  This set of ideas, as well as the Mesopotamian creation myth, are discussed in detail in my first book, J. B. Peterson, *Maps of Meaning: The Architecture of Belief* (New York: Routledge, 1999).

5.  Tablet 7:112, 7:115; A. Heidel, *The Babylonian Genesis* (Chicago: Chicago University Press/Phoenix Books, 1965), 58.

6.  I. H. Pidoplichko, *Upper Palaeolithic Dwellings of Mammoth Bones in the Ukraine: Kiev-Kirillovskii, Gontsy, Dobranichevka, Mezin and Mezhirich*, trans. P. Allsworth-Jones (Oxford, UK: J. and E. Hedges, 1998).

7.  J. R. R. Tolkien, H. Carpenter, and C. Tolkien, *The Letters of J. R. R. Tolkien* (Boston: Houghton Mifflin, 1981), letter 25.

8. See Peterson, *Maps of Meaning*, for an extended discussion of this symbolic world and the reasons for the various equivalencies.
9. I covered this in much more detail in J. B. Peterson, *12 Rules for Life: An Antidote to Chaos* (Toronto: Random House Canada, 2018), Rule 2: Treat yourself like someone you are responsible for helping.
10. Some of the neuropsychology of this ancient predator-detection system, whose disinhibition produces fight or flight, fear or panic, is detailed in Peterson, *Maps of Meaning*.

### RULE III: DO NOT HIDE UNWANTED THINGS IN THE FOG

1. J. Habermas, *Discourse Ethics: Notes on a Program of Philosophical Justification*, in *Moral Consciousness and Communicative Action*, ed. J. Habermas, trans. C. Lenhardt and S. W. Nicholsen (Cambridge, Mass.: MIT Press, 1990).
2. It is of some interest to note that these are all variant meanings or the *tohu wa bohu*, the chaos out of which God made order, according to the initial verses of the book of Genesis. Rabbi Dr. H. Freedman and M. Simon, eds., *The Midrash Rabbah: Genesis*, vol. 1 (London: Soncino Press, 1983), 15.

### RULE IV: NOTICE THAT OPPORTUNITY LURKS WHERE RESPONSIBILITY HAS BEEN ABDICATED

1. Those who work forty-five hours a week instead of forty (that's an increase of 13 percent in time) make, on average, 44 percent more money. W. Farrell, *Why Men Earn More* (New York: AMACOM Books, 2005), xviii.
2. J. Feldman, J. Miyamoto, and E. B. Loftus, "Are Actions Regretted More Than Inactions?," *Organizational Behavior and Human Decision Processes* 78 (1999): 232–55.
3. It is for this reason, among others, that the figure of Satan, the Christian representation of evil itself, is in fact a later development of the personality of Set. J. B. Peterson, *Maps of Meaning: The Architecture of Belief* (New York: Routledge, 1999).
4. J. B. Hirsh, D. Morisano, and J. B. Peterson, "Delay Discounting: Interactions Between Personality and Cognitive Ability," *Journal of Research in Personality* 42 (2018): 1646–50.
5. J. Gray, *The Neuropsychology of Anxiety: An Enquiry into the Functions of the Septal-hippocampal System* (New York: Oxford University Press, 1982).
6. N. M. White, "Reward or Reinforcement: What's the Difference?," *Neuroscience & Biobehavioral Reviews* 13 (1989): 181–86.

### RULE V: DO NOT DO WHAT YOU HATE

1. W. G. Clark and W. A. Wright, eds., *Hamlet: Prince of Denmark* (Oxford: Clarendon Press, 1880), 1.3.78, 17.

2. For a critical review, see H. Pashler et al., "Learning Styles: Concepts and Evidence," *Psychological Science in the Public Interest* 9 (2008): 105–99.

3. M. Papadatou-Pastou, M. Gritzali, and A. Barrable, "The Learning Styles Educational Neuromyth: Lack of Agreement Between Teachers' Judgments, Self-Assessment, and Students' Intelligence," article 105, *Frontiers in Education* 3 (2018).

4. V. Tejwani, "Observations: Public Speaking Anxiety in Graduate Medical Education—A Matter of interpersonal and Communication Skills?," *Journal of Graduate Medical Education* 8 (2016): 111.

## RULE VI: ABANDON IDEOLOGY

1. F. Nietzsche, *The Gay Science*, trans. W. Kaufmann, section 125 (New York: Vintage Books, 1880/1974), 181.

2. F. Nietzsche, *The Will to Power*, trans. W. Kaufmann and R. J. Hollingdale (New York: Vintage, 1880/2011).

3. F. Dostoevsky, *The Devils (The Possessed)*, trans. D. Magarshack (New York: Penguin Classics, 1872/1954).

4. F. Nietzsche, *The Will to Power: An Attempted Transvaluation of All Values*, trans. A. M. Ludovici, vol. 14 of *The Complete Works of Friedrich Nietzsche*, ed. Oscar Levy (London: T. N. Foulis, 1914), 102–3.

5. See J. Panksepp, *Affective Neuroscience* (New York: Oxford University Press, 1998).

6. A very interesting variant of this "Pareto principle" was identified by D. J. de Solla Price, *Little Science, Big Science* (New York: Columbia University Press, 1963), who indicated that half the work was done—or half the value accrued—by the square root of the number of people involved.

7. T. A. Hirschel and M. R. Rank, "The Life Course Dynamics of Affluence," *PLoS One* 10, no. 1 (2015): e0116370, doi:10.1371/journal.pone.0116370. eCollection 2015.

8. F. Nietzsche, *On the Genealogy of Morals*, trans. W. Kaufman and R. J. Hollingdale, and *Ecce Homo*, trans. W. Kaufman, ed. W. Kaufman (New York: Vintage, 1989), 36–39.

9. In the USSR, for example, deadly action was taken against those whose parents or grandparents were deemed "class enemies" because of their relative economic prosperity. See A. Solzhenitsyn, *The Gulag Archipelago*, abridged ed. (New York: Vintage, 1973/2018).

10. *Monty Python's Flying Circus*, season 3, episode 2, "How to Play the Flute," October 26, 1972, BBC.

## RULE VII: WORK AS HARD AS YOU POSSIBLY CAN ON AT LEAST ONE THING AND SEE WHAT HAPPENS

1. B. E. Leonard, "The Concept of Depression as a Dysfunction of the Immune System," *Current Immunology Reviews* 6 (2010): 205–12; B. E. Cohen, D. Edmonson, and I. M. Kronish, "State of the Art Review: Depression, Stress, Anxiety and the Cardio-

vascular System," *American Journal of Hypertension* 28 (2015): 1295–1302; P. Karling et al., "Hypothalamus-Pituitary-Adrenal Axis Hypersuppression Is Associated with Gastrointestinal Symptoms in Major Depression," *Journal of Neurogastroenterology and Motility* 22 (April 2016): 292–303.

2. Failure to inhibit aggression properly from an early age appears to characterize about 15 percent of children. S. M. Côté et al., "The Development of Physical Aggression from Toddlerhood to Pre-Adolescence: A Nation Wide Longitudinal Study of Canadian Children," *Journal of Abnormal Child Psychology* 34 (2006): 71–85.

## RULE VIII: TRY TO MAKE ONE ROOM IN YOUR HOME AS BEAUTIFUL AS POSSIBLE

1. N. F. Stang, "Kant's Transcendental Idealism," *Stanford Encyclopedia of Philosophy* (Winter 2018), ed. E. N. Zalta, plato.stanford.edu/archives/win2018/entries/kant-transcendental-idealism.

2. E. Comoli et al., "Segregated Anatomical Input to Sub-Regions of the Rodent Superior Colliculus Associated with Approach and Defense," *Frontiers in Neuroanatomy* 6 (2012): 9, doi.org/10.3389/fnana.2012.00009.

3. D. C. Fowles, "Motivation Effects on Heart Rate and Electrodermal Activity: Implications for Research on Personality and Psychopathology," *Journal of Research in Personality* 17 (1983): 48–71. Fowles actually argued that the heart beats to reward, but also that the safety that beckons in escape from a looming predator was just such a reward.

4. E. Goldberg, and K. Podell, "Lateralization in the Frontal Lobes," in *Epilepsy and the Functional Anatomy of the Frontal Lobe*, vol. 66 of *Advances in Neurology*, eds. H. H. Jasper, S. Riggio, and P. S. Goldman-Rakic (Newark, Del.: Raven Press/University of Delaware, 1995), 85–96.

5. R. Sapolsky, Personal communication with the author, September 11, 2019. I've told this story to a few audiences, erroneously substituting zebras for wildebeest. Such are the vagaries of memory. But wildebeest is the correct animal.

## RULE IX: IF OLD MEMORIES STILL UPSET YOU, WRITE THEM DOWN CAREFULLY AND COMPLETELY

1. J. B. Peterson and M. Djikic, "You Can Neither Remember nor Forget What You Do Not Understand," *Religion and Public Life* 33 (2017): 85–118.

2. P. L. Brooks and J. H. Peever, "Identification of the Transmitter and Receptor Mechanisms Responsible for REM Sleep Paralysis," *Journal of Neuroscience* 32 (2012): 9785–95.

3. J. E. Mack, *Abduction: Human Encounters with Aliens* (New York: Scribner, 2007).

4. R. E. McNally and S. A. Clancy, "Sleep Paralysis, Sexual Abuse and Space Alien Abduction," *Transcultural Psychiatry* 42 (2005): 113–22.

5. D. J. Hufford, *The Terror that Comes in the Night: An Experience-centered Study of Supernatural Assault Traditions* (Philadelphia: University of Pennsylvania Press, 1989).

6. C. Browning, *Ordinary Men: Reserve Police Battalion 101 and the Final Solution in Poland* (New York: Harper Perennial, 1998).

7. I. Chang, *The Rape of Nanking* (New York: Basic Books, 1990).

8. H. Ellenberger, *The Discovery of the Unconscious: The History and Evolution of Dynamic Psychiatry* (New York: Basic Books, 1981).

9. H. Spiegel and D. Spiegel, *Trance and Treatment* (New York: Basic Books, 1978).

10. J. B. Peterson, *Maps of Meaning: The Architecture of Belief* (New York: Routledge, 1999).

11. M. Eliade, *A History of Religious Ideas*, trans. W. Trask, vols. 1–3 (Chicago: University of Chicago Press, 1981).

12. See Strong's Hebrew concordance for the King James Version—a tool that lists all the occurrences of a given word (twenty in nineteen verses in the case of *tohuw*).

13. H. Zimmern, *The Ancient East*, vol. 3 of *The Babylonian and Hebrew Genesis*, trans. J. Hutchison (London: David Nutt, 1901).

14. E. Neumann, *The Great Mother: An Analysis of the Archetype*, trans. R. Manheim (New York: Pantheon Books, 1955); E. Neumann, *The Origins and History of Consciousness*, trans. R. F. C. Hull (Princeton, N.J.: Princeton University Press/Bollingen, 1969).

15. D. E. Jones, *An Instinct for Dragons* (New York: Psychology Press, 2002).

16. See, for example, Psalm 74, Psalm 104:24–26, and Isaiah 27:1.

## RULE X: PLAN AND WORK DILIGENTLY TO MAINTAIN THE ROMANCE IN YOUR RELATIONSHIP

1. J. Gottman, *What Predicts Divorce? The Relationship Between Marital Processes and Marital Outcomes* (Hillsdale, N.J.: Erlbaum, 1994).

2. C. G. Jung, *Mysterium Coniunctionis*, vol. 14 of *Collected Works of C. G. Jung*, trans. G. Adler and R. F. C. Hull (Princeton, N.J.: Princeton University Press, 1970), 407, doi:10.2307/j.ctt5hhr0d.

3. M. Eliade, *Shamanism: Archaic Techniques of Ecstasy*, trans. W. R. Trask (Princeton, N.J.: Princeton University Press, 1951).

4. C. G. Jung, "The Philosophical Tree" in *Alchemical Studies*, vol. 13 of *The Collected Works of C. G. Jung*, trans. G. Adler and R. F. C. Hull (Princeton, N.J.: Princeton University Press, 1954/1967), 251–349.

5. C. G. Jung, "Gnosticism as Dealing with the Feminine," in *The Gnostic Jung: Including Seven Sermons to the Dead*, ed. S. A. Hoeller (New York: Quest Books, 1982), 114–18.

6. Defined as inability to conceive within one year of trying: W. Himmel et al., "Voluntary Childlessness and Being Childfree," *British Journal of General Practice* 47 (1997): 111–18.

7. Statistics Canada, "Common-Law Couples Are More Likely to Break Up," www150 .statcan.gc.ca/n1/pub/11-402-x/2011000/chap/fam/fam02-eng.htm.

8. Excepting, perhaps, in the first year. M. J. Rosenfeld and K. Roesler, "Cohabitation

Experience and Cohabitation's Association with Marital Dissolution," *Journal of Marriage and Family* 81 (2018): 42–58.

9. US Census Bureau, 2017. Data represent children living without a biological, step, or adoptive father. Also see E. Leah, D. Jackson, and L. O'Brien, "Father Absence and Adolescent Development: A Review of the Literature," *Journal of Child Health Care* 10 (2006): 283–95.

## RULE XI: DO NOT ALLOW YOURSELF TO BECOME RESENTFUL, DECEITFUL, OR ARROGANT

1. J. L. Barrett, *Why Would Anyone Believe in God?* (Lanham, Md.: AltaMira Press, 2004).
2. P. Ekman, *Emotions Revealed*, 2nd ed. (New York: Holt Paperback, 2007).
3. A. Öhman and S. Mineka, "The Malicious Serpent: Snakes as a Prototypical Stimulus for an Evolved Module of Fear," *Current Directions in Psychological Science* 12 (2003): 5–9.
4. J. Gray and N. McNaughton, *The Neuropsychology of Anxiety: An Enquiry into the Function of the Septo-Hippocampal System* (New York: Oxford University Press, 2000).
5. L. W. Swanson, "Cerebral Hemisphere Regulation of Motivated Behavior," *Brain Research* 886 (2000): 113–64.
6. All these ideas find their empirical demonstration in J. B. Hirsh et al., "Compassionate Liberals and Polite Conservatives: Associations of Agreeableness with Political Ideology and Moral Values," *Personality and Social Psychology Bulletin* 36 (December 2010): 655–64.

## RULE XII: BE GRATEFUL IN SPITE OF YOUR SUFFERING

1. This was covered in detail in Rule 8: Tell the truth—or, at least, don't lie, in J. B. Peterson, *12 Rules for Life: An Antidote to Chaos* (Toronto: Random House Canada, 2018).
2. I discussed this play previously, both in J. B. Peterson, *Maps of Meaning: The Architecture of Belief* (New York: Routledge, 1999), 319–20, and Peterson, *12 Rules for Life*, 148.
3. J. J. Muehlenkamp et al., "International Prevalence of Adolescent Non-Suicidal Self-Injury and Deliberate Self-harm," *Child and Adolescent Psychiatry and Mental Health* 6 (2012): 10–18.
4. J. W. Von Goethe, *Faust*, trans. George Madison Priest (1806).
5. D. Benatar, *Better Never to Have Been: The Harm of Coming into Existence* (New York: Oxford University Press, 2008).
6. Jordan B. Peterson and David Benatar, *The Renegade Report*, January 9, 2018, podtail.com/en/podcast/the-renegade-report/jordan-b-peterson-david-benatar.
7. Jesus, on the Cross, quoting the opening words of Psalm 22.
8. I mention this briefly in the Coda to *12 Rules for Life*.

# Index